E-learning and teaching in library and information services

E-learning and teaching in library and information services

Barbara Allan

facet publishing

Published by
Facet Publishing
7 Ridgmount Street
London WC1E 7AE

Facet Publishing (formerly Library Association Publishing) is wholly owned by
CILIP: the Chartered Institute of Library and Information Professionals.

First published 2002

British Library Cataloguing in Publication Data

A catalogue record for this book is available from the British Library.

ISBN 1-85604-439-4

Typeset in 10/13pt Revival 565 and Zurich by Facet Publishing.
Printed and made in Great Britain by MPG Books Ltd, Bodmin, Cornwall.

Contents

E-learning and teaching in library and information services

List of tables

List of figures

Every effort has been made to contact the holders of copyright material reproduced in this text, and thanks are due to them for permission to reproduce the material indicated.

Acknowledgements

Every effort has been made to contact the holders of copyright material reproduced in this text. I would like to thank all the individuals, organizations and webmasters who gave me permission to reproduce screenshots of their diagrams or web pages in the book. In particular I would like to thank:

BECTA, British Educational Communications and Technology Agency
Cincinnati and Hamilton County Public Library
Coaching and Mentoring Network
De Montfort University Library
Free Pint
Gilly Salmon, Open University Business School
Information Services, University of Birmingham
Infopeople Project, California State Library
Infopeople Project, Institute of Museum and Library Services, USA
Joint Information Systems Committee (JISC)
Learndirect
Murphy Library, University of Wisconsin–La Crosse
Netskills, Computing Service, University of Newcastle
OnLINM, Flexible Learning Development Unit, University of Leeds
RDN, Institute for Learning and Research Technology, University of Bristol
Stories on the Web, Birmingham Library and Information Services
Three Rivers Regional Library Service, Colorado
University of Hull
Wilberforce College, Hull.

Thank you to Dina Lewis: our e-learning experiences and discussions and your reflective questioning have helped shape this book. Thank you to Nick Bowskill at Sheffield University, who offered me a role model of excellence in e-tutoring while I was a student on the Med NCL2000 programme, where many of my fellow e-learning colleagues also offered support and a vast range of ideas. In particular I must thank Margaret Freeman whose friendship, good humour and willingness to experience virtual socializing has had a great impact on this book. I would also like to thank all the e-learning students who have helped to inform my ideas and practice. Thank you to the many people in the information and library profession who have shared ideas and training materials, answered queries and generally discussed their e-learning experiences with me. Your examples are included in this book and, as requested, I have changed names to preserve your anonymity. Thank you to Gabrielle Hayes, whose superb work on the WISE programme gave me the freedom to concentrate on this book. Finally, thank you to Denis and Sarah for providing me with their constant support during this project.

1

Introduction

Introduction to this book

The aim of the book is to provide an overview and guide to the rapidly developing field of e-learning and teaching in library and information services (LIS). E-learning is becoming an increasingly important approach to user education, information literacy and also staff development. Increasingly information workers are becoming involved in the whole business of e-learning and teaching, from designing and developing materials and programmes, through to supporting individual and group learning using virtual learning environments. This book provides practical guidance to the development and use of online learning and teaching materials and programmes, and also their delivery.

This book is aimed at library and information workers who are either involved in or thinking about becoming involved in online learning and training; this may be with their customers or colleagues. In addition, the book will be of interest and relevance to those with a responsibility and/or interest in staff development such as managers or supervisors of staff, staff development or personnel officers, trainers or consultants, or other change agents. They may be employed in library and information work in the public, private or voluntary sectors.

This book is based on information and knowledge obtained and developed from:

- the author's experiences as an e-tutor to information service staff and also other learners
- her experiences as an online student in the context of an MEd in Networked Collaborative Learning at the University of Sheffield
- visits (both real and virtual) to a wide range of library and information services e-learning provision
- professional networks and conferences, and also the literature.

While the author is an enthusiast about the possible uses of e-learning and teaching, she also acknowledges that it is only one tool in the librarian or information specialist's toolkit. This book is not intended to be read as a prescriptive guide to e-learning and teaching. It presents current ideas and models of good practice, and underpins these with developing theories of online learning and teaching. The book contains a range of e-learning examples and case studies, and these are meant to demonstrate current practice in a wide range of library and information units: from small ones operating on a minute budget through to large academic information services with access to sophisticated virtual learning environments. Research for this book into the use of e-learning in LIS demonstrated the thousands of examples of good practice that are to be found around the world. Trips to professional association home pages invariably led to interesting and exciting practice in all types of libraries. It is frustrating to only have space to present a relatively small number of these examples.

What is e-learning?

Networked technologies such as the internet and world wide web are dramatically changing education and training as they enable people to access information and communicate with others across terrestrial boundaries, cultures and on a global scale. They offer the potential for sharing high-quality learning resources, exchanging information and working in learning groups. The basic tool for accessing a virtual classroom is a personal computer (PC) with access to the internet. As increasing numbers of people either have their own PC with internet access or have access to this equipment via their library, workplace, local school or college, or internet café, then it means that this form of education and training is becoming easily accessible and increasingly important.

The term 'e-learning' is used in a variety of ways by different authors, and the literature shows that it is often used interchangeably with terms such as online learning, computer-based learning (CBT), web-based training (WBT), online resource-based learning (ORBL), NCL (networked collaborative learning), CSCL (computer-supported collaborative learning) and others. Rather than get involved in an academic debate about the different meanings of 'e-learning' this book uses the term in a similar way to the Chartered Institute of Personnel and Development, whose definition emphasizes the importance of connectivity:

Learning that is delivered, enabled or mediated by electronic technology, for the explicit purpose of training in organisations.

> *It does not include stand-alone technology-based training such*
> *as the use of CD-ROMs in isolation.*
>
> (CIPD 2002)

In the context of this book this definition is developed as follows:

> *E-learning involves learning that is delivered, enabled or*
> *mediated by electronic technology, for the explicit purposes of*
> *training and/or education. It does not include standalone*
> *technology-based training such as the use of CD-ROMs in*
> *isolation.*

E-learning includes a wide range of activities and processes such as:

- use of interactive learning packages involving text, graphics, audio, video and animation
- enhancement of traditional programmes by providing access to additional resources and information
- enhancement of a programme by providing additional support, e.g. using synchronous and asynchronous communication applications such as e-mail, discussion groups, chat rooms and video conferencing
- delivery of an integrated programme where much of the learning is through online activities supported by communication tools.

These learning activities and processes can be used to enable both training and e-tutoring. Training is often used to refer to learning that is associated with the development of very specific skills and behaviours, and typical examples include training in the use of specific ICT packages, information skills training and reference skills training. It also includes training activities that involve the development of specific skills, e.g. through instruction or coaching. In e-learning, training may take place through the use of web-based training programmes, where the learner typically follows a pre-specified learning process that includes opportunities for practice and assessment and feedback activities. It also takes place through blended approaches that involve learners experiencing a mixture of face-to-face and online learning activities.

The traditional face-to-face teaching model involves a teacher or lecturer transmitting knowledge to students; in e-learning this has been largely superseded by teachers becoming facilitators and helping students to learn for themselves. In an e-learning context the e-tutor often takes on a facilitator's role, and this shift in role is often referred to as moving from the 'sage on the stage' to the 'guide on the side'. This concept is explored in much more detail in Chapter 6. Many library and information workers are involved in e-tutoring in an educational context where they may be delivering information skills and ICT to students on programmes from GCSE and A Levels through to Masters level programmes. These LIS workers are also be likely to be involved in information and ICT training programmes for academic and support staff.

Robin Mason (2002) describes three forms of e-learning: web-based training, supported online learning and informal e-learning. The following table summarizes the key characteristics of these approaches:

Table 1.1 *Three forms of e-learning*

Web-based training	Supported online learning	Informal e-learning
Content-focused	Learner-focused	Group-focused
Delivery-driven	Activity-driven	Practice-driven
Individual learning	Small-group learning	Organizational learning
Minimal interaction with tutor	Significant interaction with tutor	Participants act as learners and tutors
No collaboration with other learners	Considerable interaction with other learners	Multi-way interactions among participants

E-learning in information work involves all three approaches and this is exemplified in the following examples:

Web-based training

Jane, a reference librarian, participated in an online html course provided by Learndirect. This programme provided individual guidance on using html, and this was supported by a tutor. This web-based training course gave her the skills and confidence to work on the information unit's new web pages. She found that she was able to study at a time and pace that suited her own situation, but sometimes found that she needed additional technical support. She used help from her e-tutor and also from one of the systems librarians in her workplace.

Supported online e-learning

David overcame the challenges of running an induction programme for

2500 students by delivering it online. This enabled students to access high-quality learning materials and also to revisit them at later stages in their course. The programme was an assessed part of a study skills module, with an online multiple choice test. He provided online support via a discussion group and FAQ list. He found that the development of the programme was extremely time-consuming and although the majority of students were positive about the experience, a small and very vocal group were unhappy and would have preferred a traditional face-to-face learning experience.

Informal e-learning

Rebecca, an academic services manager in a university, used discussion groups and noticeboards to keep up to date with current learning resource issues. She also took part in an online project management programme, and this involved working on a real-life project and using a discussion group to share ideas and gain feedback. This helped to inform her professional practice and also provided support. She found that she needed to be disciplined in her approach to informal e-learning and learnt to set aside a small amount of time to it on a regular basis. Otherwise she found that other pressures of work meant that this was a low priority and often missed. She commented that it was often easier to attend a traditional course that could be diaried.

Inevitably the exaggerated claims of early e-learning enthusiasts have not been met and, at the time of writing in 2002, there appears to be a developing consensus that e-learning does not offer a replacement to traditional approaches to learning and teaching. Instead it offers an approach that may be blended with more traditional methodologies. Increasingly a blended approach, involving the use of e-learning as a prequel or sequel to face-to-face events, appears to be popular.

Blended approach

Barbara designed and delivered a project management course to six information workers located in London, Glasgow and Manchester. The programme started with a one-day workshop and this was followed up through e-learning activities in the workplace using virtual communication tools. The group met again for a half-day workshop at the end of the course. The use of virtual communication tools saved time and travel costs, and it enabled individuals to carry out practical activities in their workplace. Barbara found that the time taken to develop and support the online programme was much greater than the previous face-to-face version of the course.

Benefits and disadvantages of e-learning

There are many benefits to online learning and teaching and they include:

1 Flexible delivery – students can choose their place and time of study as the internet and WWW are open 24 hours a day.
2 Learning resources can be relatively easily developed using a variety of standard packages.
3 One can make use of, and link into, other resources available on the internet.
4 Online delivery is relatively cheap as there are no printing or distribution costs.
5 Flexible communications – students, tutors and LIS staff can communicate both in real time and asynchronously. It can bring together people from across the globe.
6 It can enable both one-to-one and one-to-many communications, e.g. tutor and individual learner, or tutor and whole groups.
7 Learners can form both formal and informal learning communities.
8 It doesn't have the negative associations often associated with formal educational settings.
9 It is easy to track learner activity and progress.

However, there are also some major disadvantages of online learning and teaching and these include:

1 Many people find it daunting, especially at first.
2 The student and tutor need reliable access to a computer and the internet.
3 The student and tutor need basic information technology skills.
4 Training is required for both tutor and student.
5 The development of high-quality learning materials is time-consuming and expensive.
6 Online tutoring can be more time-consuming than face-to-face tutoring.
7 Learning is a social process and many people enjoy face-to-face interactions.
8 The use of the large virtual learning environments is expensive and may demand additional equipment and specialized staff.

9 Some learning environments require state-of-the-art computers and the most up-to-date browser.

10 Blended solutions can be expensive as they may involve the development of expensive online learning resources, and providing technology-based support as well as face-to-face support.

The author is not suggesting that online learning and teaching is likely to replace face-to-face training and education. However, it is rapidly becoming an important additional delivery method and it offers opportunities to some people that are not readily available by any other means. It also offers an important method of enhancing learning support for face-to-face programmes.

Developing infrastructures in the UK

Governments and other agencies across the globe are investing large sums of money in e-learning. In the UK the government has invested heavily in a large number of schemes and this pattern is mirrored in other countries. Examples of schemes include:

The People's Network (www.peoplesnetwork.gov.uk)

This was set up by the UK government in the late 1990s to ensure that all public libraries have computers for public use linked to the internet and the National Grid for Learning (see below) by the end of 2002. The People's Network scheme includes an impetus to train public library staff in ICT skills and this is lottery-funded through the New Opportunities Fund. Public library staff are being trained to the standard of the European Computer Driving Licence to create content for the network and to digitize library resources. The programme covers eight core areas:

1 a grounding in core ICT fundamentals
2 understanding how ICT can support library staff in their work
3 health and safety and legal issues in the context of ICT
4 knowing how to find things on behalf of users
5 using ICT to support reader development activities
6 using ICT to support users to ensure effective learning
7 ensuring effective management of ICT resources in libraries
8 knowing how to use ICT to improve professional efficiency and reduce bureaucratic burdens.

Once everyone within a library has achieved the core training outcomes, then there is funding available to train staff to more advanced levels and these cover the five roles identified in the Library and Information Commission's report *Building the new library network* (1998):

1   network manager
2   information technology gatekeeper
3   information consultant
4   information manager
5   educator.

The National Grid for Learning (www.ngfl.gov.uk)

This is another UK government initiative that aims to connect all schools, colleges and universities to a portal or gateway website for lifelong learning. The content of the grid can come from a variety of sources, including schools, colleges, LEAs, government departments, educational organizations and training providers, and businesses. The National Grid for Learning will provide library staff with access to a wide range of quality learning materials and resources.

The National Learning Network

This investment programme in further education information and learning technologies (ILT) and funding is focused on infrastructure (hardware and connectivity), staff skills and learning resources. It is funded by the Learning and Skills Council (LSC) and it is closely associated with the University for Industry, which provides the Learndirect e-learning system. The infrastructure for the National Learning Network is provided by JANET (Joint Academic NETwork), which has linked university networks since the 1980s, and its extension to the further education sector now enable colleges to benefit from enhanced access to resources. In addition it means that Learndirect e-learning provision is now available to universities as well as colleges.

Another NLN initiative is the development and financial support of Information and Learning Technology (ILT) Champions in colleges. Their role is to encourage and mentor staff to use technology in the management and delivery of the curriculum, and to encourage good ILT practices and strategies within the post-16 sector. ILT Champions are also responsible for the commissioning of new electronic learning resources and the transformation of existing content into a form suitable for the internet, intranet or managed/virtual learning environment

(M/VLE). Susan Eales (2002) writes: 'some senior managers have appointed a member of library staff as ILT champion because of their knowledge and experience of all curriculum areas and their support role within the college.'

Other initiatives

Historically, the academic communities in colleges and universities have led the field in the development of e-learning within the UK. The Joint Information Systems Committee (JISC) has led the way in supporting the development of the necessary infrastructure, and also of research and development projects. JISC's role has been crucial in the funding and development of the JANET network and enabling further education colleges to take advantage of this high-speed, high-bandwidth infrastructure.

A long list of projects and collaborative ventures supported by JISC and other national initiatives has enabled the development of a vibrant and innovative e-learning community with information workers. The impact of these initiatives, and also of regional or local activities, has resulted in the development of a significant number of large-scale and smaller-scale online learning projects within the LIS sector. For further information and news of current developments see www.jisc.ac.uk.

A search of the literature and recent conference proceedings indicates that there are a growing number of applications of e-learning and teaching in library and information work. These examples can be grouped under the following headings:

- Information literacy
  — library induction programme
  — information searching
  — basic IT skills
  — research skills.
- Initial professional development
  — induction programme
  — initial LIS qualifications
  — initial teaching and training qualifications.
- Continuous professional development
  — masters programmes
  — management skills, e.g. project management, financial management
  — coaching and mentoring
  — networking.

Examples from each of these areas are used to support and demonstrate e-learning and teaching in the following chapters.

Developing technologies

The focus of this book is on e-learning through a range of virtual communication tools and virtual learning environments. The book covers many standard approaches to e-learning and focuses on those that are commonly available to library and information workers. As always the technology is developing rapidly, and a recent e-mail (Davies, 2002) to the VLE discussion group provides a useful list of developing technologies:

- battery technologies (for mobile devices)
- digital paper, digital ink
- embedded systems
- flexible displays
- image recognition
- intelligent agent technologies
- quantum computing
- security in mobile communications
- synchronous audio
- technologies to support assessment
- technologies to support e-commerce
- technologies to support virtual laboratories
- technologies to support virtual environments for learners
- ubiquitous computing
- voice portals
- wearable devices
- web services technologies
- wireless, mobile communications technologies.

It appears that the future of e-learning is going to include m-learning (mobile learning) based on hand-held sets such as mobile phones, and increased use of the voice via virtual communication tools. Over the next few years it is likely that the use of e-learning will develop to take on board these newer and developing technologies. However, although the technologies are changing, the basis of e-learning is likely to remain founded on communications between students, their peers and tutors.

The structure of the book

The book is divided into three main topics:

- e-learning tools and technologies
- e-learning and teaching
- e-learning and the LIS profession.

E-learning tools and technologies

Chapters 2–4 are concerned with online tools and technologies and cover the following topics:

2   virtual communication tools
3   integrated learning environments
4   web-based training materials.

It is beyond the scope of this book to describe the internet in any detail, and this topic is covered by other resources, e.g. *The advanced internet searcher's handbook* (Bradley, 2002).

Chapter 2 considers the development and use of virtual communication tools in learning. It considers a wide range of communication tools from simple e-mail to virtual worlds. The following tools are briefly described and then discussed with reference to current practice in LIS:

- e-mails
- discussion lists
- newsgroups
- bulletin boards
- webforms
- polling
- instant messaging
- chat or conferencing
- internet telephony
- videoconferencing
- virtual worlds
- web-based access to virtual communication tools.

Chapter 3 introduces integrated learning environments and briefly describes learning portals. It provides an overview of virtual learning environments (VLEs) and managed learning environments (MLEs). VLEs are often available to library and information staff working in colleges or universities and they offer a range of learning and teaching tools and resources:

- dissemination of interactive multimedia learning resources
- online assessment, including diagnostic tools, formative and summative assessment
- access to a wide range of information resources
- e-mail
- noticeboards
- discussion groups
- conference rooms
- personal management tools, e.g. diary, online portfolio
- student management tools, e.g. monitoring of student activity, student assessment results.

This chapter also considers commercial communication software tools such as Lotus Notes and Exchange 2000, and these enable information workers to create integrated learning environments for specific groups of employees or for specific topics. They may also be used for professional development activities such as action learning sets. Another option is to obtain free access to or subscribe to a host organization that offers virtual learning environments complete with a standard set of tools. This approach to virtual learning is often used in workplace libraries and information centres and in libraries in the voluntary sector. One of the key messages in this chapter is that, while e-learning may take place on a very large scale as part of a relatively well-funded development activity, many individual information workers have developed respectable and highly successful online learning programmes based on readily accessible software that is available over the internet.

Chapter 4 provides an overview of web-based training materials, and this is supported with examples from a wide range of libraries and information services. This chapter also covers the important topics of evaluating training materials and provides guidance on managing e-learning centres.

E-learning and teaching

This section contains the following topics:

5   models of e-learning and teaching

6   e-tutoring
7   successful e-learning
8   design of e-learning programmes and activities
9   e-learning activities.

Moving into e-learning and teaching requires a change in approach to learning and teaching. While many of the skills and techniques used in face-to-face programmes are relevant to online work, the virtual classroom involves different approaches to learning, and e-tutors are likely to find that they need to develop their e-learning practice. There is a growing literature of good practice in this area and there are also emerging models of e-learning and teaching. Chapters 5–7 are concerned with the underlying principles of online learning and teaching, and the skills required to become an effective e-learner or an online tutor. These are exemplified using example learning activities, programmes and courses.

Chapter 5 explores different models of learning and knowledge in the context of e-learning. It starts with an introduction to individual approaches to learning, exploring the context of learning, models of learning and learning styles, and the importance of reflection on learning. One approach to learning is to consider it as a social activity, e.g. involving groups of students learning information skills, or groups of library and information staff working together in different ways. An important concept in e-learning is that of collaborative and co-operative learning. The use of communication tools enables people to work and learn co-operatively or collaboratively. In co-operative learning individual learners are working towards their own goals with the help and support of their peers. In contrast, collaborative learners are working towards a shared goal and an end product which is a group rather than an individual goal. The latter form of learning can be very powerful as it enables the e-tutor to capitalize on the strengths of online learning and the importance of people in the learning process.

Other approaches to learning that take into account the importance of social activity include those of the cognitive apprentice and communities of practice. These two concepts are particularly important in the context of continuing professional development. Cognitive apprenticeship is concerned with individuals learning from more experienced practitioners or experts. While this may involve face-to-face activities such as coaching or mentoring, virtual communication tools offer an important method in which one-to-one communications may take place. Communities of practice are increasingly seen as important vehicles for individual and professional development. Understanding this framework enables library and information workers to develop communities and engage with them.

E-learning may be used to support different approaches to learning and teaching, and two approaches that are commonly discussed are behaviourist and constructivist. These approaches are explored in Chapter 5 and then referred to again in Chapters 8 and 9. Library and information workers who use virtual learning environments may use behaviourist, constructivist or a mixed behaviourist/constructivist approaches to learning and teaching depending on the learning outcomes and the philosophy of their programmes. While the different approaches all have their advocates, what is really important is for practitioners to adopt and use an approach that is appropriate to enabling their learners meet the learning outcomes of the programme.

Chapter 5 concludes with a review of Gilly Salmon's five-stage model of e-learning (Salmon, 2000) and this provides guidance for the design and facilitation of e-learning programmes. This model was developed as a result of her work with Masters level students in the Open University Business School, and it provides a framework that synthesizes and integrates ideas such as social aspects of learning and knowledge construction. This model is explored in some detail as it provides a useful framework and guidance on the types of activities online tutors will be involved in during the course.

The role of the information worker has expanded to include e-tutoring, and Chapter 6 explores the reasons why library and information staff get involved in e-learning. It explores the basic conferencing skills needed by e-tutors and issues that they need to be aware of when committing to getting involved in e-learning. This chapter also explores the practical idea of co-tutoring as one way in which e-tutors can gain support for their work. Chapter 6 includes a review of the key features of successful e-tutors and it also explores the development routes currently available for online tutors.

Chapter 7 explores the experiences of an e-learner and the factors that enable successful e-learning in a networked learning situation involving learning groups. It explores this issue from a number of perspectives: skills required to become an e-learner, preparing to become an e-learner, learning to learn and e-learn, and e-learning experiences. This chapter concludes with practical advice to new e-learners.

Many information workers are involved in the development of e-learning interactive learning materials and/or whole e-learning programmes. Chapter 8 provides practical guidance on the design and development process and it covers five distinct stages: analysis, design, development, implementation and evaluation. This chapter also provides guidance on the development and use of assessment tools such as quizzes or questionnaires within e-learning materials or programmes.

Information workers who are experienced trainers will have developed a toolbox of learning and teaching methodologies such as activities, exercises, group work, role play, use of media and multimedia techniques. As they move into e-learning and teaching, they will find that they modify their current practice to incorporate new techniques to enable them to develop and facilitate a range of e-learning activities. Chapter 9 explores a wide range of e-learning activities and it also considers online assessment activities.

E-learning and the LIS profession

Chapter 10 looks at the implications of e-learning for the library and information profession. Individual workers may find that e-learning has an impact on learning opportunities, employment opportunities, the development of new skills, new roles and responsibilities, possibilities for teleworking and the life/work balance. E-learning is also having an impact on individual LIS services as the increased use of ICT and web-based learning technologies has created opportunities for the provision of new services and resources to customers. It is also having an impact on the role of the LIS within the organization, such that some academic library and information services are now responsible for e-learning within their organization.

The final chapter provides guidance on resources (both web-based and print-based) to enable the reader to follow up specific ideas on e-learning. As the number of publications on e-learning is rapidly increasing, the chapter also includes an indicative list of resources that a reader may use to get started in their research into further information.

E-learning tools and technologies

2

Virtual communication tools

Introduction

The purpose of this chapter is to explore a range of virtual communication tools and their application as an e-learning tool for library and information workers. As a result of reading this chapter, readers will have an overview of the diverse range of virtual communication tools and their use in supporting their customers or end-users. The chapter also explores their use as a tool for development in the workplace.

The tools covered include e-mail, mailing lists, newsgroups, bulletin boards, webforms, polling, instant messaging, chat or conferencing, internet telephony, videoconferencing and virtual worlds. Some of these tools are available within integrated learning environments and these are considered in Chapter 3. They are mentioned here too as they are widely available on a range of websites and learning portals relevant to information workers.

It is hard to imagine working in the information world without access to electronic communication tools such as e-mail and discussion lists. Virtual communication tools are widely used in libraries as a means of communicating with users, and they provide an important channel for many information workers to communicate with their colleagues, and network across the profession and with other professions. Virtual communication tools are becoming increasingly important as a means of staff development.

Virtual communication tools are also important in enabling information professionals to exchange information and ideas, work together on a common theme or issue, and also work in collaborative teams. While this is a well established aspect of library and information professional practice, it has received a new impetus in recent years with the recognition that these professional communities of interest and communities of practice are an important source of individual, team and professional development. The terms 'communities of practice' and 'communities of interest' were coined by Wenger (1997) and this concept is described and discussed in some detail in Chapter 5. Virtual communication tools are increasingly becoming an important tool in the development and maintenance of these communities.

Virtual communication tools are of two main types:

1   **Asynchronous tools** that enable people to communicate at a time that suits them. Individuals post a message that is held by the system. This message can be read and responded to as and when the recipient comes online. Asynchronous communications take place over time rather than at the same time.
2   **Synchronous tools** that enable people to communicate when they log onto the same system at the same time, i.e. they are immediate and live communications. Unlike with face-to-face communications, a transcript or record of the communication process is available in most systems.

These tools are listed with their key characteristics in Table 2.1 and their application to learning and development in library and information units is considered with reference to specific work-based examples.

Table 2.1 *Characteristics of virtual communication tools*

	Type of communication	Asynchronous/ synchronous	E-learning applications
E-mail	1 to 1, 1 to many	asynchronous	exchanging information detailed instruction follow-up, e.g. training sessions, coaching or mentoring sessions knowledge construction training delivery, e.g. use of e-mail networking
Mailing lists	1 to many	asynchronous	exchanging information knowledge construction networking
Newsgroups	1 to many	asynchronous	information source networking
Bulletin boards	1 to many	asynchronous	exchanging information detailed instruction discussions collaborative or project work knowledge construction follow-up, e.g. training sessions, coaching or mentoring sessions
Webforms	1 to 1	asynchronous	exchanging information

Polling	1 to 1, 1 to many	asynchronous	collecting information
Instant messaging	1 to 1, 1 to many	synchronous	exchange information detailed instruction
Chat or conferencing	1 to 1, 1 to many	synchronous	exchanging information detailed instruction discussions collaborative or project work knowledge construction follow-up, e.g. training sessions, coaching or mentoring sessions
Internet telephony	1 to 1, 1 to a few	synchronous	exchanging information detailed instruction discussions knowledge construction training events, meetings
Videoconferencing	1 to 1, 1 to a few	synchronous	exchanging information detailed instruction discussions knowledge construction training events, meetings
Virtual worlds	1 to 1, 1 to many	synchronous	training events role play knowledge construction exploring future possibilities

E-mails

E-mails are a common and simple method of exchanging information. E-mail is regularly used by information workers for both formal and informal learning and teaching activities. Many library and information workers provide e-mail support to students, e.g. as part of an electronic reference service or as a support mechanism within an information literacy programme. Formal approaches to the use of e-mail involve setting up and running short courses via e-mail. E-mail is also often used as an important communication tool in formal coaching or mentoring processes.

E-mail can be used to deliver staff training programmes. It is relatively cheap and can be used to provide training to large numbers of people in diverse locations. For example, the American Association of School Librarians offers a four week e-mail-based course in learning to use the internet as a curriculum resource (www.ala.org/ICONN/onlineco.html, accessed 26 April 2002). It can also be used as an instruction medium within a particular organization, e.g. to overcome the challenges of training staff who work different schedules, this is explored in the case study that follows:

E-mail training by e-mail: case study at City College, Norwich

The increase in numbers of computers in the Library and Learner Centre meant that staff were spending an increasing amount of time either in front of a screen themselves, or helping students use computers. Conventional face-to-face training involving attendance at a half-hour session was difficult for some staff (particularly those who worked part-time) to attend and they were also time-consuming for the trainer. These difficulties in timetabling training for staff led to an investigation into alternative methods of delivery. The trainer decided to use e-mail to deliver the training to achieve two main objectives: to allow trainees to do the training at a time convenient to them; and to deliver the training to a larger group, i.e. to move beyond learning support services to the wider college staff.

The outline of the course (originally for six weeks, but spreading to seven) covered:

*   addressing messages quickly, and going on holiday
*   getting receipts, and different mailbox views
*   keeping your mailbox tidy
*   attaching files to e-mail
*   the personal address book
*   sending e-mail to groups of people (personal distribution lists)
*   sending web-page locations using e-mail.

The trainer was an internal member of staff who stated:

> *The course was offered by an experienced (computer-literate) user rather than an IT-trained specialist. The ethos was to be light-hearted rather than dense and technical. As an example, the initial message rated IT skills and knowledge on a scale of 1 to 3 anoraks, and set the course at the 1-to-2 anorak level.*

The course started with an introductory e-mail that suggested how the training could be used, and emphasized its flexibility. The trainer suggested that each e-mail should be printed out, as he felt it was important to make the user feel comfortable. He also stressed that the e-mails could be tackled once a week when sent out, or could be stored up and completed at the convenience of the trainee. The e-mails were written in a friendly style to help personalize the learning process.

Six of the seven e-mails involved a task to be completed, usually by sending an e-mail back to either the trainer or the group. For example, the evaluation of the course was sent out as a Word attachment, which had to be saved, opened, completed and reattached to be sent back. The way people used the training meant that they worked co-operatively within their staff rooms, and with colleagues, to complete the course. The training also generated a lot of discussion about using IT.

Evaluations of the programme were very positive; 82% found the training very useful and 18% found it useful; 20% found the training very convenient and 80% found it convenient. A large number of responses mentioned an increase in confidence, and lessening of fear, e.g. 'It has broken down the phobia of using the system.' Some people emphasized the need for further practice in using the skills in order to feel fully competent, and some mentioned that the humour had been important in motivation and keeping interest.

This case study was written up by Phil Ackroyd and it is available at http://ferl.becta.org.uk/ (accessed 19 February 2002).

Informal e-mail communication between staff, where information and ideas are exchanged, is possibly one of the most popular means of keeping up-to-date and solving small queries that arise every day in the workplace. This may be in the form of reference or other enquiries that may be sent to a named individual, an expert or a virtual reference desk. A quick survey of library websites indicates that many of them provide e-mail access to a virtual reference service. It can also be used to support informal coaching arrangements and this is explored in the next case study:

E-mail as part of a coaching process

The author was recently involved in coaching a colleague whom we shall call Jane, who wished to progress from her position in a workplace information unit in the food industry. The overall aim of the coaching process was to enable Jane to be successful in interviews. The structure of the coaching process was a blend of face-to-face and online elements. This was for pragmatic reasons, i.e. pressure of time and the need to complete the process within four weeks.

The first coaching session was face-to-face and involved identifying specific outcomes, and time was also spent looking at the interview process and good practice. Jane left with a series of specific actions to complete. She kept in touch by e-mail with the author, who gave her constructive feedback on her *curriculum vitae*. The next stage involved a practice interview session and it was impossible to arrange a time to meet. So, they went online and held the interview using chat software. This enabled the author to set up a 'formal' interview process and lead the questioning process. Another colleague supported this activity by playing the part of the second interviewer. This was a challenging process for all three. It required extremely detailed preparation as they keyed in and saved the interview questions in a Word file, which enabled them to cut-and-paste individual questions into the chat session. The actual interview was extremely intensive and required great concentration. In this respect it mirrored the experience of a face-to-face interview. Overall it was a very effective activity and one of the benefits was the transcript, as this enabled them to identify extremely good answers and also answers that could be improved. They discussed these by e-mail over the following few days.

The final part of the coaching process involved preparation for a presentation. Again, much of the preparatory work was carried out by e-mail and this resulted in the production of a professional presentation. The final part of the coaching process involved a practice presentation session and this was carried out face-to-face. After three interviews Jane was offered a new position. She was thrilled.

Overall this was an extremely intensive process that would have been much easier to carry out face-to-face. However, the pressures of two clashing schedules and heavy workloads meant that this wasn't possible and the blended solution worked well. One benefit of the procedure was that both parties gained experience and skills in working through e-mail.

Mailing lists

As well as sending e-mails to individuals it is possible to send them to groups using mailing lists, which are also called discussion lists or list-servs. These different names refer to the same process whereby you can send an e-mail to a large group of people rather like using the CC facility. The process is managed by a hosting service that maintains a list of all the different discussion lists and the people who subscribe to them. It is run using a mail server, which is a piece of software that stores a mailing list of e-mail addresses to individuals. Two common mail server programs are *Listserv* and *Mailbase*. This software will copy your message to all the people on its mailing list (see Figure 2.1).

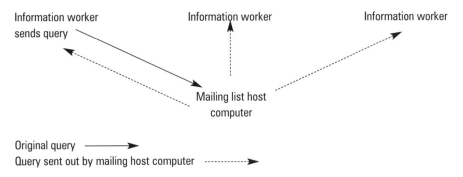

Fig. 2.1 *Diagram showing the operation of a mailing list*

There are thousands of mail lists (or discussion lists) available on the internet, and each is devoted to a particular topic and aimed at a specific audience. Mail lists can be used in a variety of ways and, in general, they provide a forum for:

- requests for factual information
- requests for advice and opinions or experiences
- information about new websites, products, publications
- assistance with software or hardware problems
- advice on buying or using new systems
- conference and meeting announcements
- staff development announcements
- information about vacancies.

Joining or leaving a mail list is a simple matter of sending an e-mail. Information about these lists is available from a number of sources including:

- *Topica* at www.topica.com/
- *Catalist* at www.Isoft.com/catalist.html
- *JISCmail* at www.jiscmail.ac.uk (see Figure 2.2)
- *Liszt.com* at www.liszt.com

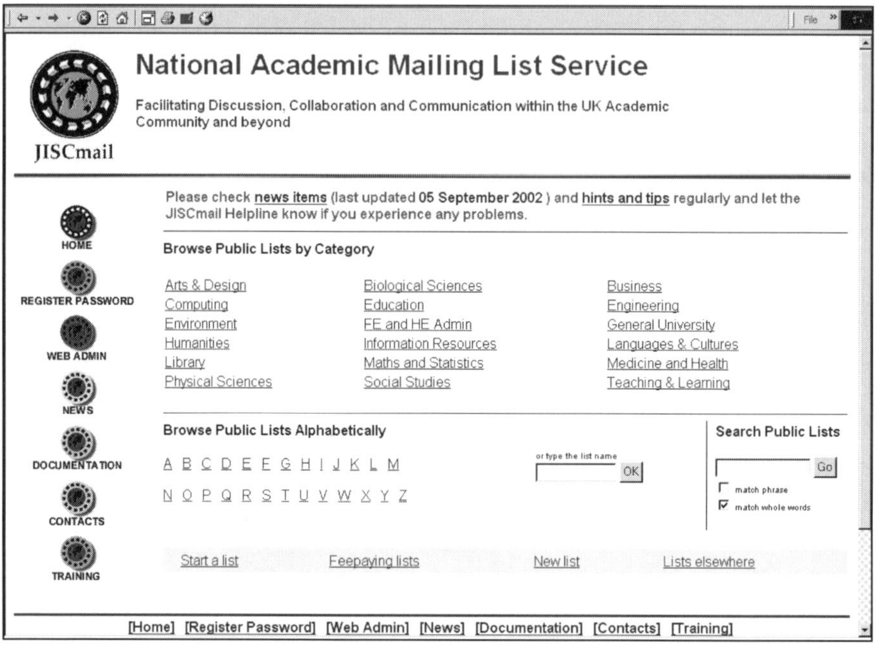

Fig. 2.2 *'JISCmail' home page*

- *Reference.com* at http://reference.com (also provides information on news-groups).

There are a number of different types of mail lists. Some are open to anyone who wishes to join, while others are closed to a specific clientele. Some discussion groups are moderated – i.e. messages are vetted before being posted to the list – while others are unmoderated. Many discussion lists maintain a database of previous discussions and these can be a useful source of information and advice. Some discussion lists develop a FAQ as this enables new members to tap into key questions and answers without established list members needing to re-visit old topics. In order to survive and thrive, discussion lists depend on four vital ingredients: content, participation, IT-support and management. If one of these elements goes wrong, then the mailing list can fizzle out.

Some lists are very active and may generate 100+ messages a day. Two useful facilities for managing this situation include digest messages and mail filtering:

1   **Digest messages**. Many discussion lists have the ability to send subscribers

a digest message. This collates all the messages received that day and sends it out as one e-mail. An index or contents page may be included in the digest.

2   **Mail filtering**. Most e-mail software has a facility for filtering mail into folders. This means that incoming mail, e.g. from a discussion list, is directed into a separate folder. This keeps one's main in-tray clear.

Table 2.2 summarizes the advantages and disadvantages of mail lists:

Table 2.2 *Advantages and disadvantages of mail lists*

Advantages	Disadvantages
Accessible from workplace	Information may not be from a credible or authoritative source
Many of them are completely open, i.e. anyone can join (closed lists exist too)	Time-consuming and time-wasting, e.g. reading irrelevant messages
Quick and easy method of communication	May be overwhelmed by e-mails
Provides access to a wide group of people	Discussions may be on very specific topics and not relevant to your particular interests
Speedy response – sometimes within minutes!	Discussions may go off-topic
Practical method of keeping up-to-date	Discussion lists are sometimes dominated by a few people
Used to access practical experience and expertise	Personal disputes may dominate or sour a discussion list
Good method of networking	
Based on e-mail, so doesn't require specialist software	

Examples of mail lists

Professional associations are often a useful source of information about discussion lists. For example, CILIP (the Chartered Institute of Library and Information Professionals; www.cilip.org.uk) currently provides a wide range of e-mail lists, including:

*   *Solo* – aimed at solo information professionals
*   *Lis-educ* – a JISCmail list for those involved in the provision of information to those involved in education and teacher training
*   *lis-cilip-reg* – a JISCmail list for librarians working towards their Charter
*   *Workplace* – available for information professionals in workplace libraries.

These e-mail lists all offer professional staff the opportunity to share ideas and information, and also to network with each other. For staff working in isolation – e.g. solo information and many workplace information professionals – they do offer a valuable opportunity to break down the isolation. They also offer an opportunity to gain professional help of the kind that is available from experienced colleagues in large libraries and information services – e.g. specific queries, say, about copyright issues, are likely to be answered with sound professional advice. For information workers who are working towards professional qualifications, they offer an opportunity to share ideas and experiences about the qualification process, and again they can offer a valuable source of support and motivation. This is particularly important to people who are relatively new to the profession and who have not yet built up their own network. The e-mail discussion list offers a valuable ready-made network.

The American Library Association (ALA) provides an extensive list of their mailing lists, including both open and closed lists. Examples of open lists include:

- *YALSA-L* – provides news and information about the ALA and a channel of communication for feedback to the ALA
- *YA-URBAN* – aimed at LIS staff in large urban public library systems who serve young adults.

Closed lists are often related to specific projects or committees – for example:

- *YALSACOM* is a closed list for committee chairs, committee members and boards of directors for committee business.

Access to New Zealand library discussion lists is available via www.vuw.nz/ dlis/ssbubl/currawar/ediscgp.htm (accessed on 28 February 2002) and this provides hotlinks to other library discussion lists, e.g. Thornton and Bonario's library-oriented lists and electronic serials, and Australian electronic discussion groups via *OZLISTS*.

E-mail mail lists are available for different groups of library and information staff across the world. Some groups may be focused on a relatively small interest area. For example, Libraries and Information for Health Network Northwest (LIHNN) provides an e-mail discussion list via JISCmail. The archive of this list for February 2002 shows contents ranging from 'Another successful ECDL librarian' (celebrating the success of an individual), through book requests, to information about forthcoming courses and events. This e-mail discussion list obviously plays a key role in the organization and administration of local training events. It also enables health information workers to keep up-to-date with new developments. For example, a new librarians' portal (www.nelh.nhs.uk/librarian/; accessed 2 February 2002) aiming to support librarians in their evolving role is advertised via the discussion list.

Mail lists are an important source of staff development and are examples of communities of interest, i.e. they enable people to keep up-to-date and to network with other professionals interested in the same theme or topic. They offer an important source of professional help and support. The author subscribes to a number of different discussion lists, such as a virtual learning environment list at vle@jiscmail.ac.uk and a training and development list at UKHRD on network@list.ukhrd.co.uk. The latter service is managed by a publisher (Fenman) and is a good example of a list that provides a daily digest with a back-up database (accessible via www.fenman.co.uk). Subscribers are involved in training and development in both public- and private-sector organizations. The list provides a professional support network in the field of training and development. Individual requests for information and advice for running particular training sessions, sourcing e-learning resources, or requests for training activities on a particular topic, are likely to be replied to with a range of offers of information and advice. The author used their database while developing a new course on time management for library and information staff. A quick search on 'time management' resulted in more than 30 hits and a number of innovative training activities. These enabled her to develop a varied programme that included a number of activities that had been pre-tested by other trainers. One of the advantages of this resource is that it is provided by people working in the field, so it offers an approach that is often down-to-earth and practical.

Evaluation of mail or discussion lists

In 1996 Bill Downey carried out a survey of users of the mail lists (Downey, 1996) on *Deliberations* (www.lgu.ac.uk/deliberations – a site concerned with learning and teaching and used by information professionals in colleges and universities). He obtained the following responses to the question 'How valuable have you found it to be a member of various lists and what benefits do they bring?':

'You gain a sense of your intellectual community through electronic communication.'

> *'The physical location of your workplace becomes less important/irrelevant and isolation from your peer group bearable.'*
>
> *'It is an easy way to keep informed. Through "lurking", you can keep abreast of what people are thinking and discussing.'*
>
> *'Excellent for making new contacts.'*
>
> *'The most valuable lists have a technical orientation/are on support issues. Here questions can be asked and the "right" answer given.'*

Although many people clearly gained a wide range of benefits from using the mail lists, there were also significant barriers to electronic communication, as shown in the following quotations:

> *'No time to participate actively in lists. The age of information overload is here.'*
>
> *'Rude e-mails sent back to you in response – or even worse to the list. Opinions that are expressed in unpleasant or personal ways.'*
>
> *'A lack of netiquette. Once you have been on the receiving end, you think twice about contributing again.'*
>
> *'Feelings of guilt associated with reading and answering e-mail at work. It is not considered a legitimate use of work time but as an indulgence/a frivolous activity. Also seen as a displacement activity and not proper work. But there is also guilt associated with not reading/responding.'*
>
> *'Pressure on the lists to provide the right answer – which militates against discussion. Lists do not allow for proper intel-lectual discourse.'*

These responses show that there can be some discomfort with this form of electronic communication, and a sense of guilt may accompany every stage of the process. Some people feel that reading or answering your e-mail at work is a less-than-legitimate or meaningful activity, while deleting messages without reading them or never contributing to the lists is also guilt-provoking. Joining a list for most people implies a certain obligation to it. Membership of a professional discussion list is not an easy process. Many people are reticent about contributing something that is not a polished message, and this inhibits more spontaneous and conversational discussions (see Table 2.3 for guidance).

Table 2.3 *Making best use of mail lists*

Dos	Don'ts
Spend some time getting to know the group and its interests before sending your first message.	Use it for personal messages to individuals who subscribe to the discussion list.
Keep to the topic.	Send a message or response if you are feeling angry/upset by something you have just read.
Send clear and concise messages.	Get involved in personal disputes.
Use short quotations from previous messages to keep the context clear.	Use it to advertise.
If you ask for information then consider summarizing responses for the whole group.	Forget that it is a public forum.
Be polite and consider other people's feelings.	

The Spire Project, based in Australia, provides access to further information and ideas about mail lists, which are accessible on http://cn.net.au/discuss.htm (accessed 28 February 2002). Phil Bradley (1999) provides a clear and useful summary of discussion lists, and this was used as a resource in preparing this section.

Newsgroups

Newsgroups or Usenets are similar to discussion lists in that they provide an opportunity to share news with like-minded people. There are more than 50,000 newsgroups in existence and they are one of the largest public information resources in the world. An advantage of a newsgroup over e-mail is that it presents messages in hierarchical threaded lists. The user can read and post messages in a single environment rather than by a series of e-mails arriving at different times.

Newsgroups work in a similar way to discussion lists. An individual will send a message to a central source, which then copies it to individuals and/or other newsgroups. In this way messages can be sent all around the world extremely quickly. The main technical differences between discussion lists and newsgroups is that the newsgroup servers exchange postings between them, see Figure 2.3 and Table 2.4.

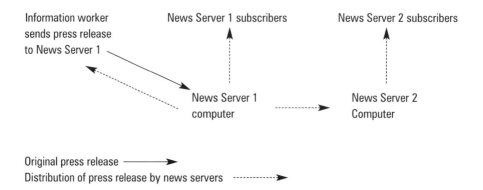

Fig. 2.3 *Diagram showing the operation of a newsgroup*

Table 2.4 *Advantages and disadvantages of newsgroups*

Advantages	Disadvantages
Quick and easy method of accessing up-to-date information	Can waste a lot of time
Provides access to huge audience	May be overwhelmed by e-mails
Extensive range of newsgroups that meet both serious and frivolous interests	Information may not be from a credible or authoritative source
	If you post a message, then your e-mail address is likely to be picked up and used, e.g. by internet marketing companies
	Many messages are off-topic, e.g. advertisements
	Newsgroups are used as a means of distributing pornography

Joining a newsgroup involves downloading and installing a newsreader and linking this into the ISP's news server. The newsreader provides access to identifying and subscribing to different newsgroups. Once a subscription is set up, then new postings from the newsgroups are received each time the user logs onto the ISP. There are many different newsreaders and the majority of them are free. *Internet Explorer* and *Netscape Navigator* have newsreader tools built into them. *Dejanews* is a website that enables you identify and subscribe to newsgroups without downloading software. It is available on www.dejanews.com. Other useful sources of information on newsgroups are http://reference.com and http://sunsite.unc.edu/usenet-I

Newsgroups are classified according to their subject, and the top level of the hierarchy is:

- **comp** computing topics
- **misc** miscellaneous topics
- **news** general news information
- **rec** hobbies, sports, arts
- **sci** science
- **soc** social newsgroups
- **talk** political issues.

Examples of newsgroups include: comp.infosystems, www.authoring.html, misc.education and news.admin.censorship, and a useful tool for finding newsgroups is http://groups.google.com/. Phil Bradley (1999) provides a clear and useful summary of newsgroups and this was used as a resource in preparing this section.

Bulletin boards

Bulletin or message boards provide a facility for discussion under various topic headings and not in real time. They allow individuals to respond to topics or threads in the group, or to begin a new topic or thread by posting a comment or question. Any messages sent to a discussion group are permanently visible to everyone who has access to it.

There are millions of message boards available on the internet. Many news-oriented websites, search engines, virtual communities and specialist interest sites provide bulletin boards. Many library and information services provide bulletin boards within their websites as a means of enabling their customers to discuss ideas and share information. Some sites provide bulletin boards for LIS professionals and provide opportunities to share good practice, discuss 'hot' topics or gain support.

Discussion groups are a key component of many e-learning programmes, and people using a discussion group can come together in different groupings and explore a topic. They may work online to produce a group product such as a presentation or report. One of the advantages of using discussion groups is that they are asynchronous and so different people can log in and respond to messages or create new messages at a time that suits them. Discussion groups are discussed in the context of integrated learning environments in Chapter 3.

A wide range of software packages enable the use of bulletin boards within websites. Some are open to anyone to use, while others are closed to a particular audience. Sometimes online registration is required before you can access a bulletin board. A typical bulletin board provides the following features:

- indexes
- a basic search facility, e.g. by topic, author, keywords
- tools to enable you to view bulletins in a hierarchical format (this is often called threaded or unthreaded) where they are sorted by date/time
- facilities to enable messages to be selected, saved and downloaded
- facilities to indicate whether or not the user has read a particular message, e.g. red flags for unread messages.

While many bulletin boards are closed groups, e.g. for staff working within a particular organization, others are public. It is therefore important to be aware that some people who use them may be using a false name and may have ulterior and possibly even sinister motives for using the bulletin board.

Free Pint

An example of a general bulletin board for library and information workers is on the *Free Pint* (People interested in net tips) website, where the Free Pint Bar enables individuals to post questions and comments. The Student Bar helps students on information courses with academic queries, job search and general career queries. It can be accessed at www.freepint.com.

Webforms

Increasingly, libraries are moving to webforms that individuals must fill in online to ask their question or to provide information. Webforms have a number of e-learning applications, and common uses include:

- reference services
- administration of services such as mentoring programmes
- as a tool for obtaining information from participants on an e-learning programme.

Webforms are often used as a means of providing a reference service within a library or information unit. Examples of libraries with webforms for reference services include:

- *Ask The Librarian* offered by the Madden Library at California State University, Fresno

- *Ask Us Virtual Reference Service* offered by University of Michigan Library staff
- *EARL – Ask a Librarian* provided by UK public libraries.

Webforms may be used as a tool within staff development processes – for example, a mentoring scheme, where they may be used as a tool for enabling mentors and mentees to apply to be part of a mentoring programme. An example of this type of application is considered in Chapter 4.

Webforms are also sometimes used within e-learning programmes, e.g. as a means of evaluating the programme or obtaining information from participants. Webforms have the advantage that they include a series of prompts enabling the designer to ask specific questions and so obtain structured information from the respondent. They can also be printed out by the respondent, who may want to use the printed record within a portfolio of evidence.

Polling

Polling enables you to quickly set up a survey or questionnaire and obtain feedback from a wide range of people. It has a wide range of uses in e-learning, including:

- obtaining feedback from e-learners or e-tutors
- setting up and running simple assessment activities
- organizing meeting times, e.g. online chat or face-to-face session.

An example of its use is described in Chapter 3. Polling software is available from a number of sources, including www.soomerang.com (accessed 3 May 2002).

Instant messaging

Instant messaging enables you to send and display a message on someone's screen in a matter of seconds. Instant message systems often have friend or buddy lists that watch to see when one of the people on your list comes online so that you know the instant when you can start messaging them. For some people this may sound like a nightmare scenario, although it does offer the opportunity to provide immediate access to help and support. Examples of when instant messaging may be used in LIS include the provision of additional support to staff who are using new systems. It means that staff who are working on a busy reference or help point may message a colleague with a question and obtain an instant response. It obviously depends on both people being online with the relevant instant messaging systems in place. One real advantage of this type of communication is that it doesn't take members of staff away from their service point and users don't need to know that additional help is being requested. One trainer can support a number of people using this type of system.

Examples of instant messaging software include *ICQ* ('I seek you') available from www.icq.com and *AOL Instant Messenger* available from www. newaol.com/aim. The AOL message system currently has two features for sending and receiving messages and about 12 features for rejecting or erasing unwanted messages. The key to successful use of instant messaging within the library or information unit is for all parties to have discussed and agreed how it will be used. It is important to set clear boundaries around its use, otherwise it can become a major irritant and a distraction.

Chat or conferencing

Chat or conferencing software enables users and the information workers to hold a 'live' discussion by sending each other short written messages. The live discussion could be between a librarian and user, or it could be between two or more members of staff in the same or different libraries. Chat software may be used to support individual users, provide quick advice and guidance to a member of staff, e.g. someone at a remote library, or as a coaching tool.

Chat software normally enables public and/or private conversations to take place and, depending on the software, these may be with individuals or groups. Chats may take place in public chat arenas or else in private. Some chat software enables individual chat rooms to be set up so that different people can meet in different virtual places. Virtual learning environments include chat or conferencing software that enables these synchronous conversations to take place, and they may be supported by tools such as whiteboards. Whiteboards are the electronic equivalent of a blackboard and allow one or more users to write or draw on the screen while others watch.

Chatting online has a number of advantages as it can be a private form of communication, it is immediate and the text can be saved for future reference or training purposes. Chatting online can be helpful for people with hearing or speaking impairments, and it can also ease communication among those working in a second language. In addition, the text of a chat session may be used for training purposes. As with most tools there are disadvantages to online chat; these include the absence of non-verbal signals and the need to learn how to send and be comfortable with short telegraphic messages between two or more people. Some people don't feel comfortable with this form of communication, and there is the potential danger that the other person may log off and 'disappear'. However, an increasing number of people are becoming very experienced with this form of communication and there is an entire internet subculture built around chat.

Staff training plays a key role in making sure that staff are comfortable with this form of communication. It can take a while for someone to become comfortable using 'chat' and this is graphically described in the following example:

> *When we first started using 'chat' at the reference desk, it was weird, really weird. It was scary. The computer bonged at us whenever someone hit the chat Web page, and I had a tendency to jump immediately to the screen that told me what IP address this visitor was coming from and what browser he was using, not that any of that mattered. Then I'd just sit there, staring in anticipation at the screen . . .*
>
> *Despite the strangeness of communicating via chat, it didn't take long to get accustomed to it. We discovered that users tended to send many short messages rather than one long paragraph. The transcripts didn't make complete linear sense, but while you're in the conversation, it's understandable. It certainly eases the anxiety of empty waiting time . . .*
>
> Broughton (2001 p1)

Kelly Broughton was writing as reference co-ordinator in the Jerome Library at Bowling Green State University in Ohio, USA, and using software called *HumanClick* that enables the user and the librarian to exchange chat messages. In addition, the software may enable the librarian to:

- pre-store messages (canned messages) that can be added to the software and made available from a drop-down list
- show things online to the user, e.g. by 'pushing' web pages that will open up on the user's screen, e.g. from a database
- fill in an online form, e.g. a database search form or an interlibrary loan form, and e-mail the chat session to the user or another librarian
- refer the user to another member of the LIS
- maintain logs of transactions for later analysis.

The facility to 'push' web pages is extremely useful in chat-based information skills training, as it enables the information worker to provide visual examples to support the text message:

> *This is an enormous advantage. It is extremely difficult to teach someone by only using the written word. Nothing to point to. No facial expression to discern. Nothing to observe if they could really do it on their own . . .!*
>
> Broughton (2001 p1)

As a result of the positive impact of using the *HumanClick* software, the library obtained a new product that is specifically aimed at libraries called *Virtual Reference Desk*. This offers an extensive range of features including transcripts with URLs, statistical reports for libraries, queuing and customization features, and training. It also offers co-browsing and other collaboration features that allow library staff to escort users around the web and provide a personalized training service. In the future they hope to add voice and video features.

Chat or conference software provides a facility for a group of people to get together and work in a virtual space by chatting online. This facility is becoming increasingly popular as an e-learning tool as it enables large and small groups to work together with or without a tutor. As with one-to-one chat, it does take a while to become comfortable with working in this type of environment. There is the potential for chaos if everyone 'speaks' at once, and the following processes – very similar to those used in formal face-to-face meetings – are often used as a means of managing the process:

Tips for using chat or conference rooms

1   Appoint a chairperson.
2   Signal when you want to speak using a '?'. The chairperson then invites you to speak.
3   Send short messages.
4   If you want to send long messages, then split them into chunks and indicate that a message continues, either with (more) or by using a series of full stops . . .
5   Limit your conference room sessions, e.g. to no more than an hour or one item of business. Most people find chat sessions demand high levels of concentration.

Tips for joining a conference

1   When you enter a conference room and other people are already present, then you will not be able to see the discussions that took place before you arrived.
2   Indicate your presence with a 'Hello'.
3   Wait a minute or two so that you can understand some of the context of the conversation.
4   Once you feel ready, then plunge in and get going.

It does take time to tune into group sessions and to be able to follow the conversation. This is illustrated in the following transcript from a conference session that took place as part of a project management course. Names have been changed to protect the privacy of the individuals.

A conference session from a project management course

Clare is the tutor and Helen and Jane are two information specialists working in higher education, while George and Anthony work in the computer industry. In this session you can see that the messages are short and informal. Spelling errors and abbreviations are acceptable. The tutor adds some non-verbal input, e.g. 'nods@G', as this can help the session move along.

Jane has joined #prm@ulh.
Clare says: Hi Jane
Jane says: Hi - sorry I'm late.
George: Hi Jane
Clare says: OK - it's any question time
Helen says: Can you explain a bit more
Helen says: about what is required for the second assessment!
Clare says: It's basically your project plan using MS Project
Clare says: See p. 38 of your guide
Clare says: Any specific queries about asignment 2?
Helen says: The assigment mentions a financiaL plan...
Jane says: p.24 of the Guide says a report of up to 1500 words excluding appendices. What would go in the report?
Clare says: nods@G
Clare says: I'lL respond to H and then J
Clare says: H do you want to finish your ?

Helen says: Is it necessary to include...

Helen says: As it's not really relevant in my context.

Clare says: H it's ok to miss it out but justify why you are doing that

Helen says: Thanks!

Clare says: J - what goes into your report is basically the right hand side of the list on p. 38/39

Clare says: A or G any ?s

Jane says: But that seems mainly to be MS project reports - I don't know that I'd need anywhere near 1500 words for the other bit

Anthony says: Wish i'd looked at p38 b4

Clare says: Yes, J it is mainly MS Project reports.....

Clare says: but you need to summarise key aspects with printouts e.g. in an Appendix

Jane says: Clare, in your emaiL you say themes 2 and 3 - should that be themes B & C?

Clare says: J - yes.

Clare says: Tony - look at p.38 later and send in any queries. I think it will make...

George says: C alL this is extremely useful, could it be kept on the VLE intact for future ref?

Clare says: better sense when you look at the page

Clare says: G - I'lL get a copy for you...

Clare says: IT permitting

Jane says: OK - I think I understand the assignment - the wordy bits would just backup and justify the reports?

Clare says: J - that's rigth. The words set the context and connect it together.

Clare says: Any more queries/comments?

Jane says: Fine. Thanks.

Jane says: Can I echo 2 of G's comments? a) a copy of this would be usefuL and for those not here. b) I would like more help using MS Project, particularly in tracking a project.

Clare says: J what kind of help would be most useful?

Helen says: As a complete beginner to MS Project....

George says: We alL have gone about 1/3 of the way in the unit . Might it be helpfuL if we had a face to face plenary to present our project briefly to each other and get feedback on whether or not it comes across to any and alL third parties as if they were project clients/stakeholders at that?

Helen says: I would find another lab session useful
Clare says: Thanks G. Would anyone else find another lab session useful?
Jane says: Another practicaL session if poss. where we could try updating the projects with yr guidance
Clare says: OK. When?
...
Jane says: Got to go. Bye.
Clare says: Bye Jane
Jane has left 194.80.48.88.

Further information about chat in libraries is available on www.le.ac.uk/li/distance/eliteproject/elib/chat.html.

Internet telephony

Synchronous communications now includes internet telephony, which is the ability to make phone calls via the internet. The advantage of internet telephony is that it enables individuals to make long-distance phone calls through the computer and the internet without paying expensive long-distance phone charges. However, it requires relatively up-to-date computers with access to a fast modem and large RAM memory, otherwise the sound quality can be poor.

Individuals using the internet for phone calls need to obtain a microphone for the computer and also to install internet telephone software. Increasingly organizations are combining internet telephony, e-mail, traditional phones, voice mail and facsimile transmissions into a powerful new unified messaging services.

Videoconferencing

Videoconferencing has been available for years, but previously required specialist and very expensive equipment installed in specialist rooms. In recent years videoconferencing packages have been developed for use on standard desktop computers. The use of desktop videoconferencing doesn't appear to be widespread in LIS but its use is increasing. One library that has used desktop videoconferencing for reference services is Emory University, Atlanta, GA, USA, and an evaluation of their work concluded that users were less enthusiastic about the system than anticipated but that 'desktop video does have potential in library settings where there is remote access to information' (Pagell, 1996, 25).

Videoconferencing and general reference work

In a joint project at the University of Michigan, the Shapiro Undergraduate Library and the Residence Hall Libraries collaborated in using a desktop videoconferencing program to provide reference services to students located in residence halls across the campus. Evaluation of the project showed that students used it to ask general reference enquiries rather than in-depth research requests. Those students who used the service were positive about it and said they would consider using it again. The librarians who participated in the project were enthusiastic about the potential of the technology.

One of the major problems was the inconsistent quality of the audio and video – some evenings the performance was so poor that it was better to communicate by telephone. Another problem for library staff was the lack of technical support or knowledge, and this indicates the importance of having easy and reliable access to technical specialists. One point raised in the evaluation was that some students and a few staff were quite self-conscious while on camera. Some students even refused to go on camera.

This example shows the importance of technical issues in enabling desktop videoconferencing to be used successfully in libraries. At the time of writing in 2002 it appears to be used infrequently, but as the technology improves in quality and drops in price, it becomes another option for library and information workers to communicate with each other and their customers. In the meantime innovative projects such as that at the University of Michigan offer a route forward for developing professional practice in desktop video conferencing.

Further information available on www.ala.org/acrl/paperhtm/a09.html (accessed 9 May 2001).

Videoconferencing and childrens' librarians

A 1999 survey on children's service needs by the Nebraska Library Commission showed that librarians who work with children wanted:

- informal discussion meetings to share ideas and concerns about events that are part of the yearly library calendar for youth
- opportunities to interact with colleagues from other parts of Nebraska
- continuing education events that don't require excessive travel
- events that are reasonably priced.

In response to the survey, the Nebraska Library Commission Youth Advisory Board suggested that one way of tackling this issue was to introduce interactive videoconferences. This involved setting up 10 initial videoconference site locations and these were chosen so as to minimize travel requirements. There was no charge for attending events. Participants could interact with their colleagues from around the state using the videoconferencing facilities. The dates of the meetings were set to allow plenty of time for follow-through and implementing ideas shared at the videoconference. This example demonstrates the potential for a blended training solution based on the use of face-to-face sessions and videoconferencing.

Further information available from:

www.nlc.state.ne.us/libdev/travelnearbor.html (accessed on 28 February 2002).

Videoconferencing and health information

In the USA, the National library for Medicine and the National Network of Libraries of Medicine are important resources for improving internet access and providing related training to the public health workforce. As part of their current programme the University of Nevada is providing on-site internet training to public health professionals in health departments, rural health centres, state health divisions and the Nevada state laboratory. They have selected a blended approach to training and the on-site training is supported by training via a state-wide videoconferencing system. This helps to maximize the benefits of face-to-face training and also to reduce time lost from the workplace due to travel.

Videoconferencing and supporting people with disabilities

In the UK, the introduction of the Disability Discrimination Act is continuing to result in many development projects to help support people with disabilities. Many public and educational libraries support their staff in gaining skills and expertise in using sign language, e.g. British Sign Language. E-learning offers new possibilities for the provision of support and services to this group of clients. City College Manchester worked on a videoconferencing project in the late 1990s funded by QUILT. The aim was to train all staff working with deaf students at the college to become confident in using videoconferencing technology to help support these students. This project was started by communication support workers and tutors and then developed by other staff within the college. One of the useful benefits of this project was the development of guidelines on using this medium with people whose hearing is impaired:

1 Wear plain clothing which contrasts with your skin .
2 Use a dark blue screen as background.
3 Communicating through BSL via videoconferencing is very tiring because there is quite a loss of information, so keep your eyes relaxed with the right clothing and background.
4 Set up the linkup first. This takes ages and is better planned a week in advance. If deaf students are going to access the equipment independently, make sure you have a textphone number for the people at the other end – they will need it to check the linkup arrangements.

Virtual worlds

Some of the earliest forms of internet synchronous activity were online games through the creation of virtual worlds. These are often referred to by names such as MOO, MUD, MUXe, MUSE or MUSH. These names related to various forms of 'multiple user' environments, which often involve individuals assuming a character and then getting involved in virtual role play. Virtual worlds are often used as a form of e-learning within universities, where they have been adapted as an educational tool. Nowadays it is possible to access three-dimensional virtual worlds and to act out or explore a particular character or process.

Starting points for exploring these virtual worlds include:

- *MUing for Beginners* at www.cwrl.utexas.edu/moo/
- *MOO Links* at http://ebbs.english.vt.edu/moo.html
- *MUD Connector* at www.mudconnector.com
- *MUD Central* at www.mudcentral.com
- *MUD Cows FAQ* at www.moo.mud.org/moo-faq/.

Access to virtual communication tools

Previous sections presented a series of virtual communication tools that may be used for customer or staff training and development. While some of these tools are used on a standalone basis, many of the tools are commonly brought together to provide a range of communication options from one access point. Chapter

3 explores integrated learning environments, which typically include e-mail, bulletin boards, chat or conference rooms. Many organizations and groups use websites with virtual communication tools as a means of disseminating information, enabling individuals to make contact with other people, and also sharing ideas and concerns.

Many libraries and information units provide web-based access via their home page to bulletin board, e-mail and conferencing software, and these are used to host a variety of activities such as discussions about a particular book or theme, or a visit by a guest speaker. They offer a route for engaging people with the products and services offered by the library. An example of this type of service aimed at children is *Stories from the web* (www.storiesfromtheweb.org/; accessed 25 April 2002); this and other examples are explored in Chapter 4.

Many websites aimed at library and information professionals also offer access to a range of virtual communication tools and learning resources. For example, the Special Libraries Association (SLA) in the USA offers *Virtual SLA*, which provides access to discussion lists, chat rooms, information and members-only resources. It is available on www.sla.org/content/interactive/index.cfm; accessed 3 April 2002). This site provides useful guidelines for hosting chat rooms as well as an instruction guide for setting up a chat room. Another good example is the *Free Pint* site (see Figure 2.4).

Free Pint

Free Pint (people interested in net tips) provides a website that brings together a variety of facilities and resources for information workers. It was founded by three UK-based information workers – William Hann, Rex Cooke and Simon Collery – and it is disseminated fortnightly to nearly 50,000 subscribers. The *Free Pint* website is a lively and user-friendly site. It provides a free e-mail newsletter with tips on internet searching and website reviews. The site includes an archive of newsletters, and also a number of bulletin boards such as the Free Pint Bar and Student Bar. Overall, this site is a useful source of information on the internet and it provides a valuable service in helping students in networking and getting started with their careers. It can be accessed at www.freepint.com.

One of the advantages of virtual communication tools is that they are easily and cheaply accessible to all information workers. This means that solo information workers such as those working with voluntary or community groups can use this type of facility to create web-based access to information, resources and support for their customers.

Figure 2.4 *'Free Pint' home page*

An information worker and pre-school provision

One information worker involved in the provision of books to the under-fives set up a website for parents, librarians and support staff. She built up this website from scratch and introduced a basic discussion and chat facility. Her choice of a do-it-yourself site meant that the site was simple to use and uncluttered by an extensive range of facilities. She said it took her about two weeks to put the site together, and that although she had minimal technical skills these had developed as her project progressed. The end result was a simple and attractive website that was used by parents, librarians and support staff to exchange information and ideas about using books with the under-fives. The discussion group was often used by parents as a support service as people helped each other by discussing different ways of coping with young children.

In the voluntary sector a diverse range of sites are available. These may be managed and provided by one organization or they may be provided by a host organization. For example, the *Hull Daily Mail* newspaper provides an online website called *Beehive* (www.thisishull.co.uk), and this is an online network devoted to local community and voluntary groups. The network provides a way for non-profit-making organizations to share ideas and information on the internet. This site provides access to a wide range of bulletin boards on themes from arts and culture through to youth groups and organizations, and it also provides facilities for local organizations to create and upload their own website. The online help sheets and guides are simple and easy to use. The *Beehive* site is part of a UK national network of community sites. Similar services aimed at the community and voluntary groups are offered by other agencies. For example, the East Sussex Local Authority provides the *eSussex* website at www.essussex.org.uk (accessed 3 May 2002), and in addition to information this provides a range of virtual communication tools such as chat and bulletin boards. This type of site is often set up and maintained by library and information workers. Further information about community networking is available from: www.communities.org.uk (accessed 3 May 2002).

Some websites are linked around a particular theme or topic, and the following example explores the use of websites linked with communication tools to support mentoring.

Use of virtual communication tools to support mentoring

Mentoring is a process that enables library and information staff to learn by association with a role model, who is often a more experienced and senior member of staff. It is typically used to develop specific skills, for new recruits, for support and development and also for career development. The internet provides a tool for:

- enabling mentors and mentees to identify each other and establish a mentoring relationship
- discussions about mentoring
- disseminating training materials on mentoring
- disseminating information about mentoring.

The internet provides an ideal environment for identifying and locating a mentor, and individual library services or professional groups may set up sites to enable mentors and mentees to register and then identify a mentor/mentee. The University of Georgia Libraries have established a mentor programme which encompasses 'counseling and guidance, collaboration, research assistance, and professional development needs.' It is hosted on a website (www.libs.uga.edu/mentor/informa-tion.html; accessed 28 February 2002) that provides access to a mentoring resources web page containing many resources and links to mentoring information. The scheme is open to all library staff who have a skill or interest which they would like to share or learn about. Individuals can sign up as a mentor or guide and include their information on a database. Staff who are seeking a mentor can search the database using a range of criteria. This scheme is very open in that the mentoring relationship can be a one-time event or an ongoing process. It is up to the individuals concerned to come to an agreement that will meet their needs. Information exchange between participants is confidential.

The Association of College and Research Libraries (ACRL), a unit of the American Library Association offers a new member mentoring programme that is advertised via the internet on www.ala.org/acrl/mentoringprogram.html (accessed 28 February 2002). This scheme is open to new ACRL members and the mentors need to have been active ACRL members for more than five years.

ACRL see the mentoring scheme as an important professional development route: 'It is increasingly important for new librarians to develop professional relationships with experienced senior librarians whose advice and direction will help guide them.' ACRL recognizes that mentoring is a mutually beneficial process 'in addition to the fun and satisfaction of helping a new professional, experienced librarians and leaders who serve as mentors will gain a fresh perspective on academic library issues and concerns.'

A free downloadable learn-to-mentor toolkit is available from the National Mentoring Partnership on www.mentoring.org/training/TMT/ (accessed 28 February 2002). Further information on mentoring is available from DeShane and Mahaley (2001) Mentoring an annotated bibliography, 2nd. Edition. www.slabf.org/mentorbib.html.

Summary

Virtual communication tools offer new approaches to delivering library instruction, training programmes and also professional communications. The examples selected in this chapter demonstrate that information workers often use virtual communication tools as a means of providing additional support and/or overcoming time and travel issues associated with attending face-to-face programmes. In some instances virtual communication tools are used to offer new services to specific groups of staff or customers. They are also an essential means of continuous professional development either through formal programmes or by informal learning. Communities of interest and communities of practice often use these tools to share and develop their professional knowledge.

3

Integrated learning environments

Introduction

The purpose of this chapter is to provide an overview of integrated learning environments. These are web-based learning environments that provide a range of tools and facilities for learners. In some respects they can be considered as a 'one-stop shop' for a particular learning experience. Integrated learning environments are available in a wide range of forms: web-based 'learning portals', virtual learning environments, and also alternatives such as messaging and collaboration systems.

Reading this chapter will enable library and information workers to explain the concepts of a learning portal, a virtual learning environment and a managed learning environment. It also provides guidance on the key features of common virtual learning environments, with examples of how they are used in practice. Finally, this chapter identifies alternative routes such as commercial communications software and also using a host site to providing integrated learning environments.

The learning portal

Portal
... n. a gate or doorway, esp. a great or magnificent one: any entrance.

Chambers Twentieth Century Dictionary (1975)

A learning portal provides access to a range of e-learning facilities and resources, including web-based training materials, news and information, support, guidance, virtual communication and also administration tools. The content of a typical learning portal includes:

- A learner management system
  - — student enrolment and collection of fees
  - — student tracking, e.g. usage and progress
  - — student outcomes
- Web-based training materials
  - — virtual communication tools
  - — development software
  - — access to information and learning resources.

Examples of learning portals include:

- www.learndirect.co.uk (see Figure 3.1)
- www.trainingzone.co.uk
- www.click2learn.com
- www.learn2.com
- www.digitalthink.com
- www.easycando.com

Fig. 3.1 *'Learndirect' portal*

- www.headlight.com
- www.enlighten.com.

External portals are accessible to many organizations while an internal portal is limited to a specific organization and is made available via a corporate intranet. The internal portal is likely to provide the following facilities:

- a corporate university
- internal training and development programmes
- virtual communication tools, e.g. to support internal training programmes and schemes such as mentoring or online communities of practice
- corporate news and documents
- access to specific and relevant external portals
- access to web-based information sources and training opportunities.

While some organizations design and produce their own learning portal – for example, *OnLINM* at the University of Leeds, while the *Virtual Campus* was originally designed for in-house use at the University of Lincoln, a large number of organizations use commercially available systems such as *WebCT* and *Blackboard*. These are often called virtual learning environments and they are explored in the next section.

Learning portals may also be set up in relationship to a specific topic or theme such as coaching or mentoring. Examples include:

- www.coachingnetwork.org.uk (see Figure 3.2)
- www.libs.uga.edu/mentor/information.html
- www.mentoring.org/training/TMT/.

Virtual learning environments

Recent years have seen an explosion in the range of tools and programmes for supporting online learning and teaching. This has resulted in the emergence of a virtual learning environment (VLE) and, more recently, a managed learning environment (MLE). Although these two terms are often used interchangeably, there is a distinct difference between them:

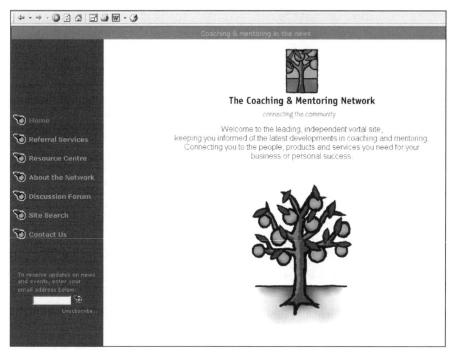

Fig. 3.2 *The 'Coaching & Mentoring Network' portal*

VLEs are web-based toolkits that facilitate learning through
the provision and integration of online teaching and learning
materials and tools. These materials and tools usually consist
of most or all of the following: facilities for electronic
communications such as discussion lists, bulletin boards and
chat rooms, facilities for groupwork online; online learning
materials; links to remote resources; course timetables and
reading lists; online assessment tools; and an administrative
area, including a log-in access function.

INSPIRAL (2001)

MLEs include all the functions of a VLE, while integrating
other information systems and processes of the institution, such
as student record databases.

INSPIRAL (2001)

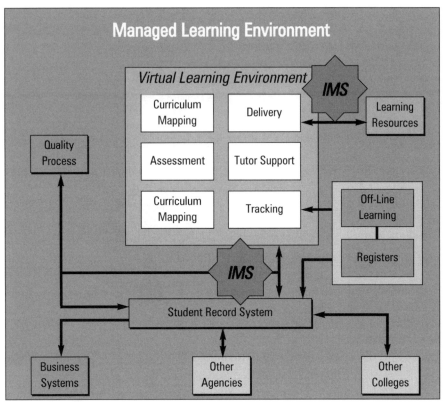

Fig. 3.3 *The relationship between MLEs and VLEs*

So, VLEs are a subset of MLEs and this relationship between VLEs and MLEs was illustrated by BECTA and JISC and is presented in Figure 3.3.

The next stage in the development of virtual learning and information environments is the linking of VLEs and MLEs with digital and hybrid libraries. This will provide an integrated learning environment, enabling library and information workers to collaborate even closer with educators. The feasibility of this development is currently being actively researched in the UK. An example of this research is the INSPIRAL project funded by JISC (Currier, 2001).

VLE Facilities

Virtual learning environments (VLEs) provide all the facilities that are required to enable learning to take place in virtual space. In many respects they replicate many of the facilities seen in physical learning situations, as shown in Table 3.1:

Table 3.1 *Comparison of virtual and traditional learning environments*

Virtual environment	Traditional equivalent
Learning materials and resources	Resources available within a library and information unit
Online assessment	Examinations
Notice or bulletin boards	Noticeboards
Discussion forum and conference rooms	'Rooms' where tutors and learners work together
Virtual cafés	Cafés
Help desk	Help desk
Monitoring and tracking systems	Registers, tutor records

VLEs are currently revolutionizing how colleges, universities and increasingly schools deliver their learning and teaching, and they are widely used across the world. They support the learning and teaching process within a single software environment. Common examples of virtual environments include *Blackboard* (see Figures 3.4 and 3.5), *WebCT* and *Virtual Campus*. These learning environments are typically owned by the whole institution, who employ specialist staff to manage and administer these large and complex systems. Some of the advantages and disadvantages of VLEs are described in Table 3.2.

Table 3.2 *Advantages and disadvantages of VLEs*

Advantages	Disadvantages
Anywhere and anytime learning	Cost of the commercially available systems such as *Blackboard*, *WebCT*
Opens access to a wider range of learners, e.g. teenagers, housebound, older people	Set-up time, finding, buying and writing courseware
Opens access to workplace learning, e.g. can be fitted around staff rotas	Time taken to learn how to use the VLE
Provides support for distance learners (including peer-group support)	Learners need access to PC and internet
Easy to manage a group of students	Need tutors or facilitators with e-tutoring skills
Controlled environment for learners	Inappropriate use of VLE
Easy administration of virtual classroom	Suspicion and cynicism about this form of learning
Provides an up-to-date and professional image	Technical problems that mean the system is down

VLEs typically provide access to the following tools, which may be organized in such a way that learners only have access to the tools linked to their particular programme of study:

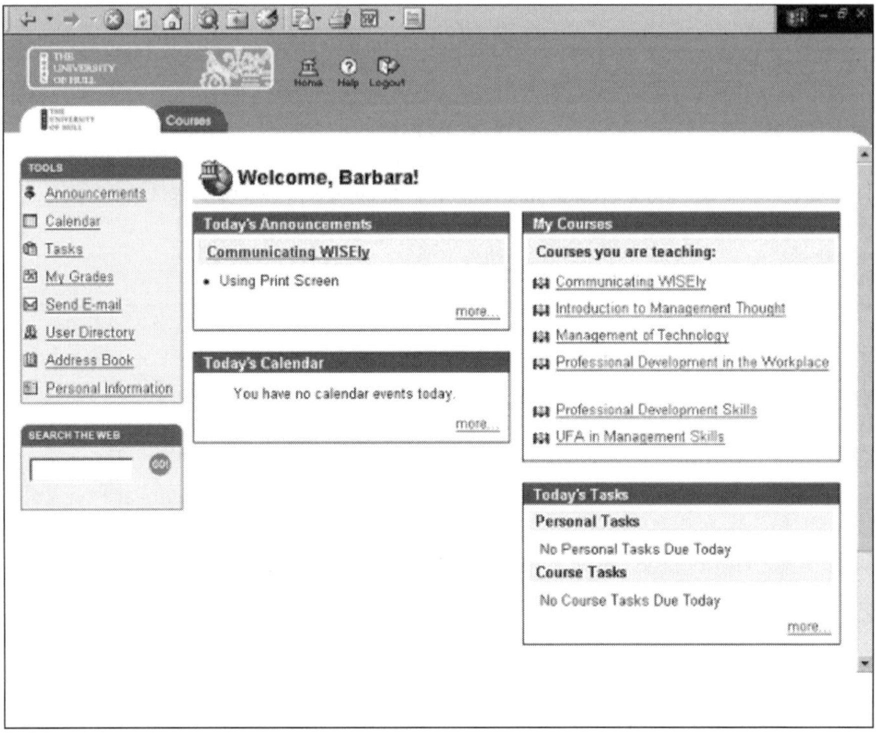

Fig. 3.4 *Home page in 'Blackboard'*

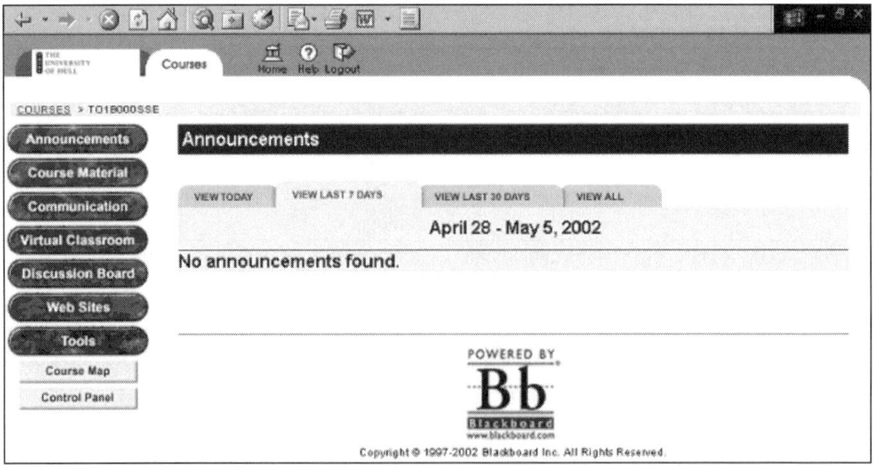

Fig. 3.5 *Facilities available for a particular group of students using 'Blackboard'*

- structured learning programmes
- information sources
- communication tools
- assessment tools
- personal management tools
- administrator and tutor tools.

Structured learning programmes include resources such as self-study materials, multimedia packages, and also online assessment tools, questionnaires and inventories. These may be developed in-house or as part of a collaborative project, and the suppliers of VLEs often provide a standard bank of learning and training materials. Web-based training materials are described in some detail in Chapter 4.

The majority of VLEs are designed in such a way that the course tutor can provide access to information sources via direct or hot internet links. Clicking on these links results in the learner having immediate access to the resources via the screen. Examples of information sources include:

- information directly related to a programme of study
- information about the organization or department
- national newspapers and information sources
- search engines.

Early users of virtual learning environments frequently used them in a limited way as a means of disseminating information to students. This could be information about topics such as using the library, searching the internet, or standard methods of referencing. Nowadays, the use of virtual learning environments has broadened and the use of their communication tools is becoming central to e-learning. The communications facility normally provides access to the following tools (see Figure 3.6):

- noticeboards, which are used by library staff, tutors and instructors to disseminate notices and files to students
- discussion groups, where students and/or tutors can communicate by leaving messages for each other
- conference or chat rooms, where a group of students and/or tutors hold a live chat session.

The use of these communication facilities is a vital part of e-learning and is briefly outlined in examples later in this chapter and also in subsequent chapters.

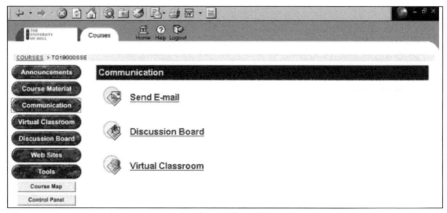

Fig. 3.6 *Access to virtual communication tools on 'Blackboard'*

Table 3.3 summarizes these tools and also explores their use by library and information workers.

Table 3.3 *Use of VLE communication tools by library and information workers in educational organizations*

Tool	Brief description	Application in library and information services (LIS)
E-mail	Many VLEs provide e-mail facilities. These may be limited to e-mailing members of a particular group and sending messages within the VLE, i.e. not external to it.	A user sends an e-mail with an enquiry and the information worker replies by e-mail or other means
Notice or bulletin boards	As their name suggests, these enable e-tutors to post notices to their learners. Some systems enable the attachment of files.	LIS staff use noticeboards to inform users of changes in services, news items (e.g. about information resources) or other news.
Discussion groups	These provide a facility for discussion (much like an internet newsgroup) under various topic headings and not in real time. They allow the students to respond to topics or threads in the group, or to begin a new topic or thread by posting a comment or question. Any messages sent to a discussion group are permanently visible to everyone who has access to it.	These may be used to promote interest and a sense of community between users; e.g. some public libraries run discussion groups on current news topics and/or books. They are commonly used in courses, as they enable students and tutors to discuss new ideas, problems or projects. See Chapters 3 and 9.

Conference or chat rooms	Conference rooms provide a 'real time' conferencing facility (much like internet chat or a face-to-face seminar). Many conference rooms are text-based, although others provide facilities for sound and images too. They offer opportunities for one-to-one and also small-group discussions.	Conference or chat rooms are commonly used for small group tutorials, peer learning activities (e.g. two librarians working at different sites), mentoring discussions, and also general socialization. See Chapters 3 and 9.

An important component of all learning processes is assessing learning and the achievement of the learning outcomes of the programme. E-learning offers a wide range of assessment opportunities and these are discussed in some detail in Chapters 8 and 9. One form of assessment is the use of question sets such as multiple choice questions to test specific knowledge, and a particular strength of VLEs is that they provide assessment tools that enable e-tutors to:

- create interactive learning activities
- diagnose student knowledge and skills
- monitor student progress
- formally assess student learning.

E-tutors need to design and plan their assessment activity, and this can then be input into the assessment tool to develop a set of questions. The types of questions that are normally available include:

- select current answer from drop-down list boxes
- select current answer using radio button responses
- fill-in-the-blanks
- input short text
- select true or false statements.

Responses are automatically assessed and appropriate feedback is given to both the student and the tutor. Tutors will have access to summaries of their students' performance and these can normally be transferred onto spreadsheets in office applications. Assessment tools enable the tutor:

- to create questions using a set of question types;

- to arrange questions into sets to be delivered together;
- to assign attributes to the question set, such as
  — whether the questions are presented in a random order
  — whether the question set is time-constrained
  — the pass mark for the question set;
- to provide feedback on a per-question and/or question-set basis
- to provide a copy of the feedback that the student can view at a later date, using the diary facility.

Online assessment tools are extremely useful for e-tutors who are involved in assessing the learning of large groups of students. Their application in a library context is described in the next section of this chapter.

The personal management facility enables individual learners to keep a diary, update their user details (if the VLE is part of a MLE, then this will update all relevant records), keep track of online results from self-diagnostic tests and formal assessments, and also change their password.

The tools facility is normally only available to specific users such as library and information staff, tutors and instructors, and system administrators. They enable individuals to:

- create and manage a group of students
- update and manage the virtual learning environment
- set up and create online assessment tools and activities
- monitor student activity, e.g. login, length of time online, results of online assignments
- view enrolment information.

The layout of the tools facility in *Blackboard* is demonstrated in Figure 3.7.
VLEs typically allow different types and levels of access:

- student or guest access
- tutor access
- administrator or manager access.

Each of these types of access enables the user to work in and manipulate the virtual environment. For example, students are typically allowed access to specific learning materials and resources, they will be able to communicate with other students in their group, and take specific online assessments. Tutors normally have access to student tracking information, e.g. details of logins and online work, and

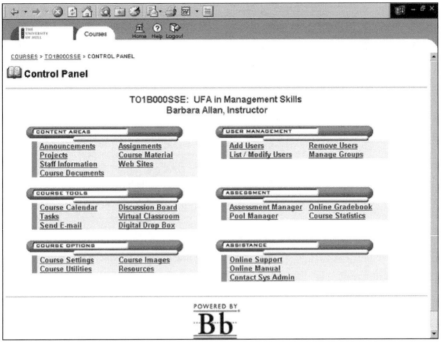

Fig. 3.7 *'Blackboard' tools facility*

assessment results. Administrator or manager access privileges enable them to add new courses and provide access to the system to students and tutors.

Learning to use a VLE

As can be seen above, VLEs provide an extensive list of facilities, and individual library and information workers will need to spend some time exploring and learning how to use the facilities available in their organization's VLE. Typically a VLE contains online tutorials for students and also for tutors or instructors. Working through these is likely to take a couple of hours and will provide a good overview of the system and its capabilities. In addition, the home websites of these VLEs often provide excellent tutorial and demonstration features, as well as product news and FAQ sections.

Kent (2001) describes a co-ordinated approach in which IT trainers and liaison librarians worked together to develop a *WebCT Training Pathway* 'to bring together the range of *WebCT* related materials already available into a coherent structure, to develop a support site web interface and to develop training courses.' (See Figure 3.8.) They offer a blended approach of training sessions, drop-in

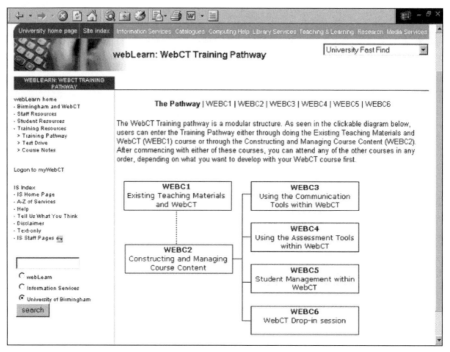

Fig. 3.8 *'WebCT Training Pathway'*

sessions and web-based learning activities to enable staff to develop their knowledge and skills about using *WebCT* to support learning and teaching.

VLEs and library and information workers

VLEs are increasingly being used by library and information staff as a means of supporting their end-users and also as a tool in the staff development process. Library and information specialists can take a variety of roles within the VLE environment – e.g. strategic, operations, learning and teaching – and this is explored in some more detail in Chapter 10. In colleges and universities they offer a shared learning environment where information specialists, tutors and lecturers, and technical staff can work together to provide an integrated learning environment for students.

The adoption of VLEs by many colleges and universities has led to many library and information services now offering wide-ranging support to staff and students to enable them to utilize e-learning fully. This is often carried out through a range of different services, including help-desk (e-mail, phone, face-to-face), training sessions, drop-in surgeries, materials development and management, and co-tutoring. The library and information services tradition of providing student services for extensive opening hours and operating after hours means that they are ideally placed to offer help desks. This model is used at Flinders University in Australia (McBain and Rowe, 2001), where typical help-desk queries include:

- log in problems
- access problems, e.g. difficulties in navigating within *WebCT*
- course management, e.g. adding students to a course
- problems with particular tools within *WebCT*
- remote-access problems.

In addition to offering help-desk support, many library and information workers are involved in other aspects of supporting student learning via a VLE. These staff are often involved in the content of programmes, e.g. developing learning resources, providing guides to web-based resources, and maintaining and updating the learning environment. Library and information workers are increasingly becoming involved in collaborative work with academic staff and subject specialists in supporting student learning via a VLE using e-mails, discussion groups or conferences. They may be involved in the following activities:

- providing support to individual students, e.g. responding to queries using e-mail or discussion groups
- providing support to specific courses, e.g. managing the VLE and the provision of access to information resources
- providing support to groups of students, e.g. running assessed information skills units.

The following examples demonstrate some of the learning and teaching activities that library and information staff are involved in when using VLEs.

Information skills module for postgraduate students

At Hull University, staff from the Brynmor Jones Library provide a course on information searching skills for postgraduate students and this is delivered via their VLE Blackboard (Pennie 2001). This programme is based on a training materials model of e-learning and there is an option for students to have their work assessed and gain academic credit for the unit.

E-learning information services staff development programme

Information services staff at the University of Birmingham, UK, are involved in an innovative online course that enables them to experience and develop skills as e-tutors. This course uses *WebCT* and the following communication tools:

1   Noticeboards – the main method for tutors to disseminate information to the group.
2   Discussion groups – the 'virtual classroom'. Participants use them for whole group and small group discussions. The course includes a number of group projects and members of each group work together in discussion groups. This enables individual group members to access the discussion group at a time and place to suit them. They fit their course work and course communications in and around their work.
3   Chat rooms – sometimes tutors lead chat room sessions, while at other times tutorless groups meet, e.g. to discuss their work together. Guest speakers can also take part in chat sessions.

It is worth noting that this programme also includes a number of face-to-face workshops, which are held at key stages of the programme, e.g. induction, mid-programme review and final evaluations. This programme is described in more detail in Chapter 6 and example learning activities are included in Chapter 9.

NVQs and e-learning

The University of Lincoln Learning Resources department is committed to staff development, and their staff development activities include a National Vocational Qualification (NVQ) route. A small number of staff opt to take NVQs each year. Each NVQ candidate works with an internal assessor (an experienced member of the department who is also a qualified NVQ assessor). Sometimes candidates and assessor are based on different campuses, perhaps 50 miles apart.

The university's VLE (the *Virtual Campus*) provides noticeboards, discussion areas and conference rooms. This can be used by NVQ candidates and assessors as a communication channel. As many of the candidates are part-time, it enables them to communicate with each other and their assessor at times that fit into their work schedule. One of the advantages of using the discussion group is that a permanent record of discussions is held online and, in some instances, this acts as a FAQ database. It can also be used as evidence in the candidate's portfolio.

Use of *WebCT* in assessing an information skills unit

Grave, L. et al. (2001) report the work of Sally Patalong of Coventry University, describing how she uses the *WebCT* assessment tools as a means of assessing the learning outcomes of 700 computing students who are studying an information skills unit. The sheer size of the task meant that marking written exercises was not feasible. The information skills unit was delivered using a blended approach and the assessment involves the use of multiple choice questions at four stages during the module. The information skills assessment counts for 10% of first-year marks for that module. Student evaluation of the module and the online assessment was generally positive.

OnLINM at Wilberforce College

Wilberforce College is a member of the *OnLINM* Consortium along with 12 other colleges in Yorkshire and Humberside. The *OnLINM* VLE (www.onlinm.ac.uk/), which was developed by Leeds University, allows users to build a virtual college with learning floors for each subject area, complete with learning rooms within which resources can be placed for students to access. Individual tutors or library staff can provide a diverse range of learning resources and activities in the learning environment. The environment itself is built around visual images of a college and this helps provide a familiar feel to students. An example of the *OnLINM* environment is shown in Figure 3.9.

Staff and students can access the system by any internet-linked machine. Students can therefore access the resources from any machine in college and from any internet-linked machine elsewhere. Access within college tends to be from the Learning and Resource Centre adjacent to the library. The assistant librarian is trained in *OnLINM* and has attended one of the initial training courses at Leeds University. They also have a designated IT technician, who provides technical support for staff and students using the *OnLINM* system.

Trevor Buttery (2001) describes the strengths of the system, which include:

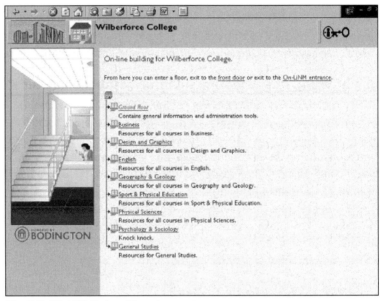

Fig. 3.9 *'OnLINM' virtual learning environment*

1   Differentiation can be built into course materials by the application of access rights.
2   All learning materials are password protected.
3   A wide range of learning materials in different forms can be made available for students, including:
— multiple-choice questions that mark themselves and give group and individual feedback immediately
— short-answer questions
— discussion rooms
— website links
— pigeon-hole facilities
— powerpoint demonstrations
— a receptacle for storing lesson notes/worksheets.

One weakness in the current system is that *OnLINM* at present will not link to any MIS system. This means that MIS support is time-consuming and difficult (e.g. generating passwords, maintaining staff usernames, checking access rights etc. Another problem is that, in general, the access control is clumsy and staff need a high level of skill to master it fully.

Other forms of integrated learning environment

The previous section focused on commercial virtual learning environments, which are now well established within the post-16 education sector. These large VLEs are expensive and generally require specialist staff to implement and support them. They are therefore not accessible to smaller libraries and information units. At the time of writing there are viable alternatives to the VLE: using commercial communications software packages or using communication tools hosted by another organization.

Commercial communications software packages

Many organizations now use commercial communications software packages that offer a mix of e-mail, messaging, bulletin board and conference room facilities. A common example is *Lotus Notes*, which integrates e-mail and business software for the internet and also corporate intranets. *Lotus Notes* provides a range of facilities, including e-mail, calendaring, group scheduling and a to do list; integration with the Lotus Domino R5 server makes *Notes R5* a powerful communications tool, enabling organizations to use a range of facilities, from standards-based messaging to built-in collaborative applications like discussions and document libraries. Because *Lotus Notes* can be used with other business software, it means that it can be used to create integrated learning environments within companies and other organizations. One advantage of this approach is that it means employees are familiar with these electronic tools and use them as an everyday part of their work. So when they use them for e-learning applications, this isn't viewed as a separate activity requiring the need to learn and use specialized software.

An action learning set using *Lotus Notes*

Action learning involves a small group of people coming together (either face-to-face or using virtual tools) to work on a particular problem or live issue. It is described in more detail in Allan (1999). Commercial communication software tools offer a way for library and information workers to come together in action learning sets. A group of information workers in the financial sector set up an action learning set to explore ways in which they could improve their unit's internet searching training programmes. The group originally met on a day's training course in London and as a result of this decided to set up a learning set using a common tool: *Lotus Notes*. The action learning set was used as a vehicle for developing and testing new courses, obtaining feedback on training materials, and also sharing and identifying solutions to practical problems encountered during the training programmes. Learning set members worked together using *Lotus Notes* for about six months and then formally closed the learning set as they began to move forward in different directions. During the time that the learning set existed, it provided a valuable forum for learning and development.

Another example of this type of system is *Microsoft Exchange 2000*, which offers an infrastructure for messaging, bulletin boards or discussion groups, contact and task management, and document management. It has built-in content indexing and search facilities to help users find and share information quickly. It also enables data and videoconferencing including realtime conferencing, document authoring, whiteboarding, text discussion and file transfer. One of the real strengths of the system is that it provides management tools. For example, the conference management service keeps track of scheduled conferences and provides administrators with control of attendee access to conferences. Another strength is that information in *Exchange 2000* can be accessed using *Office 2000*, web browsers, *Microsoft Windows Explorer*, cellular phones and hand-held computers. This means it is accessible to e-learners and e-tutors in the workplace, at home and also on the move. This type of system was designed for large-scale use within organizations, and it offers an alternative to the VLE for a variety of information units.

Use of *Microsoft Exchange*

Harry, an information worker in an insurance company, set up a pilot information service based on the use of *Exchange 2000*. He identified and set up a number of experimental services: an instant messaging service from 9 to 10 am every morning; and a user forum in a discussion group. The discussion group was used by a number of internal customers as a means of raising problems and making suggestions, while Harry used the group to discuss new ideas and possible initiatives. He found that the user forum was a more lively group and attracted more interest than the face-to-face sessions he had attempted to organize twice a year. He also used the service to disseminate documents and guides to the information service. When he evaluated the new service, he found that it was popular with his customers, who liked the way in which the information service had come to their desktop rather than them being expected to visit or phone the unit.

Cheaper alternatives

A growing number of commercial and voluntary organizations provide access to integrated communication or learning environment and these often provide many of the facilities that are offered by the commercial VLEs. Access to this free or low-cost resource is important as it enables information workers in a diverse range of situations such as workplace libraries, school libraries and voluntary organizations to create and participate in the benefits of online learning and teaching, and also of professional communities of practice. The host organization provides and maintains the technical facility, and individuals or groups have access to its technical resources. Examples include www.intranets.com and www.quickteam.com. Further information is available from CDE Software Evaluation (see page 255).

Using these systems is relatively easy and it can take less than 15 minutes to create this type of learning environment. All that is required is for an individual to take on a subscription (often available for free for 30 days) and then to be provided with access to a named site. One or more people within the group may have administrator rights, and they can ensure that membership is established for the whole group. They will have access to the following types of features: administration tools, calendar, document facility, discussion facility, instant messaging, internet links, and a help facility. These are briefly described, and the advantages and disadvantages of using this approach are summarized in Table 3.4.

Table 3.4 *Advantages and disadvantages of alternatives to a VLE*

Facilities	Advantages	Disadvantages
General points	Free, simple, easy to use Access to online help and support Available to anyone with internet access.	As it is free, users can often feel inundated with advertising materials. No real power over upgrades or the development process. What happens if they go out of business?
Administration of site	Simple, easy to use, and the ability to choose the number of of administrators, e.g. one or everyone.	Cannot personalize intranet, e.g. with logo or graphics.
Calendar	Access to a calendar.	
Document facility	Provides a shared document facility. Simple, easy to use, takes a wide range of files and has a familiar folder structure. Can add useful descriptive comments/messages.	Sometimes document size is limited and very small, e.g. 50K.

	Password facility enables differential access.	
Discussion facility	Provides an asynchronous discussion facility. Simple, easy to use, with a facility for viewing threading structure. Password facility enables differential access.	Sometimes lacks a new message or flag alert system.
Instant messaging	Provides synchronous (real-time) discussion facility. Simple relatively easy to use and enables one-to-one and group conferencing.	Sometimes tricky to use. Sometimes lacks group conferencing facilities and only has one-to-one chat chat facilities. Sometimes cannot make a copy of the transcript.
Internet links	Simple, easy to use and provides easy access to people's 'favourite' internet sites. Can add useful descriptive comments/message.	Sometimes no indexing/hierarchical features. Sometimes difficult to structure, so that if too many links were made, then it would time-consuming to search through a serial list.
Help facility	Simple online help system, clear and readable, with access to additional support often available via e-mail.	

The following example demonstrates the use of an alternative VLE by a group of library and information staff who call themselves 'The Escape Committee'.

'The Escape Committee'

'The Escape Committee' was established in 2000 with the aim of providing a group of librarians with a forum for helping each other to progress within their career and move to a new position. Membership was by invitation and all communications are confidential (in the following account names have been changed to protect the identity of individuals).

The Escape Committee provides members with:

- an informal network of like-minded librarians
- information, support and advice

- feedback on job applications, *curriculum vitae* etc.
- opportunities for exchanging information about new vacancies
- opportunities for personal and professional development
- friendship and fun.

Members of The Escape Committee include:

- Anna – a law librarian who wants to progress to a team-leader role
- Barbara – recently made redundant from a university information services position, and now looking for any professional post within 50 miles of her home
- John – an information officer working in a local authority, but wanting to move back into a workplace library position, preferably in a Blue Chip company
- Anne – having recently completed her Masters in information studies, and now wanting to progress from a library assistant role to a professional post
- Tina – wanting to get out of librarianship and thinking of working as a webmaster.

The following scenarios provide a picture of how different members of The Escape Committee use the intranet site to help them communicate with each other. The software used was free and came from the site intranets.com. At the time of writing a charge had been introduced to use this site.

Scenario 1
The Escape Committee members all have busy time schedules and sorting out face-to-face meeting times used to be very time-consuming. Members used to joke that it took a whole meeting to organize the next meeting. Using the polling facility, they now sort out their meeting times online.

Using the polling facility. One person sets up the online poll and this takes a few minutes. Group members are all alerted by e-mail to the poll and they log into the site. They then click on the times that they are available to meet in a particular week, and the software works out the most popular times. The results are available on the intranet site.

Scenario 2

Members of The Escape Committee decided to share their CVs and letters of application via the site. Each person has his or her own document folder and stores personal information there. Anyone in the group may access the documents, and they give each other feedback or copy good ideas, e.g. on the layout of letters.

Using the document facility. This is very like saving files in folders using a standard software package.

Scenario 3

Barbara has an interview for the post of college librarian next month. The Escape Committee helped her to put her application together and gave her feedback on her covering letter and application form. Barbara used the discussion facility to discuss her forthcoming interview and also to obtain advice on current issues in further education college libraries.

Using the discussion facility. Useful features include:

- password facilities on the intranet site
- password facilities on discussion facilities
- the ability to keep an online record of discussions, which means that Barbara can print out discussions and read them at her leisure, e.g. on the journey to the interview.

Scenario 4

The Escape Committee members work in a variety of organizations. It is often inappropriate to discuss their 'escape' plans with their immediate colleagues or managers. The online discussion facility enables group members to improve their practice by:

- asking for advice, help or support
- sharing ideas and experiences
- giving support
- reducing potential feelings of isolation.

Summary

This chapter provides an introduction to integrated learning environments. These are extensively used in colleges and universities and provide facilities for students, tutors and library staff to work together and provide an information-rich virtual learning environment. Virtual learning environments provide the following facilities: structured learning programmes, access to information sources, communication tools, assessment tools, personal management tools, administrator and tutor tools. Traditional VLEs are expensive and alternative approaches are available through the use of commercial communications software, e.g. those integrating messaging and collaboration systems, and also accessible groupware available from community sites. These approaches enable library and information workers to create small-scale learning environments that include virtual communication tools.

4

Web-based training materials

Introduction

The aim of this chapter is to introduce web-based training materials and their use within library and information services. The chapter is divided into three sections. The first introduces web-based training materials and identifies the characteristics of good-quality learning packages, and also their advantages and disadvantages. This includes a brief overview of technical aspects of interactive learning packages, which will help the reader who is new to this field to obtain an overview of technical issues and an understanding of some of the jargon.

The second section provides an overview of different examples of web-based training materials that are currently used within the library and information profession. They are organized under the following headings:

- information literacy, e.g. library induction programme, information searching, basic IT skills
- initial professional development, e.g. induction programmes, initial professional qualifications
- continuous professional development, e.g. mentoring.

The challenge with this section was how to select a diverse range of packages from a multitude of good examples. The examples given demonstrate packages that have been developed in-house, by commercial organizations and also through regional or national collaborative projects in a number of different countries.

The final section considers the role of library and information workers in providing access to web-based training materials. E-learners are likely to access e-learning opportunities in a variety of locations, including at their desk or in a learning centre, or at home. The advantages and challenges arising from this choice are briefly outlined. Many library and information services provide e-learning facilities using specialist e-learning centres or general ICT facilities (ICT training room, internet café, general reference room), and this chapter explores practical aspects of managing and supporting e-learning centres.

Web-based learning materials

Web-based learning materials may be used in a variety of learning situations:

- as a standalone learning experience used by a learner working independently
- as a package integrated within a face-to-face programme
- as a means of providing additional practice on a specific skill or theme.

They may be used by students working either with or without a tutor or librarian's support in a further or higher education programme. Web-based learning materials are used for staff development by LIS and they may be used by individual library and information workers working in their own time as a means of progressing their career. Interactive learning packages often use a mixture of welcoming text, talking heads, online activities and exercises, and video clips to deliver tutorials or training courses to library and information customers and staff. They are commonly used as a means of delivering library and information service induction programmes, IT skills, information searching skills and also training on specific products and services, e.g. database services. Today a variety of software tools make it relatively easy (although still very time-consuming) to develop learning packages involving text, graphics, audio, video and animation.

Interactive learning materials are often developed and linked to the library and information service home page or a linked page, e.g. Public Library of Cincinnati and Hamilton County home page and De Montfort University in the UK. They are often made available through a learning portal and many college and university virtual learning environments provide access to interactive learning packages. For example, many organizations that use the *Virtual Campus* use training materials provided by the supplier (Teknical) such as interactive learning packages covering key skills qualifications (see www.teknical.com). Some organizations provide access to interactive learning materials through their intranet service or a special website such as a training or staff development website. Web-based training materials may be available to registered users, e.g. students enrolled in a college or university, or they may be available to anyone with access to the internet. *TONIC* and the *Virtual Training Suite* are examples of training materials that are freely available over the internet. They are described in more detail below.

The best examples of interactive learning packages are those that:

- arouse the learner's interest
- use clear language
- structure the content in manageable chunks
- provide a variety of routes through the materials
- use supporting images and diagrams
- give opportunities for learners to practise, e.g. activities and quizzes
- give personalized feedback.

The checklist in Table 4.1 can be used to evaluate externally provided training materials and also internal web-based training materials.

Table 4.1 *Evaluation of web-based training materials*

Evaluation criteria	Interactive learning material
1 Do the aims and learning outcomes match your specific aims and learning outcomes?	
2 Are the materials easy to access and quick to download?	
3 Do they arouse the learner's interest?	
4 Do they use clear language?	
5 Is the content structured in manageable chunks?	
6 Is the content relevant and are there appropriate examples?	
7 Does the package provide a variety of routes through the materials?	
8 Does it use supporting images and diagrams?	
9 Does it give opportunities for learners to practise, e.g. activities and quizzes?	
10 Does it give personalized feedback?	
11 Is it up-to-date?	
12 Is it from a credible author(s)/organization?	
13 Will you be able to obtain permission to use it?	
14 Other notes.	

Examples of good practice are described later in this chapter. The worst examples are those where traditional print-based materials are presented via the web or where tutors and instructors post up their *PowerPoint* presentations and label them as examples of e-learning. This is rather like signing up for a dynamic training event and finding yourself in a training room in the company of a print-out. Other bad examples provide an over-enthusiastic mixture of sound, vision and activities that can overwhelm information workers (and also their PCs).

The development of quality interactive materials is an expensive process and, as a result, many packages are developed as part of collaborative projects, often at a national level. Examples of products developed in this way include the *Net-skills TONIC* tutorial and the *Virtual Training Suite*, and these are described later in this chapter. One essential element that is missing from this form of e-learning is the human touch – automated feedback, however positive, can come across as sterile and insincere. As a result, many library and information trainers and tutors integrate these packages into face-to-face training sessions (Amber, 2001).

Multimedia interactive learning packages

This section provides an overview of basic technical features associated with the development and use of multimedia interactive learning packages. This is a fast-moving technical field, and it is worthwhile remembering that these features are becoming more sophisticated and easier to use as new technical tools are developed. Relatively simple-to-use software packages allow text, document files, images, sound, animation and video to be integrated into web-based training materials:

1 **Text**

    This is the simplest and most familiar method of presenting information. Chapter 8 briefly considers design issues, and further information (e.g. on accessible learning materials) is available from The Web Accessibility Initiative at: www.w3.org/TR/WAI-WEBCONTENT/

2 **Document files**

    Document files are widely used as a means of distributing documents on the internet, and many learning packages use this format as a way of disseminating additional resources. The standard format used is called PDF (Portable Document Format) and these files are created and read in *Adobe Acrobat*. E-learners need to have the *Adobe Acrobat Reader* available on their own PC, but it can be downloaded from the internet at no charge (http://adobe.com). *Access Adobe* enables PDF files to be accessible to people with visual impairments – it translates PDF into HTML or into a text e-mail, making it readable by someone unable to access PDF in the usual way. *Access Adobe* is available on http://access. adobe.com/.

3 **Images**

    A simple method of enhancing learning materials is to use visual images. Common image file formats are GIF (Graphics Interchange Format), JPG (Joint Photographic Experts Group) and PNG (Portable Network Graphics Format). Images can be included as a background as well as in the foreground of the screen. Clipart provides access to a wide range of images.

4 **Sound**

Audio files can be played as clickable links or as background audio that starts as soon as a page is loaded or on the closedown of a section. There are two main formats: digital formats and synthesized audio formats. It is possible to integrate sound as:

— discrete sound clips – the whole file must be downloaded before the component can play
— live audio streaming – parts of the file are played as the rest of the file is downloaded (a much faster process than using discrete sound clips)
— live audio – learners can listen to what is being delivered as it actually happens.

There are many different sound formats, and popular examples include WAVe format (.wav), MIDI (.midi or .mid), AIFF (.aiff), AU (.au), MPEG (.mpg), Rich Music Format (.rmf) and RealAudio (.ra or .ram).

5 **Animation and video**

Movement, animation, sound and video components all add vitality to interactive training packages. They are used to provide real-life examples (e.g. of someone carrying out a practical activity), demonstrate complex points, add interest, include interactivity and provide a professional image. Animation may be used in assessment activities, e.g. where an e-learner is asked to identify and click on a specific location.

Plug-in software such as *RealPlayer* and *Shockwave* use compression and streaming technologies to enable multimedia data to be sent smoothly and quickly over the internet. *Shockwave* provides access to high-quality multimedia, animated graphics and sound components. It is very powerful, and text, graphics, animation, video and sound sequences can be combined together relatively easily and downloaded quickly. *RealPlayer* enables live video streaming, thus providing access to moving pictures. However, it can make heavy demands on the learner's PC. E-learners need to download and install these plug-ins to enable them to access these parts of the interactive package. Many packages provide materials in alternative formats such as HTML, and this enables everyone to access all parts of the learning resources. Benjes-Small and Just (2002) provide guidance on the use of plug-ins and other web browser tools for library and information professionals.

There is a balance between providing a state-of-the art multimedia presentation and providing e-learning materials that are accessible to a wide range of people using technology that may be dated. Media-rich interactive learning materials are

often provided by organizations that supply e-learning opportunities to specific groups of learners who have access to top-of-the-range PCs and broadband networks. In contrast, information workers in the public and voluntary sector are more likely to be working with a range of customers, many of whom have limited access to PCs and the internet. In these situations it is important to use relatively simple learning materials and particularly ones that download quickly.

Advantages and disadvantages of web-based interactive training materials

There are many advantages to using web-based training materials and these include:

- learners can work through materials at their own time, place and pace
- learners can follow their own route through the materials
- they can be used by large numbers of learners
- they use many of the elements of CD ROM-based learning but add enhanced communication options
- learning materials are relatively easy to update
- they can make use of resources already available on the internet
- they can be created using very basic web-based technologies
- they can include multimedia, e.g. text, graphics, audio, video and animation.

The disadvantages include:

- learner reluctance to use technology
- the time required to develop materials
- dependence on the availability of a PC and the internet
- some learning packages require state-of-the art computers
- some packages demonstrate an over-enthusiasm for technical effects and lose sight of the needs of the learner.

Web-based learning and training opportunities

The aim of this section is to demonstrate how web-based learning opportunities are used within libraries and information services both for staff development and for informing and training their customers. It is impossible to do justice here to the vast range of interactive learning packages that are available to library and information workers. So an indicative range of packages has been selected that demonstrate good practice within the profession and also in the wider world.

Information literacy

The concept of information literacy has grown in importance as ICT and global communication systems mean that we are living and working in an information-rich world. Information literacy is high on the agenda of many organizations concerned with learning and teaching. Increasingly it is seen as essential for everyone, as learners, employees and citizens, to be information-literate and also effective users of ICT. The growth in e-learning and the use of integrated learning systems is an important driver to ensuring that library and information workers and their customers are information-literate.

A key watershed in the development of information literacy was the publication of a report by the American Library Association Presidential Committee on Information Literacy (1989). This identified:

> *the need for all people to become information-literate, which means that they are not only able to recognize when information is needed, but also able to identify, locate, evaluate and use effectively information needed for the particular decision or issue at hand.*

The ALA report expressed the need for all students to be competent in six general areas:

- recognizing a need for information
- identifying what information would address a particular problem
- finding the needed information
- evaluating the information found
- organizing the information
- using the information effectively to address a particular problem.

This list forms the basis of many information literacy programmes world-wide. It has been developed into the Standards for Information Literacy developed by the American Association of College and Research Libraries (ACRL) and has been adopted in an adapted form by the Council of Australian University Librarians.

In the UK, a lead-body on information literacy was the Sconul Task Force on Information Skills (Johnson, 2001), who thought that information literacy within higher education should include the idea of an individual who is able to

contribute to the synthesis of existing information, to develop ideas building on that synthesis, and to be able to create new knowledge. The Sconul Task Force developed the Seven Pillars Model, which defines information literacy as the ability to:

- recognize a need for information
- distinguish ways in which the information gap may be addressed
- construct strategies for locating information
- locate and access information
- compare and evaluate information obtained from different sources
- organize, apply and communicate information to others in ways appropriate to the situation
- synthesize and build upon existing information, contributing to the creation of new knowledge.

Information literacy programmes are considered below under the following headings:

- library induction
- internet skills packages
- basic ICT skills
- access to internet resources for web creation
- other initiatives.

Additional information on the concept of information literacy in the context of library and information work is available from Martin and Rader (2002).

Library induction

The first point of access for many library and information users is the home page on the world wide web. In parallel with the practice of displaying advisory leaflets and guides near the entrance of a physical building, an increasing number of library and information services provide a range of user education facilities through their home page. Nipp (1998) provides a useful overview of innovative uses of the home page, and this section will explore a number of different examples.

Public Library of Cincinnati and Hamilton County home page

The Public Library of Cincinnati and Hamilton County home page is packed with useful information organized under headings such as: What's New, Catalog & Collection, In the Spotlight, Internet Resources, KidSp@ce, General Information, Service information, Meet the Director, Programs & Exhibits. This is demonstrated in Fig. 4.1.

One click away is a wealth of user instruction packages. For example, 'How to use the catalog' provides a simple and readable guide to the catalogue, which is supported by examples of what will be displayed on the screen. The webtools section includes guides on search engines, metasearch engines, subject directories. Kidsp@ce provides a lively entry point for younger people and it is offered in a text-only format, making it more widely accessible. Another section presents tutorials, resources for parents, search engine reviews and techniques for effectively searching the internet, and includes the following links:

* Child Safety on the Information Highway
* Learn the Net
* The Librarian's Guide to CyberSpace for Parents and Kids
* New User Tutorial
* Safekids.com

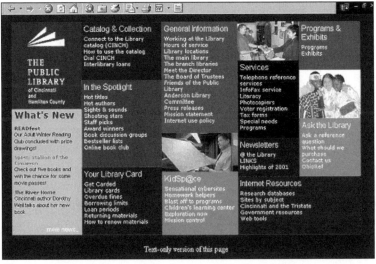

Fig. 4.1 *The Public Library of Cincinnati and Hamilton County home page*

- Search Engine Watch
- Search Engine Showdown
- The Spider's Apprentice
- Yahoo! How-To
- Web Search Guide.

This is a very useful site as it is packed with relevant user education and tutorials, and all the ones tested were only one click away from the home page. The guides provided by the library were simply produced and were chiefly based on the use of text and screen images, e.g. of the catalogue screen. The overall impression is of a very professional website and one that will encourage its readers, and particularly young people and their parents, to use the library. It can be viewed at http://plch.lib.oh.us/ (accessed 15 January 2002).

Murphy Library University of Wisconsin–La Crosse

The Murphy Library Information Skills Tutorial is part of a comprehensive information literacy program at Murphy Library University of Wisconsin–La Crosse. It is easily accessible from the home page of the library (see Figure 4.2).

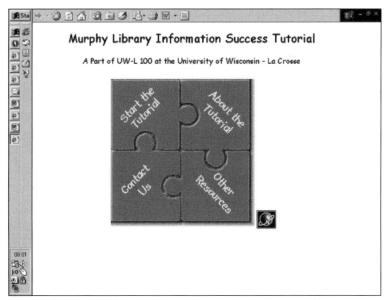

Figure 4.2 *Murphy Library University of Wisconsin–La Crosse home page*

This online tutorial is made up of six modules, each of which should take about 15 minutes to complete. The tutorials are clearly presented and provide key points on the following topics:

1   information resources
2   research skills
3   finding books
4   finding periodicals
5   web information
6   the lifelong learner.

Each module has a number of linked pages, each leading to the next. At regular intervals there are simple questions that must be completed to move forward. These are written in a friendly style and they are presented in an uncluttered screen. At the end of the tutorial successful students may obtain an online certificate of completion.

The pathway through the tutorial is clearly structured and supported by a glossary and map screens. The tutorial includes hotlinks to relevant documents and sources, e.g. there is a section on plagiarism with links to: *The Student's Guide to Avoiding Plagiarism* and also *Academic Disciplinary Procedures*. There is a screen where users can submit feedback by e-mail, and the language is informal throughout the tutorial.

The Murphy Library Information Skills Tutorial is part of a comprehensive information literacy program at UW–La Crosse and it contains links to a number of US information literacy links of interest such as: Information Literacy Competencies and Criteria for Academic Libraries in Wisconsin; The Nine Information Literacy Standards for Student Learning; Information Literacy Competencies by the National Information Literacy Institute.

The Murphy Library University of Wisconsin–La Crosse can be accessed at http://perth.uwlax.ed/murphylibrary/tutorial/ (accessed 15 January 2002) and the home page provides instructions for guest access.

De Montfort University Library

De Montfort University Library provides a range of information sources, guides for new users and tutorials via its home page, which can be viewed at www.library.dmu.ac.uk/ (accessed 20 January 2002). For example, the home page provides access to a range of tools to help students improve their study skills. The study skills page provides to a range of useful resources and guides, as shown in Figure 4.3.

As with many library and information services, the De Montfort University library internet resources are in fact hot links to tutorials and guides developed elsewhere, and these are reproduced in Figure 4.4.

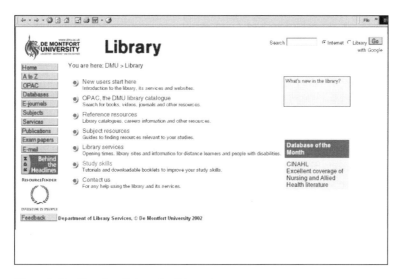

Fig. 4.3 *De Montfort University Library home page*

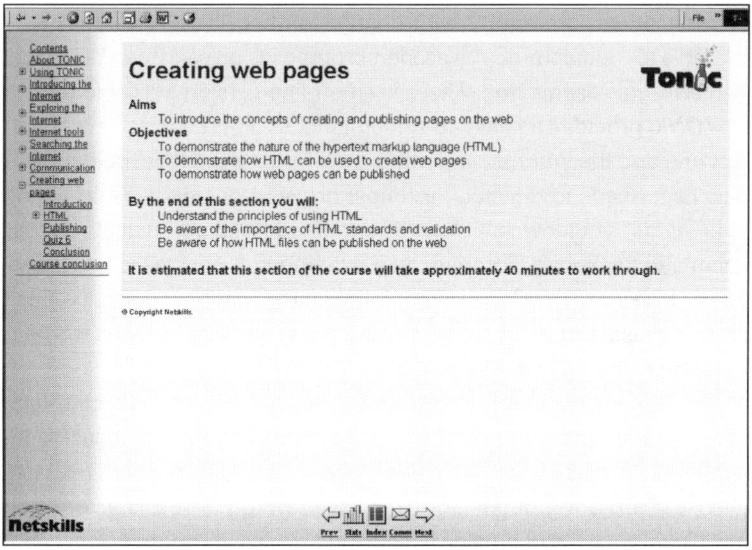

Fig. 4.4 *De Montfort University Library hot links to tutorials and guides*

Internet skills packages

A vast number of interactive learning packages for developing internet skills are available on the internet or via individual websites. Many of these packages are made freely available. Their quality varies from extremely poor through to excellent. Some of the best examples are those produced as part of a collaborative venture involving information workers from a range of different organizations. Key examples that are often held up as models of good practice include *TONIC* and the *RDN Virtual Training Suite*. These are both freely available for non-commercial academic purposes and were originally produced with support from JISC.

Netskills

A good example of an excellent package is *TONIC* developed as part of the Netskills project based in the UK. Netskills is an internet training service that helps those in higher education to develop their internet skills to make effective use of both internet and Intranet technologies for teaching and learning, research, administration and marketing activities. The service provides workshops, online tutorials and training. One of the early products was *TONIC*, which has evolved into the *TONIC-NG* online tutorial system that was developed by Netskills and DESIRE. *TONIC* was produced with help from JISC and made available for the benefit of the UK higher and further education communities. It was developed for the UK education community with central funding. It is currently freely available for non-commercial academic purposes on www.netskills.ac.uk/TonicNG/cgi/sesame?tng. There is an off-line version available too.

 TONIC provides an easy-to-understand, structured overview of networking and the internet, and offers step-by-step practical guidance. A new user needs to register – a simple process that involves providing your name, your own password, e-mail address and selecting your occupation area, e.g. librarian, staff developer. It only takes a few seconds. Once into *TONIC*, the learner is presented with clear guidance. Each topic is presented in the following structure: aims, objectives, learning outcomes, timing (see Figure 4.5).

 The learning materials are extremely easy to follow and work through. They are arranged in a linear menu-driven form, but the alphabetical subject index enables you to move directly to specific topics. Short, readable chunks of text are supported by clear line drawings. Two characters, Ron and Linus, are used to provide a question-and-answer session about connecting to the internet.

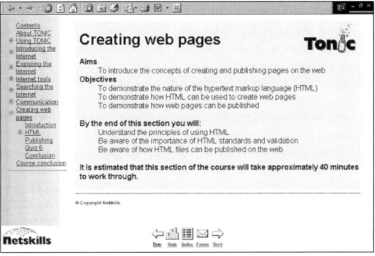

Fig. 4.5 *Example page from 'TONIC'*

There are optional quizzes that you can use to test your knowledge on specific subjects, and the feedback is clearly structured and very user-friendly. If you get the answer wrong, you are clearly presented with the right answer. Colour (red and green) is used to highlight your answers and you are also given a score for the quiz. It is not surprising that this package is widely used within libraries and information units, as it provides an excellent starting point for people to begin to get to grips with the internet and communication technologies. Although the content is biased towards the academic community, its content is relevant to anyone who wants to know about using the internet for research.

> *I didn't know very much about the internet when I started working at the university library. As part of my staff development I used TONIC. It was great as it clearly told me about the Internet. There wasn't too much to read and I liked the drawings. I found Linus and Ron a bit annoying and would have preferred someone different. Preferably women. I liked the way you were told how long it takes to read through each section. The quizzes were OK but I didn't like getting red crosses – just like school. One of the good things about it is that I can work at my own pace and go back over bits when I felt like it. We have the Internet at home and my daughter who is 16 has done the TONIC course too. She found it really helpful for her GCSEs.*
>
> Karen, Library Assistant, University Library

RDN Virtual Training Suite

Another example of a national initiative designed to teach internet information skills to students, lecturers and researchers in higher and further education in the UK is the *RDN Virtual Training Suite* (VTS) (see Figure 4.6). The content of tutorials within the *Virtual Training Suite* has been authored by a team of academics and librarians based in 30 universities, museums and research institutes across the UK. This type of collaborative effort in the development of interactive learning packages is very popular as it enables high-quality materials to be produced and developed using expertise from different professional groups such as library and information workers, lecturers and education developers. The *RDN Virtual Training Suite* project was financially supported by JISC, a strategic advisory committee serving The Higher and Further Education Funding Councils of England, Scotland and Wales.

The *Resource Discovery Network (RDN)* was designed for use within further and higher education and it is also used by many researchers and LIS staff in workplace information units, public libraries and also government libraries. It provides 40 online subject-specific tutorials, it is free and requires no registration. It can be accessed at www.vts.rdn.ac.uk/. It provides a set of 'teach yourself' web-based tutorials, each of which offers internet information skills training in a particular subject area. The tutorials offer a subject-based approach to Internet skills training, enabling the user to:

- **tour** key internet sites
- **discover** how to improve internet searching
- **review** the critical thinking required to use the internet
- **reflect** on how to use the internet for studying, researching or teaching.

Each tutorial takes around an hour to complete, and includes quizzes and interactive exercises. Special features include a 'links basket', where learners can collect their favourite links to key sites, quizzes and exercises, a glossary of internet terms, and print and download options.

In 2002 the RDN extended its range to include some tutorials specifically aimed to support subject curricula, student induction, staff development and training in IT Key Skills within the further education sector. The skills covered map onto part of the Key Skills specifications for Information Technology as defined by the Qualifications Curriculum

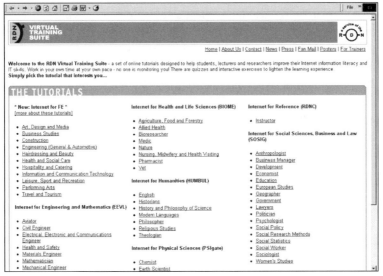

Fig. 4.6 *'RDN Virtual Training Suite'*

Authority (www.qca.gov.uk). Teaching packs offer case study examples of how these tutorials can be used in different courses at levels 1–3, ranging from A Level to GNVQ and AVCE. The 11 tutorial titles are:

- Internet for Art, Design and Media
- Internet for Business Studies
- Internet for Construction
- Internet for Engineering (General and Automotive)
- Internet for Hairdressing and Beauty
- Internet for Health and Social Care
- Internet for Hospitality and Catering
- Internet for Information and Communication Technology
- Internet for Leisure, Sport and Recreation
- Internet for Performing Arts
- Internet for Travel and Tourism.

The site provides an extensive range of supplementary resources for trainers, and these provide useful guidance for LIS staff and others on using these resources. Many of the materials available on the *Virtual Training Suite* may be downloaded in Microsoft Word format and/or Rich

Text Format. It also includes a trainer's PowerPoint presentation that can be downloaded too. The site even includes a poster that can be downloaded and used for advertising sessions. This is an impressive resource that is used by a large number of LIS staff to help deliver information skills and internet searching skills to their staff and student customers.

An independent evaluation of the *Virtual Training Suite* was conducted in January 2001 by Lin Amber of the University of Bristol Library. Lin noted:

> *Overall, users regarded the tutorials highly. The most frequently noted strengths were their good structure and ease of use, and the high quality of the content. Download and print options also proved popular. Criticisms mainly related to functionality issues, such as particular browser requirements in order to use all the tutorial features and an inability to use case-insensitive answers in the tutorials' quizzes. Other aspects of the tutorials received mixed comments, including the length of the tutorials and the level of interactivity they offered.* Amber (2001)

The evaluation clearly demonstrated that the positive features of the tutorials were clearly felt to outnumber negative ones. The results of the evaluation showed that librarians chiefly used the *Virtual Training Suite* to support independent learning and library user-education programmes.

Web-ezy

Charles Sturt University (CSU) in Australia is a leading provider of distance education with a commitment to flexible online delivery. The library became involved in a collaborative project to develop software to provide a shell for creating customized web-based library and information skills. Their product is called *Web-ezy* and it is used within their own library. It is accessible from the home page at www.csu.edu.au/division/library. Initial evaluation of the library and information skills package suggests that students make 'just in time' use of the module around assignment deadline times. The software package means that library staff are freed 'from some repetitive routine instruction while giving students the independence to choose where, when and what information skills they want to develop.' (Bishop and Henderson, 2001)

Basic ICT Skills

Many library and information services support a range of ICT training activities, often through a blended approach of hands-on workshops supplemented by e-learning tools. An example of a simple web-based training package on using a mouse is found on the Tucson–Pima Public Library site (http://tppl.org/), and this basic package was designed for people who have never used a computer. In response to community needs it is available in two languages, English and Spanish, and the welcome page includes clear directions about asking a librarian for further information on local computer classes.

For library and information workers wanting to develop their ICT skills, there are a wide range of e-learning opportunities. For example, information workers wanting to develop their web creation skills will have opportunities to learn through face-to-face and/or e-learning options and either specialist courses focused on the needs of library and information workers or general training programmes.

Library 101 Web Pages

In the USA, the Central Colorado Library System (CCLS) serves over 850 university, college, school district, public, hospital, cultural, educational and governmental libraries. These libraries, located in nine counties in the Denver metropolitan area, serve 56% of Colorado's population. They provide a range of face-to-face and also e-learning programmes, including *Library 101 Web Pages*, which enables library staff to create and design a basic web page using *Netscape Composer*. Access to this site is at www.colosys.net/.

Library 101 Web Pages covers a range of html topics such as adding links, creating tables and lists, inserting images and more! Information and guidance to the learner is presented in a readable and light-hearted manner. Navigation through the site is simple and intuitive, and library staff are advised to contact their supervisor for support. The home page to this module provides a friendly and accessible entry point (see Figure 4.7 overleaf).

HomeMaker for Libraries

Another example of a web-based training package for librarians is *HomeMaker for Libraries* on www.kn.pacbell.com/wired/libmkr/ (accessed on 26 April 2002). This site provides very simple instructions and example templates to enable library workers to create their own web-

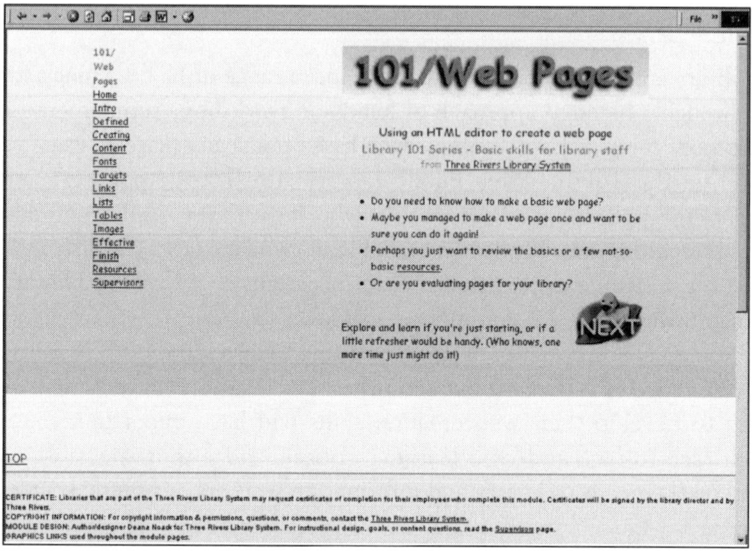

Fig. 4.7 *'Library 101 Web Pages'*

site. This site advises librarians on the process of gathering information about their library, and it provides a useful checklist to help in this process. It also provides guidance on serving, managing and editing web pages. The overall approach in this website is extremely prescriptive, and this is likely to inspire confidence with solo librarians working in schools or voluntary organizations who have been asked to produce a website but don't know where to start. Following the instructions and using the provided templates makes it a relatively easy task.

Access to internet resources for web creation

A large number of web-based ICT courses on web creation are available and many of them are free. Access to information on these resources is available from websites set up by individual libraries, professional groups or individual enthusiasts. The Library of Congress provides an internet resource page on www.loc.gov/global/internet/training.html (accessed 28 February 2002), which covers an extensive range of resources and is aimed at anyone accessing their website. In contrast, the International Association of School Librarianship provides an annotated list of websites that can be used to help individual school librarians create a webpage. This site is available on www.iasl-slo.org/creatingweb.html (accessed 26 February 2002). Anne Clyde, based at the University of Iceland, has created a website of internet resources for web creation and this is available at www/hi.is/~anne/internet3.html (accessed 26 April 2002). The Central Colorado Library System (CCLS) provides examples of courses on creating websites and using html on their website. These examples were provided by Christine Hamilton-Pennell and are available on the enticingly-named section 'Midnight at the Internet Cafe: Web-Based Learning: Online Tutorials and Self-Directed Courses' on www.colosys.net/. Examples from this site include:

- *JavaScript World*, www.jsworld.com/
- *Knowledge Hounds*, www.knowledgehound.com/
- *Learn2.com*, www.learn2.com/
- *Learn2University*, www.learninguniversity.com/
- *Tutorials.com*, www.tutorials.com/.

Other initiatives

Many library and information units are involved in special projects that may result in web-based learning activities and/or increased library and information unit use. Margaret Kendall (2000) lists examples of projects that use interactivity as a means of integrating ICT into use of the library for other purposes. Examples of projects quoted include:

- websites concerned with specific authors, themes or genres of literature
- genealogy websites
- use of e-mail to access other information and advice services provided by voluntary organizations
- citizenship information and communications.

A website that provides ideas for library and information workers to use ICT as a means of creating new communities of users is *Net notions for librarians* available on http://dspace/dial.pipex.com/town/square/ac940/netnotes.html (accessed 12 February 2002). This site is aimed at public libraries, although many of the ideas could be used in other types of library and information units. A typical example provided in the site is the work of the North Ayrshire Education Resource Service in providing information and support to local schools for their work on special projects and activities.

Another good example of this type of initiative is *Stories from the Web* (see Figure 4.8), a reader development programme managed by Birmingham Library and Information Service and originally funded by the Library and Information Com-

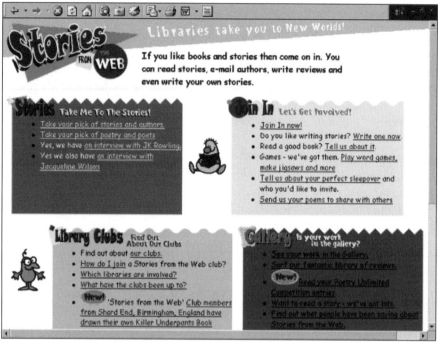

Fig. 4.8 *'Stories from the Web'*

mission. The welcoming site on www.storiesfromtheweb.org/ (accessed 25 April 2002) provides opportunities for young people to read stories, e-mail authors, play games, write reviews and also write their own stories. This is a delightful site to visit – lively, entertaining and visually interesting. Young people who get involved will develop their literacy and information skills, as well as developing a positive image of their public library.

Web-based library and information staff development activities

Induction

Web-based learning materials are a really useful means of augmenting face-to-face staff induction programmes. They enable staff to explore and learn at their own pace, and give them a break from the pressures of constantly meeting new people. They also enable staff to become familiar with the ICT systems in the library. Below is an example of an online tutorial developed for new staff in a wide range of libraries by a regional library collaborative organization.

Library 101: a learning experience for new library employees

Library 101: a learning experience for new library employees is a web-based programme that offers clear and helpful guidance to a new member of staff and is provided by the Three Rivers Regional Library Service in Colorado, USA. This internet training module provides 'first day' skills for new paraprofessional employees in public, college and school libraries. New employees work with library staff to learn about confidentiality, policies, operations and physical organization.

Topics covered include: the library, responsibilities, confidentiality, cases, resources, services, catalogue, classification. It includes guidance to supervisors, so that they know the topics that need to be covered before the staff take part in the programme as well as those covered within the programme. It is possible for successful candidates to obtain a certificate on completion of the programme. This is a very simple and accessible programme. It is readable and focuses on key ideas and the vocabulary a new employee is likely to need.

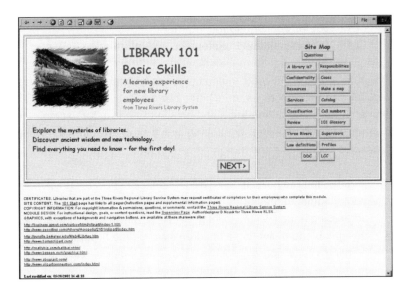

Fig. 4.9 *'Library 101'* induction programme

Initial library and information service qualifications

Many initial library and information qualifications involve a blended approach of face-to-face and online learning. An increasing number of initial qualifications are made available over the internet. This is particularly useful in library services that serve geographically distributed populations.

Community Library Training Programme

The Community Library Training Programme (CLTP) is a web-based distance education programme offered by the Public Library Services Branch of the British Columbia Ministry of Municipal Affairs; (www.bcpl. gov.bc.ca/lsb/cltp/; accessed 9 May 2001). The aim of the programme is to help public library staff develop the skills they need to serve their communities. The programme is also open to public library volunteers and board members, and, subject to space, to employees of school libraries or other British Columbia residents interested in acquiring library skills.

The Public Library Services Branch recommends that completion of the CLTP programme is the minimum qualification for anyone employed in a small or medium-sized public library. Seven courses are currently available, covering a variety of public library operations and services. Examples of courses include:

- CLTP 106: Introduction to the Internet
- CLTP 102: Introduction to Reference and Information Services.

The programme is delivered entirely over the internet, and each course requires an average of ten or more hours of work (both offline and online). Students can study at times to suit themselves and so, for example, fit it in around volunteering, workplace activities or their private lives. Examples of activities and assignments include:

- participating in a bulletin board discussion about how to attract more young adults to the library
- addressing issues related to internet access policies and procedures
- designing and delivering a children's story-time programme
- creating a collection development plan for a subject area or specific format
- evaluating an electronic reference source.

Approximately 150 students complete the CLTP courses each year. The programme is supported by tutors and Public Library Services Branch consultants.

Postgraduate Diploma/Master of Science course in Information and Library Studies

In 2000 the School of Information and Media at the Robert Gordon University (RGU) in Aberdeen began delivering their Postgraduate Diploma/Master of Science course in Information and Library Studies on an online, distance-learning basis and hosted on the RGU Virtual Campus. The Virtual Campus is used to deliver teaching materials, and these are supported by both e-mail and telephone tutorials. Students communicate with each other and with academic staff through a series of course- and module-related electronic forums and discussion groups. The submission of course work, and the provision of marks and feedback, are also done electronically. In addition, the VLE provides access to the university library catalogue and a range of online resources. An e-mail evaluation of the programme showed that 'generally respondents were very happy with the level and nature of interaction and many felt it compared favourably with prior educational experiences. The most significant problem to emerge was that of student access to resources and this was being addressed by the academic staff and library (Anderson, 2001).

Continuous professional development

Many web-based training packages, e.g. information skills and ICT skills learning resources, are used by library and information workers to develop their knowledge and skills. Typical examples of these have been presented in previous sections in this chapter.

Web-based training packages are also a useful way of enabling library and information workers to develop their management skills, and many learning portals (see Chapter 2) provide access to a range of good-quality training materials. Web-based training materials cover topics such as project management, budgeting, time management, supervision and mentoring. These resources may be provided by the parent organization or by the library or information unit. For example, Surrey County Council provides e-learning courses to employees on public finance, e-government and best value; the authority purchased these courses from the Institute of Public Finance (Sloman, 2002).

The provision of masters level programmes by distance learning often incorporates the use of web-based training materials as mentioned in the example above. Web-based training materials may be used to help the new student get to grips with learning in a virtual environment and they may also be used to deliver some of the content. Additional examples of programmes can be obtained from www.ala.org/alaorg/oa/disted.html, www.libraryhq.com/distance.html and www.cilip.org.uk.

Managing the location of e-learning

Individual e-learners may elect to study web-based training materials in a range of different locations, including their workplace, libraries or information units, specialist e-learning centres or at home. In practice most e-learners use a number of different places to study depending on their personal situation and time constraints. Table 4.2 summarizes the advantages and disadvantages of the three main e-learning locations from the perspective of the learner.

Table 4.2 *Advantages and disadvantages of different e-learning locations*

E-learning locations	Advantages	Disadvantages
Learning centre/Library and information unit	Access to face-to-face support	Environment may be noisy
	Access to a range of resources	Distraction from other learners
	Presence of other learners	Need to travel to unit
	Access to social activities, e.g. lounge area, refreshments	Time limitations
Work	Familiar environment	Interruptions
	Familiar ICT systems	Distractions
	Time flexibility	Lack of specialist support
Home	Familiar environment	Interruptions
	Familiar ICT systems	Distractions
	Time flexibility	Lack of specialist support
	Privacy	Conflict with family needs

Library and information workers who are accessing web-based training programmes may access them from all three different locations. In practice, learning at your own desk can be quite a frustrating experience as interruptions and distractions can interfere with the learning process. E-learners may find that time away from their desk and the service area in a special e-learning centre can make a huge difference to their experience of e-learning.

Library and information services provide e-learning facilities in a variety of ways, including specialist e-learning centres, general ICT training rooms, internet cafés, or general reference rooms. This means that it is important for library managers and information workers to have an awareness of the needs of e-learners in terms of providing an appropriate learning environment.

E-learning centres

There are many types of e-learning centres: at one end of the spectrum are centres set up within specific organizations to suit the needs of employees; and at the opposite end are public access centres located in libraries, internet cafés, community centres and projects, mobile projects, colleges or universities.

The use of e-learning centres is a key feature of the UK University for Industry's Learndirect network and the DfEE's network of UK online centres; these are national networks made up of hundreds of centres focused around regional hubs. They provide local access to high-quality learning opportunities. One of the aims of these initiatives is to attract into learning people of all ages through local access to networked learning resources. Library and information workers are often involved in supporting these services, e.g. within public libraries, or have obtained roles managing centres or regional hubs.

This means that it is important for library and information workers to have an understanding of e-learning and the requirements of an e-learning centre. These requirements will vary depending on the type of e-learning centre and its learners. The following list identifies the facilities required to provide a typical public-access e-learning centre:

1 **Equipment and ICT facilities**
    * individual workstations with access to high-specification ICT
    * internet access
    * video viewing
    * document reproduction facilities, e.g. printing, photocopying, scanning
    * access to specialist equipment to support individuals with special needs.
2 **Learning facilities**
    * guidance and advice
    * learning materials (electronic and print-based)
    * tutorial support including assessment
    * technical support
    * library and information support.

3   Social facilities
   - refreshments, e.g. drinks machine
   - access to newspapers and magazines
   - relaxation area
   - noticeboard
   - playroom.
4   **Administrative facilities**
   - reception
   - enrolment
   - booking system, e.g. for ICT, video, tutor support.

Managing e-learning centres

Managing an e-learning centre is familiar territory for many readers as, in many respects, it is similar to managing library and information units. It involves identifying the overall goals and outcomes of the e-learning centre, and identifying the learners and their needs. It involves ensuring that the right resources (ICT, electronic and print-based resources) are identified and made available to the e-learners by opening at appropriate times. It involves identifying a range of policies and procedures to ensure that the centre runs effectively, such as a customer service policy, an ICT policy, and health and safety. It involves ensuring that the centre is staffed by well trained, confident and enthusiastic staff who are backed up by appropriate management and technical support. It involves marketing and promoting the e-learning centre. Monitoring and evaluating the e-learning centre is an important activity and, as with library and information services, the collection of relevant quantitative and qualitative information on a regular basis is crucial to identifying areas and services that can be improved, developed or axed. For externally funded e-learning centres (e.g. those funded by government or European funds), there will be a range of standard reporting activities such as regular returns to be completed and returned to the monitoring unit. For centres that are funded by a range of agencies, the monitoring and reporting of activities can be quite complex and time-consuming, as all funders have their own standard forms, systems and procedures. Finally, managing e-learning centres also involves liaison with other centres, groups and organizations.

One key issue is staffing the e-learning centre. Many of these centres are managed by an individual person as part of a wider brief. In workplace libraries, for example, the e-learning centre may be part of the librarian's brief. In larger centres such as public libraries, colleges or universities, it may be the responsibility of one person, e.g. the ICT co-ordinator or champion. This person is likely to be supported by a (part-time) administrator and also technical support. The actual support provided to learners may come from specialist tutors or library and information staff. This implies that all staff need to understand how the e-learning centre operates and to provide basic support and assistance, e.g. to be able to handle basic ICT queries. In the UK, The People's Network scheme is providing ICT training for public library staff, who are being trained to the standard of the European Computer Driving Licence.

Summary

This chapter is concerned with web-based training materials and their use within libraries and information units. Well designed and accessible training materials provide learning opportunities for a wide range of people, and the speed of technical developments means that more advanced features involving the use of animation are becoming accessible to more people. The library and information profession has embraced the use of web-based training materials, both for their own staff and for their customers. A selection of examples show their use in training staff and customers to search for information, develop their ICT skills and use the library. They are also used for initial and continuous professional development programmes. Training materials may be designed by enthusiastic individuals, by teams within specific libraries and information units, and also by collaborative teams and groups. Finally, library and information workers are actively involved in providing access to training materials through e-learning centres and within the library or information unit.

E-learning and teaching

5

Models of e-learning and teaching

Introduction

The purpose of this chapter is to provide an overview of theories of learning that are particularly relevant to e-learning. This is an important topic as understanding the theoretical ideas that underpin learning enables information workers to design, develop and deliver effective e-learning environments, programmes and activities.

The chapter is divided into sections covering:

- approaches to learning
- learning as a social activity
- cognitive apprenticeship
- communities of practice
- knowledge and competence
- approaches to learning and teaching
- five-stage model of e-learning.

It is useful to have a basic understanding of individual approaches to learning, and the first section explores three different aspects: the context of learning; models of learning and learning styles; and reflection on learning. The information presented here is relevant to face-to-face as well as e-learning programmes, and each of these sections outlines current theories and then makes explicit links with reference to the design and delivery of e-learning programmes.

Many people learn most effectively when they are working in a supportive environment with other people. Some theoretical models of learning focus on the importance of social processes, and this is a key element in e-learning when tutors and learners are working together on collaborative activities. Understanding the importance of the social element of learning enables programme developers and tutors to identify and establish the most appropriate learning activities and processes for their learners. This has implications for library and information practitioners who are working with relatively large groups of students, e.g. information skills programmes for very large groups (350+) of undergraduates. A challenge is to provide a learning process that enables and validates social processes as well as enabling the students to achieve the learning outcomes of the programme. This may require a shift in perspective for the LIS practitioner.

This theme of the social context of learning is explored further in the sections on cognitive apprenticeship and communities of practice. The concept of cognitive apprenticeship is inspired from traditional apprenticeship and is concerned with individual learners learning from experts through work-based discussions and social interactions. For many practitioners, continuous professional development often takes place through membership of communities of practice. Key ideas about communities of practice are useful in helping individuals establish and facilitate this form of e-learning using virtual communication tools. This section of the chapter is particularly relevant to library and information workers who are involved in professional development (e.g. the development of health-care professionals within the higher education sector), and it is also relevant to those involved in professional development within the library and information sector.

Individual e-learning programmes are based on underpinning ideas about knowledge and competence. Developing a basic understanding of theories of knowledge is important, as this in turn will inform the development of an appropriate e-learning programme. This is particularly relevant to library and information professionals who are working in educational organizations where different groups of academic staff may be operating from different underlying theories of knowledge. The concept of knowledge and knowledge construction is developed further in the five-stage model of e-learning that is presented in the final section of this chapter. This model is a particularly useful one, as it takes into account the different stages e-learners are likely to experience as they become proficient within a virtual learning environment. It also integrates ideas about knowledge construction and learning as a social activity.

Approaches to learning

Ideas about how individuals learn are important for anyone wanting to get involved in developing and delivering e-learning programmes or activities. Different authors identify and give weight to different factors that will affect individual learning experiences. Curry's onion model (1983) provides a useful framework for exploring different approaches to learning, and this model has been adapted and simplified in this chapter. Approaches to learning can be viewed at three different levels:

- outer layer – the context of learning
- middle layer – learning and thinking styles
- core – the central personality dimension.

Outer layer – the context of learning

The context of learning includes factors such as the learning environment (both virtual and physical), the students, e-tutors and support staff. While some of the elements contained within these factors are outside of the control of the e-tutor or programme designer, there are some aspects that need to be taken into account during the design and delivery of e-learning (and also face-to-face) programmes.

The learning environment is crucial to learners, and while important in face-to-face situations it is even more important in e-learning situations. Entering a virtual environment can be a daunting experience for many people and providing clear guidance with minimal but key amounts of information can help allay fears and ensure that the learner becomes engaged in the learning experience. While it may be difficult for learners to walk out of a traditional training situation, it is easy to switch off the computer and move on to other activities. Unless there is easy access to help, e.g. via help menus, e-mail, phone or in person, then the new learner may give up at the first hitch or technical problem. In addition to providing a positive virtual learning environment, many library and information workers provide physical learning environments in libraries and learning centres, and it is important that these provide a conducive environment for e-learning – this involves taking into account factors such as noise level, light, temperature and the provision of appropriate furniture.

Many factors affect individual motivation to learn, and key among them is a clear reason for learning, e.g. desire to gain a new skill, obtain a new job or develop new relationships. The process by which potential learners select and enter e-learning opportunities will depend on their motivation. Providing transparent e-learning programmes that clearly identify the benefits to the learner, and also the ways in which their learning will be useful to them, will help to motivate individual learners. Increasing or maintaining one's sense of self-esteem and pleasure are strong secondary motivators for engaging in learning experiences (Zemke and Zemke, 1984), and this suggests that e-learning environments need to be easy to navigate, simple to use and enjoyable, and they should also include positive feedback.

The attitudes of e-tutors and support staff to the e-learners and the e-learning programme will also have an important impact on the learners' ability to learn.

Positive staff who are enthusiastic about, and committed to, e-learning will enable the learners to engage in their programme, while negative or cynical attitudes can really inhibit learning. It is also very important that all staff, including library and information workers who may be supporting e-learning as part of their everyday reference or help desk duties, have the appropriate knowledge and skills to support e-learners. This has important implications for the recruitment of staff, and also for their training and development.

Summary of implications for the design of e-learning environments, programmes or activities

1 Provide an accessible virtual learning environment.
2 Provide effective learner support.
3 Identify and clearly present the goals and learning outcomes .
4 If possible, link these to qualifications and/or progression in the workplace.
5 Provide constructive feedback.
6 If possible, ensure that all staff likely to be involved in the e-learning programme have the appropriate knowledge and skills, and are positive about this approach to learning.

Middle layers – learning and thinking styles

The middle layer is concerned with the learner's approach to assimilating and processing information (Curry, 1983) and many popular learning style and thinking style theories are located at this level. The author has selected three theories on the basis that they are widely used within education and training, and they are all very relevant to the development and delivery of e-learning programmes. They are the Honey and Mumford model, the NLP model, and the Felder and Soloman model.

The Honey & Mumford model (Honey and Mumford 1992), was based on the ideas of Kolb (1984) and it is now widely used in both academic and commercial learning and teaching situations. Peter Honey and Alan Mumford found that different people prefer different ways of learning but that most people are unaware of their preferences. They identified four main learning styles and produced tools for identifying them. These tools are widely available online. Learning about learning styles gives e-tutors or developers an insight into the range of learning style preferences in a group of learners. The Honey and Mumford model of the learning cycle is shown in Figure 5.1.

On entering a new virtual environment, some people will get on with it

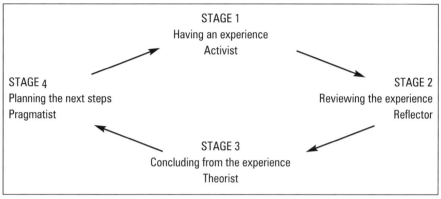

Fig. 5.1 *Learning styles*

straight away, and use trial and error to find their way around the environment – they are *activists*. *Reflectors* prefer to stand back, observe, read instructions and think things through analytically. *Theorists* prefer to work systematically on a structured programme, whilst *pragmatists* enjoy the practical application of ideas in a common-sense way. Though there are obvious drawbacks of typecasting and categorizing people, information about learning styles can be used in the design of e-learning environments, programmes and activities to ensure that they meet the different needs of individual learners.

Table 5.1 briefly summarizes the main characteristics of the different learning styles.

Table 5.1 *Summary of the main characteristics of the different learning styles (description by John Fewings (1999), Humberside Training and Enterprise Council)*

Activists

Activists are 'here and now' people who are keen to try anything once. They tend to act first and think about the problems afterwards (if at all). They are gregarious people who enjoy being the centre of attention. They are excited by anything lively and vibrant, but quickly get bored with the routine and mundane. They are creative in their thinking and come up with innovative solutions to problems, but lose interest with the implementation or long-term consolidation of plans.

Pragmatists

Pragmatists enjoy new theories and techniques. They can often see instant applications and are keen to try out their ideas in practice. They enjoy the challenge of having a problem to solve, and quickly come up with practical solutions. They are rather impatient with long-winded planning and discussion, preferring to 'get on with the job'. They are tightly focused – concentrating on the job in hand until it is completed. This can sometimes result in tunnel vision. Pragmatists are often task-oriented rather than people-oriented.

Reflectors
Reflectors like time and space to think things through carefully before coming to a conclusion. They listen carefully and gather information to help them make rational and considered judgments. They prefer to act as observers rather than be involved in the thick of things. Because they often adopt a low profile, they may be thought of as quiet or shy. Nevertheless 'still waters run deep', and their considered opinions should not be ignored. Reflectors often find it difficult to make decisions.

Theorists
Theorists have a methodical and logical approach to most things. They like to analyse ideas in a detached way, asking questions and making mental connections until they have integrated new theories into a comprehensive overview. They are not usually happy with intuitive thinking or subjective judgments. They are often perfectionists with set ways of doing things. Theorists pay attention to detail, which can be of great benefit – or may serve to slow them down and stand in the way of creativity

Another accessible learning style theory is that of Bandler and Grinder, described by O'Connor and Seymour (1994) who developed a model of communication based on very detailed observation of expert communicators, and their model is known as neuro-linguistic programming (NLP). NLP looks at how people prefer to organize and access information in their mind. They have found that individuals tend to prefer one of three main methods, or sensory modes, of taking in and learning information. The main styles are visual, auditory and/or kinaesthetic (hence the alternative designation VAK model).

Visual people prefer to take in new information in a visual form, e.g. pictures, charts or diagrams, and like to visualize information. Auditory people may prefer to listen and talk through new ideas. They frequently remember the tone and exact content of different conversations. In contrast, kinaesthetic learners like to be actively involved in doing things, and like to touch and handle things. According to Smith (1998) the following breakdown shows how these different learning styles are represented:

- visual learners 29%
- auditory learners 34%
- kinaesthetic learners 37%.

While these models offer some insight into individual preferences for information processing and general approaches to e-learning, they can be criticized as being limited in their application to learners with a more rounded learning style (Atkins, Moore and Sharpe, 2001). In addition, as many aspects of e-learning are text-based, they do not provide a detailed insight into the verbal–visual modality.

110

Felder and Soloman (1988) provide another approach to learning styles. They focus on four bi-polar references for learning along the following scales: active–reflective, sensing–intuitive, visual–verbal and sequential–global. Active learners are those who learn through activity and doing things, and enjoy working with others. Reflective learners prefer to think things through and work alone. Sensing learners prefer facts and procedures, while intuitive learners are more conceptual, innovative and focus on theories and meanings. Visual learners prefer visual representations, e.g. charts and diagrams, while verbal learners prefer written or spoken explanations. Sequential learners are linear and orderly, and prefer to learn in incremental steps. Global learners prefer to see the big picture and learn in large leaps. Papp (2002) reviews the work of Felder and Soloman, comparing it with other models of learning style, and concludes that it seems to have a more consistent and applicable predictive value than the other models.

These models of learning styles are relevant to the design and delivery of e-learning programmes, as they provide insights into the diversity of learners and their range of different learning needs. Successful e-learning programmes will structure their learning programmes so that learners can take their preferred route through a mix of different learning activities. They are also useful as a developmental tool, e.g. to enable individual learners to identify and reflect on their preferred learning styles and identify ways of improving. This is explored in more detail in Chapter 8.

Core – central personality dimension

Our personality has an impact on the way we learn and, as with learning style theories, there are many different approaches to personality. An important model is the Myers-Briggs Type Indicator (MBTI) (Association for Psychological Type, 2000), which is based on Karl Jung's theory of psychological types. It identifies preferences in the four dimensions of: extraversion/introversion, sensing/intuition, thinking/feeling, and judging/perceiving. These are then used to characterize people according to different combinations of the four dimensions, e.g. one learner could identify as extravert/sensing/feeling/perceiving, while another may come out with an intravert/intuition/feeling/perceiving profile. These profiles can then be explored and used as a basis for individual reflection in the same way as the learning style profiling tools mentioned previously. The MBTI model is widely used as a psychological profiling tool, and it is beginning to be explored in the context of e-learning (Atkins, Moore and Sharpe, 2001). The implications of this model for the design and delivery of e-learning programmes is to consider the needs and preferences of many different types of learners. One way of ensuring that these are met is to involve a diverse range of people in the design and piloting of a new e-learning programme. Feedback from different people will inevitably be based on their previous learning experiences, their learning styles and personality, and this can be used to ensure that the e-learning programme meets the needs of its intended audience.

Summary of implications for the design of e-learning environments, programmes or activities

1 Provide visual, auditory and practical experiences:
   — use visual images – diagrams, graphs, photographs, mindmaps
   — introduce auditory experiences – sound clips, discussions, telephone support
   — introduce activities – quizzes, developing and producing a product such as a website.
2 Provide different learning activities and processes:
   — for pragmatists – case studies, practical tips and techniques
   — for activists – activities, opportunities to socialize
   — for reflectors – opportunities to stand back and think, learning journals and reflective activities, opportunities to work by themselves
   — for theorists – provide background information and links to additional learning materials
   — for sensing learners – provide facts and procedures
   — for intuitive learners – provide theories and opportunities to explore meanings
   — for sequential learners – provide linear and orderly learning experiences that are arranged in incremental steps
   — for global learners – provide the big picture.
3 Provide opportunities to practise working with new skills and knowledge.
4 Provide opportunities to synthesize and integrate ideas.
5 Involve a wide range of people in the design and piloting of a new e-learning programme.

Reflection on learning

Reflection is an important human activity in which people recapture their experience, think about it and mull over it and

> *evaluate it. It is this working with experience that is important in learning. The capacity to reflect is developed at different stages in different people and it may be this ability which characterizes those who learn effectively from experience.*
> (Boud, Keogh and Walker, 1985, 19)

Reflection is a natural human activity. Typically we reflect on our daily activities, our successes and failures, relationships and careers. This reflective process may take place during other activities – walking, swimming, showering, washing up – and our thoughts and conclusions may be lost as we move onto another activity. The importance of reflective practice is that it helps learners to improve their studying and learning skills.

One study of reflective practice (Morrison, 1995) found that learners who were actively involved in formal reflective activities (e.g. keeping a learning journal) reported:

- increased motivation and confidence – in studying, learning, reflecting, questioning
- greater self-awareness leading to self-fulfilment
- better-developed professional skills and career self-awareness
- greater understanding of the links between theory and practice.

Reflective practice is used by many professional groups as the basis of their continuing professional development.

Summary of implications for the design of e-learning environments, programmes or activities

1   Provide opportunities for reflection, e.g. during and at the end of programmes or activities.
2   Encourage learners to stand back and reflect on different aspects of e-learning programmes, e.g. individual or group processes, their feelings about e-learning, implications of their experiences for their studies or work.
3   If you are involved in establishing e-learning programmes that lead to a qualification, then include reflective practice as part of the assessment strategy, e.g. use online reflective activities or learning journals.

Learning as a social activity

Learning can also viewed as a social and cultural activity, and some people argue that learning is inherently social. In this model of learning individuals learn as a result of interactions with others and what we learn depends on who we are, what we want to become and what we value. This means that learning is placed within the context of a group or a community.

Example

The author's experiences of becoming an e-learner and making new virtual friends (including visits to a virtual public house) helped motivate her to keep going with an e-learning course when external distractions were at their highest and energy was starting to flag.

Goodyear (2000) summarized this view in the following 'principles of learning' adapted from Darrouzet and Lynn (1999):

- learning is fundamentally social
- learning is integrated into the life of communities
- learning is an act of participation
- knowing depends on engagement in practice
- engagement is inseparable from empowerment
- failure to learn is the result of exclusion from participation
- people are natural lifelong learners.

These principles suggest that e-learning programmes should be designed so that they foster learning groups and communities. It is important that the e-learning environment provides virtual communication tools such as e-mail, bulletin boards or discussion groups, and chat or conference rooms. As mentioned in Chapter 2, these are standard features in VLEs and are readily available in alternatives to VLEs such as groupware. E-learning environments combined with face-to-face meetings provide tutors with different means of facilitating learning and teaching. They can be used to enable students to learn in different ways: independently, co-operatively and collaboratively.

Independent learning

Independent learning involves learners working by themselves with various levels of formal support – from no support through to support from a tutor. This is the type of learning that is often associated with interactive learning packages.

Characteristics of independent learners

Independent learners are motivated to learn. They accept responsibility for their own learning and have the confidence to approach others for help if they need it.

Independent learners are capable of managing their learning processes effectively. This includes:

- identifying and understanding their overall goal
- being clear about their learning outcomes
- selecting and using appropriate methods and techniques
- managing time, stress, other commitments
- using a wide range of learning opportunities and resources
- adapting the learning process to make use of new opportunities.

Independent learners are able to monitor and reflect critically on how and what they learn. Through this they develop an awareness that helps them to learn with increasing effectiveness. They also demonstrate a more questioning attitude to what they are learning.

Adapted from Allan and Lewis (2000)

E-learning environments can be used to support independent learning activities, based on the use of web-based training materials incorporating self assessment activities and formal assessment activities, and on the use of a wide range of information sources. It is worth pointing out that independent learning isn't necessarily the same thing as learning by yourself. Successful independent learners are likely to use help and support from a range of different people, including their peers and tutors.

Co-operative and collaborative learning

E-learners can also use a virtual environment to work co-operatively or collaboratively with each other. Such learners may be in the same or different organizations, and they may be in the same or different countries. Co-operative working includes sharing resources, exchanging information, and giving and receiving feedback. Typically, co-operative working involves individuals working towards individual goals and outcomes, but benefiting from working in a supportive group.

Collaborative learning groups are likely to involve e-learners working together towards a shared goal. This may be a goal that they have agreed and negotiated themselves, or it may be a goal set up by a tutor or other person. Examples include students working on a joint project, practitioners working together on a joint report or academic article, or colleagues working together on a joint workplace project.

The benefits of co-operative and collaborative learning include increased motivation due to sharing of ideas, support from other learners and 'sparking off ideas'. Research (e.g. McConnell, 2000) suggests that these approaches to structuring learning result in individual learners having a deeper understanding of the material and also developing high-quality thinking strategies. McConnell concludes that achievement is generally higher in co-operative situations than in individualistic or competitive ones.

One common approach to the design of e-learning programmes (see Figure 5.2) is to start off with collaborative activities, then move into co-operative activities and finally enable learners to work independently. This enables learners to develop online support networks at the start of a programme, and these will then be used as they move into more independent work. This type of approach is typically front-loaded in terms of tutor support, as the early stages of the programme require much facilitation. One risk of this approach is that there can be a high dropout rate if there are early problems with group dynamics.

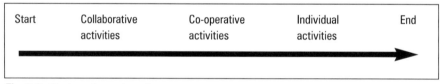

| Start | Collaborative activities | Co-operative activities | Individual activities | End |

Fig. 5.2 *Design of an e-learning programme*

Some people, for example Jensen (1995) and Garratt (1997), suggest that students will have different preferences for working together independently, co-operatively or collaboratively, and that this is another type of learning style. This suggests that some students may be less successful in programmes built around one of these styles of working and learning. The author has certainly experienced this aspect on one e-learning training event where one or two people who signed up for a programme that they perceived as involving independent learning were horrified to find that they were expected to work co-operatively and collaboratively. While developing group and team working skills is considered important

116

within most contexts, this example raises the issue of the importance of clarity about programme expectations and the importance of appropriate programme design.

Different experiences of online learning

The author asked two reference librarians about their experiences of an online course on using html. The first response was:

> *It was great. I learnt what I wanted to in my own time and at my own rate. A few of the activities were a bit confusing but I just got on with them. I got what I wanted from the course and really recommend it to others.*

The second librarian said:

> *I hated it. It was a lonely experience. The tutor was helpful but I would have preferred to have met him. E-mail wasn't the same as being face-to-face with someone. I'd never do another online course.*

The differences in the experiences of these two librarians is likely to relate to their learning styles and preferences for working independently or in a group situation.

Summary of implications for the design of e-learning environments, programmes or activities

1   Select learning processes that support the aims and learning outcomes of the programme.
2   Ensure that prospective e-learners are clear about the types of learning activities involved in independent or group learning situations.
3   Identify the sources, types and levels of support within the e-learning programme.
4   Identify the role of peers, colleagues and mentors in the e-learning programme.
5   If you are using a group learning process, then start off with collaborative group activities, as this can enhance motivation, group bonding and also generate supportive relationships that will facilitate learning throughout the programme.

Cognitive apprenticeship

The current concept of cognitive apprenticeship is based on traditional apprenticeship, and it explores learning from the viewpoint of new practitioners developing their knowledge and skills by observing and learning from expert practice. Cognitive apprenticeship may involve face-to-face and/or virtual communication processes, it is embedded into authentic work practices, and involves a range of different instructional methods as well as social activities. Collins et al. (1989) provide a framework of six instructional methods of cognitive apprenticeship:

1 Modelling, where the new LIS practitioner learns from observing and copying an expert's practices.
2 Coaching, where the new practitioner is supported through one-to-one support that is likely to include goal setting, instruction, practice and feedback.
3 Scaffolding, where the experienced practitioner provides temporary support to the learners for those parts of the task that they find difficult. This support may initially be extremely active and then the experienced practitioner may fade out, gradually removing support as the new practitioners develop their competence and confidence.
4 Articulation, where new practitioners discuss their issue or problem and explore it with the guidance of the more experienced practitioner.
5 Reflection enables new practitioners to externalize their internal thinking processes, and discuss them with the more experienced practitioner. This is likely to involve a process that includes evaluation, exploring other options or ways of behaving, and action planning.
6 Exploration, where the new practitioner is involved in work-based problem-solving. The more experienced practitioner may set guidelines, make suggestions for action, and enable the learner to understand and appreciate the complexity of the problem, the underlying issues and the LIS context.

Virtual communication tools are increasingly playing an important role in cognitive apprenticeship, and this is explored by Wang and Bonk (2001). Virtual communication tools such as e-mail, discussion groups and chat rooms provide a medium through which new entrants to the profession can learn from more experienced practitioners. This process is often managed through formal mentoring schemes. In the context of library and information professional training programmes, the concept of cognitive apprenticeship provides a framework for the development of work-based learning activities, e.g. through the use of case studies or problem-solving activities in both face-to-face and e-learning situations. Finally, the process of cognitive apprenticeship may also lead individual practitioners to become members of communities of practice as they are introduced to, and become part of, a professional community.

Summary of implications for the design of e-learning environments, programmes or activities

1   Involve work-based case studies and problem-solving activities.
2   Involve experienced practitioners, e.g. as mentors.

Communities of practice

The previous section highlighted the importance of learning as a social activity, and explored collaborative and co-operative learning. These learning groups may evolve into communities of learners called 'communities of practice'. This concept, first coined by Wenger (1997), is currently influencing the development of many professional education groups and programmes, so it is an important idea in the context of e-learning and in the development of the library and information profession. The use of virtual communication tools has enabled new forms of learning and working together, as different people come together in virtual space to form groups focused around a particular interest or issue. Communities of practice may develop as part of a collaborative project or programme, through discussion groups, or in response to a particular issue. Communities of practice may develop within a library and information department (e.g. people interested in a specific issue) or across different library and information units (e.g. special interest groups). They may be located within a particular country or region, or they may be global.

Wenger (1997) coined the phrase 'communities of practice', which is defined as:

. . . a special type of informal network that emerges from a desire to work more effectively or to understand work more deeply among members of a particular specialty or work group. At the simplest level, communities of practice are small groups of people who have worked together over a period of time and through extensive communication have developed a common

119

> *sense of purpose and a desire to share work-related knowledge*
> *and experience.*
>
> Sharp (1997)

Most people are members of a number of different communities of practice. The author, for example, is a member of two communities associated with information work, three e-learning communities of practice, a training community of practice, and a dog training community of practice. Some of these communities meet face-to-face, while others involve a mixture of face-to-face and virtual communications, and a few communities are virtual ones.

Wenger differentiates between communities of practice and communities of interest, and his ideas are summarized in Table 5.2. Library and information workers are likely to be members of both types of community.

Table 5.2 *Comparison of communities of practice and communities of interest*

Characteristics	Community of practice	Community of interest
Purpose	To create, expand, and share knowledge. To develop individual's professional practice.	To be informed.
Membership	People who share a particular interest or passion in a topic. People who become subscribers or members of a particular group, e.g. mail list, e-learning programme. They may be self-selected or members by invitation. Membership is likely to be relatively small, e.g. 6–24.	People who become subscribers or members of a particular group, e.g. mail list, e-learning programme. Membership may be very large, e.g. 12–1000.
What holds them together	Passion, commitment, identity with group. Personal relationships within the group.	Access to information and a sense of like-mindedness.
Examples in LIS	Some groups involved in collaborative project work. Professional groups supported by professional organizations. Some e-learning programmes.	Some discussion groups. Newsgroups.

Wenger et al. (2002) identify the following benefits to community members:

- help with challenges
- access to expertise
- better able to contribute to the team
- confidence in one's approach to problems
- fun of being with colleagues
- more meaningful participation
- a sense of belonging.

Participating in communities of practice also fosters professional development, as they provide a forum for expanding skills and expertise, and the network enables individual information workers to keep up-to-date. Membership of communities of practice can also lead to enhanced professional reputation, and so increased marketability and employability. Information workers who are members are likely to develop a strong sense of professional identity, and this is particularly important to relatively new entrants to the field, and also to people who are working in solo libraries or information units.

Wenger's description of communities of practice identifies different levels of participation by individual members. He identifies three levels: peripheral members, who rarely participate but are on the sidelines observing discussions; active members; core members who introduce new topics or projects, and help shape and lead the community. He suggests that there is a development route from peripheral through to becoming an active or core member. Many information workers will be familiar with this model, even if they hadn't previously conceptualized it in these terms. It is a model that appears to operate in traditional face-to-face professional groups, e.g. special interest groups of AALA, ALA or CILIP. As with traditional professional groups, the presence of a co-ordinator or facilitator can help integrate new members into the community, which will enable them to become active or core members. As with face-to-face environments, in virtual environments the use of e-buddies can be a useful means of providing support and encouragement to new community members.

Involvement in communities of practice also brings benefits to the library or information unit, and Wenger (2002) identifies both short- and long-term benefits (see Table 5.3).

Table 5.3 *Benefits of communities of practice*

Short term benefits	Long term benefits
Arena for problem solving	Ability to execute a strategic plan
Quick answers to questions	Authority with customers or stakeholders
Reduced time and costs	Increased retention of talent
Improved quality of decisions	Capacity for knowledge-development projects
More perspectives on problems	Forum for 'benchmarking' against other information or library units
Co-ordination, standardization and synergies across units	Knowledge-based alliances
Resources for implementing strategies	Emergence of unplanned capabilities
Strengthened quality assurance	Capacity to develop new strategic options
Ability to take risks with the backing of the community	Ability to forecast technological developments
	Ability to take advantage of emerging opportunities

Many of the virtual communication tools described in Chapter 3 enable the development of communities of interest and communities of practice. For example, many discussion lists are communities of interest. Examples of communities of practice may be found in:

- special interest groups, e.g. those focused around a particular issue or interest such as legal information, sports information
- some professional sub-groups, e.g. chief librarians, librarians in colleges of higher education, prison librarians
- groups focused on specific systems or activities, e.g. interlibrary loans, vendor groups, MLE or VLE groups
- groups brought together for a specific purpose, e.g. collaborative projects
- some virtual learning groups.

The e-learning in higher education programme at the University of Birmingham (see Chapter 6) is an example of a developing community of practice as staff from a range of backgrounds (library, IT, academic, educational development) work together on projects that involve individuals sharing ideas, constructing knowledge and developing their knowledge and skills by discussing and exploring ideas with colleagues. This community of practice has developed beyond the boundaries of the original programme and is having an important impact on the development of e-learning within the university.

It is true that some information professionals may be cynical about the concept of communities of practice, and consider it jargon for describing the types of networking and collaborative work that the library and information profession has traditionally excelled at. But the concept does help to focus on the importance to individuals and their employers of becoming involved with different groups and developing their own and the profession's knowledge and practice.

Wenger (2002) provides detailed guidance on the development of communities of practice, and McDermott (2000) describes 10 critical success factors in building a community of practice:

1 Focus on topics important to community members.
2 Find a well-respected community member to co-ordinate the community.
3 Make sure people have time and encouragement to participate.
4 Build on the core values of the organization.
5 Get key thought leaders involved.
6 Build personal relationships among community members.
7 Develop an active passionate core group.
8 Create forums for thinking together as well as systems for sharing information.
9 Make it easy to contribute and access the community's knowledge and practices.
10 Create real dialogue about cutting-edge issues.

Summary of implications for the design of continuous professional development processes

1 Consider whether or not you wish to develop an online learning community.
2 If you decide to establish an online community, then identify the need for a community of interest or a community of practice.
3 If you are establishing, developing and maintaining a community of interest, then consider using a mail list, bulletin board or similar tool. Establish clear boundaries and follow existing good practice in running and moderating such a community.
4 If you are establishing, developing and maintaining a community of practice, then consider using a mail list, bulletin board or similar tool. Establish clear boundaries and follow existing good practice in running and moderating such a community.
5 If you are establishing, developing and maintaining a community of practice, then consider using McDermott's 10 critical success factors.

Knowledge and competence

In recent years there has been an important debate about knowledge and learning, and this section considers three perspectives on higher education that were identified by Goodyear (2000). Each of these perspectives is concerned with developing higher-order thinking skills – i.e. applying, analysing, synthesizing and evaluating knowledge – and e-learning offers new opportunities for developing a learner's cognitive skills. The three perspectives are:

- the traditional academic view
- the vocationalist view
- the reflexivity view.

The traditional academic view of knowledge is one of a 'body of knowledge' that is transmitted to students. In this perspective, only professional academics or expert practitioners are able to add to this body of knowledge, which means they effectively have a monopoly on this knowledge. The traditional academic view places value on the disinterested acquisition of academic knowledge. Students are asked to become competent in academic discourse, with its heavy reliance on declarative conceptual knowledge, contemplative forms of analysis and use of textual (including mathematical) representations.

In contrast, the vocationalist view requires students to use academic knowledge as the content and context for developing their skills and expertise, and they will later transfer these skills into the world of work. This perspective is often linked to discussions about generic competence and employability, and students are required to develop transferable skills that can then be applied in the workplace. Goodyear argues that much of this work is oriented towards information, knowledge and communication, and so requires the skills of academic discourse.

The third perspective, the reflexivity approach, focuses on the importance of developing individual reflexivity which can be applied to any situation, and on the acknowledgement that there is no certain knowledge in the world. This approach to critical thinking and reflexivity is described by Barnett (1997a/b), who argues that reflexivity, i.e. the ability to question and apply second-order thinking, is required for dealing with the modern world, where there is no certain knowledge. Barnett argues that students who develop reflexivity will be able to manage the challenges of working in modern organizations operating within a turbulent environment.

Each of these perspectives require the ability to engage with knowledge in a different way:

1 **Traditional academic view** – knowledge is transmitted, and after experiencing a rite of passage such as a PhD or extensive professional experience, then individuals gain the right to develop knowledge and then transmit it.

2 **Vocationalist view** – knowledge is used as the context in which individuals develop skills, which can then be transferred to the workplace.

3 **Reflexivity approach** – there is no certain knowledge, and individuals must develop their thinking skills so that they can deal with living and working in a rapidly changing world.

This distinction is important in the context of e-tutoring and the development of e-learning programmes. For example, someone who is operating within a traditional academic view is likely to want to use online learning experiences to enable students to exchange and understand a particular knowledge base. Information workers who are working in this type of knowledge environment may be called upon for their skills in finding and utilizing a wide range of resources. They may be involved in developing e-learning programmes where the emphasis is on identifying and transmitting standard packages of information.

Tutors working from a vocationalist perspective may want to develop their students' transferable skills through online problem-solving tasks or project work. Many information literacy projects are based on the principle of enabling individuals to develop transferable skills that can be used in a wide range of situations. Traditionally, information workers lead the development and implementation of information literacy programmes within their organizations.

In contrast, experienced information practitioners are likely to be involved in the design and development of projects or learning programmes that place a priority on the development of higher-order reflexivity skills. Typical examples include postgraduate programmes in library and information work, action research projects, and collaborative workplace projects.

While this identification of three basic approaches to knowledge linked to three specific types of examples is an over-simplification, the key point is that information workers involved in e-learning need to identify and acknowledge the dominant perspective in their context.

Summary of implications for the design of e-learning environments, programmes or activities

1 Identify the approach to knowledge that is required in the particular e-learning programme.

2 Ensure the e-learning programme matches the underpinning theory of knowledge.

Approaches to learning and teaching

Learning and teaching online involves more than simply transferring traditional programmes to new media, or adding an e-learning component to a well established course. It involves being clear about:

- pedagogical goals
- the learning needs of students
- the capabilities and limitations of the resources
- deciding how to use the resources to achieve your goals.

There are many different models of learning, and online learning environments can be used to support different approaches to learning and teaching. Two approaches that are commonly discussed in relation to online learning and teaching are behaviourist and constructivist.

Behaviourist approaches

Behaviourist approaches are typified by learning activities and processes that can be clearly labelled, observed and measured. These are typified by:

- very specific definition of learning objectives
- material broken down into small chunks and linked in a clear logical sequence
- emphasis on knowledge and skill reproduction
- learning activities sequenced by the tutor
- frequent tests or reviews – the use of 'model' answers
- regular feedback based on students' ability to achieve outcomes set in programme
- little awareness of, or allowance for, personal learning needs, interests or negotiation.

Many interactive learning packages designed for independent learners are designed on behaviourist principles.

Constructivist approaches

One theoretical model that is becoming increasingly discussed in relation to online learning and teaching is the constructivist theory. Alexander (1999) describes the three basic characteristics common to constructivist theory as:

1   Knowledge is not a product to be accumulated but an active process in which the learner attempts to make sense out of the world.
2   People acquire knowledge in forms that make sense to them and enable them to use it in a meaningful way in their lives.
3   The construction of knowledge is based on collaboration and social negotiation of meaning. Common understandings and shared meaning are developed through discussions with peers and tutors.

This suggests that in online discussions it is important to create a learning environment that will enable students to work in learning groups and:

- exchange their own world maps or mental models
- explore their own ideas on the meaning of a topic
- identify and explore ideas between theory and practice
- share their work and academic experiences with one other.

Information workers who use virtual learning environments may use behaviourist, constructivist or mixed behaviourist/constructivist approaches to learning and teaching, depending on the learning outcomes and the philosophy of their programmes.

Summary of implications for the design of e-learning environments, programmes or activities

Identify the underlying approach to learning, e.g. behaviourist or constructivist, and ensure that the programme is congruent with this approach.

Five-stage model of e-learning

Models of online learning are still being developed, and one useful model presented by Salmon (2000) and describing an individual learner's experience is presented here. This model is particularly relevant to this chapter as it integrates many of the ideas mentioned above, such as individual approaches to learning, learning as a social activity, and knowledge construction. Salmon uses the term 'moderating' to describe e-tutoring. In this model learners start at stage 1 and then progress through the stages up to stage 5 (see Figure 5.3).

This model provides a framework for programme designers to identify the types of learning processes, activities and support that they need to include at different stages of the programme. The practical implications of this model are

Stage 5	Development
Stage 4	Knowledge construction
Stage 3	Information exchange
Stage 2	Online socialization
Stage 1	Access and motivation

Fig. 5.3 *Five-stage model of e-learning*

described in more detail in Chapter 7 and Chapter 8.

Using this model in practice some issues arise:

1 If learners don't succeed in setting up their access to the system, then they won't be able to learn via an online system. Although this is a very obvious point, it has implications for the provision of technical support to enable learner participation. Many information workers are involved in helping their customers access e-learning opportunities, e.g. in learning centres based in libraries and information units. It is vital that they are able to provide access and also support in overcoming technical issues. Similarly, information workers who are working as e-tutors are likely to have a role in this process, either at the level of referring the learner to technical support from help desks and maintaining their motivation through what can be a very frustrating time period, or by actually providing them with technical support.

2 Individual e-learners may experience situations that cause them to move back down the stages. Information workers may then be called in to help them progress. For example, people working at Stage 3 Information exchange may drop back to Stage 1 Access if they experience ICT problems. It then may be the role of the information worker to help them access the e-learning programme and move forward again.

3 Different learners may be at different stages in this development process. As in face-to-face situations, the e-tutor must manage and support learners in the same group who may be at different stages in the five-step model.

4 The underlying philosophy and programme design will have a bearing on how far learners develop along this process.

Access to e-learning

Anisha was a student on an Open University programme that required her to access a virtual learning environment two or three times a week. Her computer broke down and had to be sent off to be repaired. It was likely to be away for 2–3 weeks. After contacting her tutor, Mustafa, she visited her local public library (a small rural branch library in North Yorkshire), where she was able to book and use a computer. This enabled her to keep up-to-date with her course.

Summary of implications for the design of e-learning environments, programmes or activities

1   Use the Gilly Salmon five-stage model as a framework for design.
2   Ensure that there is technical support built into the delivery process.
3   Design activities so that they help guide and support the learner through the five stages.
4   Ensure that learners who access e-learning programmes from library and information services have access to appropriate technical support

Summary

Learning is a complex process. Different models attempt to explain and clarify the learning process. These models provide general ideas about individual and group learning, and these are important for information practitioners who are involved in providing access to e-learning programmes and/or designing, developing or delivering their own programmes. The concept of a cognitive apprentice is useful in that it makes explicit the types of instructional processes that take place as a new LIS practitioner learns from a more experienced practitioner. This process of cognitive apprenticeship may take place through a mixture of face-to-face and virtual meetings. The next step in the professional development of a new practitioner may be their involvement in (face-to-face or virtual) communities of interest and communities of practice, and these enable individuals to share, exchange and construct knowledge.

6
E-tutoring

Introduction

The purpose of this chapter is to explore e-tutoring. It will enable library and information workers who are involved in e-learning programmes to have an understanding of the role and responsibilities of e-tutors. The chapter identifies and explores the knowledge and special skills required by e-tutors, and also some of the issues they are likely to face when delivering e-learning programmes. E-tutoring often involves co-tutoring – e.g. information staff working with subject specialists – and this topic is explored from a practical perspective. The chapter concludes with an overview of staff development approaches to enabling information workers to become effective e-tutors.

Library and information staff may be involved in e-tutoring at a number of different levels:

- providing face-to-face support to e-learners who are accessing online learning opportunities using ICT in the library or e-learning centre
- supporting online learners using a virtual reference desk
- providing additional support to face-to-face programmes using virtual communication tools
- e-tutoring programmes with minimal or no face-to-face support
- e-tutoring in blended programmes.

Providing face-to-face support to e-learners who are using ICT resources in the library or information unit to carryout online learning activities is an important area of activity for information workers. For example, public libraries are an important community access point for e-learning, which means that library staff need to be able to provide the right kind of environment, basic technical help and learning support. As a result these libraries need staff with ICT skills as well as knowledge and skills in supporting e-learning. Chapters 1 and 4 mention The People's Network scheme, and this includes a strand to train public library staff in ICT skills. Public library staff are being trained to the standard of the European Computer Driving Licence to create content for the network and to digitize library resources.

The provision of virtual reference desks, and the opportunities for providing additional support to learners using virtual communication tools, are well established in academic library and information services. This type of service is becoming increasingly common in workplace libraries too, and in multinational companies information workers in different countries may co-operate to provide 24/7 (24-hours-a-day, 7-days-a-week) service, so supporting employees across all time zones and different working days. These services often require information workers to have effective virtual communication skills.

Information workers who are involved in e-tutoring, whether in programmes with minimal or no contact, or blended programmes, need to develop and use e-learning teaching and training skills. Although working in a virtual environment requires many of the same skills and techniques that work in a face-to-face environment, it also requires the development of new approaches to communicating with learners. In this chapter we will explore the key conferencing skills required for working in an e-learning environment. In addition, e-tutoring often involves working in collaborative teams and co-tutoring, and this is explored later in the chapter. Becoming an e-tutor involves a development process that may include experiencing e-learning first-hand as a student by taking part in one of the many excellent e-learning and tutoring programmes available over the internet.

Why become an online e-tutor?

Barajas and Owen (2000) describe some of the reasons why e-tutors may want to become involved in online learning:

- to gain experience of e-tutoring and e-learning
- to gain professional standing by teaching on an e-learning programme
- to offer the possibility of learning to those potential learners who would not find it possible to participate in the traditional face-to-face manner.

Informal discussions with information workers have provided additional reasons that are based on their view of their customer needs and their own professional needs:

- to improve the learners' learning experiences

- to enhance the learners' learning achievements
- to enable the learners to develop their online skills
- to enable the learners to develop their group-working skills
- to enhance career opportunities
- to change career
- to enable teleworking (working from home)
- to be involved at a relatively early stage in what is to become the future
- curiosity.

This suggests that individual e-tutors who get involved in online e-tutoring are likely to be motivated in a range of different ways, both intrinsically and extrinsically. This has implications for the motivation and development of online e-tutors.

Challenges to becoming an online e-tutor

Library and information staff may have concerns about becoming an e-tutor. Some people may be concerned that they don't have sufficient technical skills or time to learn new systems and processes. Standard virtual learning environments tend to be transparent and easy to use, but it does take time to get to know their strengths and weaknesses. The author found it took her about three hours to get to grips with the basics of systems such as *WebCT* and *Blackboard*, and she is still developing her knowledge and skills of these systems. Online tutorials are readily available but they do take time to work through and digest.

Time does tend to be an issue with respect to library and information staff working as e-tutors. They may be concerned that this is yet another activity they are asked to become involved in, and this is often on top of an already busy workload. One of the potential dangers of e-tutoring is that it can be fitted in and around other information work activities, which can mean that the working day becomes even more pressurized.

Library and information workers tend to enjoy working with customers and colleagues, and there is often a perception that e-tutoring is an impersonal activity. The reality of e-tutoring is that it can be a warm and friendly process with real relationships building up over the internet. However, unless staff have experienced this type of person-centred process, it can be hard to convince them that positive and rewarding relationships are possible online.

Another challenge is to overcome cynicism due to previous experience with off-the-shelf computer-aided learning CAL packages. Many early CAL packages (and also some later ones) offered a dry, boring and uninspiring approach to learning. While badly designed e-learning programmes can offer negative experiences, well designed ones can offer valuable and enjoyable learning experiences. Finally, for some library and information trainers whose current programmes and user education activities are working effectively, there can be the attitude of 'if it isn't broken then don't fix it.'

E-tutors and their role

Online learning and teaching is a relatively new process and one that is changing the e-tutor's roles and relationships. Goodyear (2000) provides a framework of e-tutoring roles, summarized in Figure 6.1, and this identifies a move from the 'sage on the stage' to a 'guide on the side'. In other words the e-tutor is working as a facilitator and guide rather than an authoritarian figure head.

This concept of 'guide on the side' is supported by research summarized by McCabe (1998) which suggests that in online groups there is a greater equality of participation, with online e-tutors providing a much smaller input than in a face-to-face group. McCabe quotes figures of e-tutor participation of 10–15% and 22%.

Traditional tutor roles	Online e-tutor roles
'sage on the stage'	'guide on the side'
Lecturer	Consultant, guide, and resource provider
Provider of answers	Expert questioner
Provider of content	Designer of learning experiences
Solitary e-tutor	Member of a learning team
Total control of the teaching environment	Shared control with the learner as fellow-learner
Total power over the teaching experience	Shared power with the learner

Fig. 6.1 *Change in tutor roles*

The characteristics of the 'guide on the side' are well illustrated by Hislop (2000) (see Table 6.1), who describes the characteristics of effective e-tutors. His work is based on experiences of e-tutoring an online Masters degree in information systems at Drexel University.

Table 6.1 *Characteristics of effective e-tutors*

Motivated	Motivated e-tutors have a strong interest in working to make their online class successful. They are willing to make the effort to deal with technology and a new teaching and learning environment.

Approachable	Approachable e-tutors encourage learners to interact with them. Being approachable reduces barriers to interaction in the online environment.
Visible	Visible e-tutors make their presence felt frequently in the online environment. This helps add substance to the online experience and provide glue to hold the community of learners together.
Explicit	Explicit e-tutors provide timely, detailed directions about what the learners need to do and how the class will operate. They are also explicit in addressing course content. This helps to ameliorate the limitations of the restricted communication channels in the online environment
Pro-active	Pro-active e-tutors make an extra effort to reach out to learners in ways beyond what would be necessary or typical in a traditional environment. For example, a pro-active instructor might put extra effort into contacting an inactive learner in an online class.
Discreet	Discreet e-tutors manage a class without dominating it. They facilitate online discussions while encouraging learners to provide most of the comments. They also know when to comment publicly and when to switch to private communication with a learner or learners.
Collaborative	Collaborative e-tutors are willing to work with staff and other e-tutors engaged in online education. They are also comfortable working with learners in a coaching role rather than a more hierarchical style.
Technically capable	Technically capable e-tutors have sufficient technical knowledge and adeptness to be comfortable with the online environment. Online e-tutors do not need to be technical experts, but they need basic technical skills to get started. They also need to be able to deal with the inevitable technical glitches and technology changes (with technical support help).
Credible	Learners accept credible e-tutors as experts in the subject of the course. Past research has shown the importance of credibility, particularly in technical fields, including information systems. For online classes this may be even more important, since the learner's connection to the university is embodied largely in interactions with the instructor.

What does online e-tutoring involve?

The role of an online e-tutor is to facilitate learning within the online environment. Collins and Berge (1996) have identified four main types of e-tutor activities: pedagogical, social, managerial and technical.

Pedagogical activities involve enabling learners to learn in an online environment, develop their subject knowledge, and also develop their effective learning and thinking skills. This involves a number of different activities: modelling appropriate online behaviours; supporting and developing subject learning by introducing ideas and insights; questioning and probing learners' responses; and focusing discussions, e.g. on critical concepts, principles and skills.

E-tutors also need to engage in and encourage **social activities** with their learners. This includes creating a friendly and informal environment, which is a necessity for successful online learning. It includes acknowledging learners' contributions and helping individuals to work together. It can also mean sharing experiences from outside the e-learning programme, e.g. holiday experiences, outside interests, jokes. Online socialization is the second stage in the five-stage model of e-learning described in Chapter 5, and it appears to be an essential pre-requisite for effective learning. It provides the 'glue' that helps individuals to work together as an e-learning group.

As with face-to-face groups, e-tutors need to **manage** the agenda for the discussion or conference: starting the learning group; introducing the outcomes; setting the pace; introducing and setting tasks; focusing and refocusing the discussion or conference; managing the time; summarizing the outcomes; and closing the discussion or conference. The learning group may be led by an e-tutor whose style is directive or someone with a 'light touch'.

The online e-tutor must be competent with the **technology** and enable learners to develop their competence in the particular technical environment. This means that new e-tutors need to spend some time getting to grips with the technology, and that they also need access to technical back-up from either their own organization or their supplier.

Finally, Goodyear (2000) presents a list of recommendations for e-tutors and this is presented at the end of this chapter (pages 155–7).

Working as an e-tutor

Online learning and teaching involve e-tutors (and also learners) developing new skills. The practical realities of learning online include the need to:

- distribute time
- deal with overload
- develop skills in reading and following threads
- develop an online voice
- develop skills in knowledge construction.

Online e-tutors who are involved in facilitating co-operative or collaborative learning groups need to access their virtual learning environment and, possibly, interact with their learners regularly, e.g. 2–3 times a week. This is quite different from the traditional training or user education practice of scheduled events, and it may involve some changes in time management. Managing time, and also learner expectations of online access to their e-tutor, is an important part of the initial stages in online e-tutoring.

There is concern about information and work overload of e-tutors. It is really important that new e-tutors are clear about the demands and expectations that arise as a result of this role. The author has found the following strategies very useful for managing time in a virtual environment:

- set very clear boundaries around time online
- let learners know how often you are likely to be online, e.g. 3–4 times a week
- ask learners to phone or send private e-mails for urgent actions
- set up a FAQ list.

The online e-tutor (and learner) also needs to be able to read a large number of messages and become 'comfortable in trying to make sense of jigsaws of text' (Cooper and Smith 2000). Such skills are, in many respects, a standard part of the library and information worker's toolkit – analysing large amounts of information, synthesizing the different ideas or threads (this particular skill is called weaving), managing potential uncertainties about this jigsaw of ideas, and then having the confidence and time to post comments and responses themselves.

The online skill of weaving involves moving into and out of online discussions and helping them to move forward. E-tutors need to bring together the messages on a particular topic or thread and present them in a structured way. If you imagine a party with 10 different conversations all taking place at the same time, and people moving from conversation to conversation, then the task of weaving involves creating a summary from the key points of these multi-stranded conversations. In some respects it is like a plenary session at a conference. The following list identifies some of the activities e-tutors may be involved in as they weave a discussion.

Weaving an online discussion

Typical activities involved by e-tutors:

- using open-ended comments
- leaving 'handles' for future threads
- linking responses and threads
- using names in linked comments
- standing back
- having a 'weave day'

- seeking similarities across threads
- affirming and moving discussion on
- contrasting views
- referencing back to more than just the previous comment
- sharing the flow and encouraging learners to weave themselves by modelling good practices.   (Cox et al., 2000)

In addition to weaving, Cox et al. (2000) provide some guidelines for e-tutors on involving learners in online discussions:

- start from the learners' experience
- use relevant and authentic materials, e.g. real-life case studies
- generate enthusiasm and a curiosity about each other's perspectives
- acknowledge and include different points of view
- explain why you are saying what you are saying
- summarize, then pose a question to move on debate
- bring in outside ideas.

One important online facilitation tool used in conferences and discussion groups (and also in face-to-face meetings) is that of meta-comments.

Meta-comments can help repair matters if the conference is suffering because of insufficient clarity of response, irrelevant contributions, information overload. Meta-comments are comments at a 'higher level' than the individual contributions to the substantive discussion in a conference. They are more general and probably don't refer directly to any one person or any one contribution. A timely comment like 'One of the difficulties with conferences like this is if people put in very lengthy contributions then newcomers may be put off participating' can have a marked effect on contribution styles, without needing to 'point the finger' at anyone in particular. Unobtrusively managing the flow and direction of the conference discussion without stifling the participants is a sine qua non of successful conference facilitation

(Collins and Berge, 1996)

Online e-tutors and learners need to be able to create and project their online voice, which involves developing a writing style that is appropriate to the online environment, and also confidence in posting messages. Alexander (2000) provides guidance on this topic, and he identifies the following key principles in online communications:

- going for consensus
- thanking, acknowledging and supporting people freely
- acknowledging before differing
- speaking from one's own perspective
- following netiquette principles.

E-tutors also need to develop skills in knowledge construction, and interventions by e-tutors are likely to include: appropriate questioning; acknowledging and challenging learners' ideas and perspectives; presenting alternative perspectives, encouraging independent thinking; encouraging learners to take a lead in their learning processes. The concept of 'scaffolding' is often used with regard to e-tutors providing frameworks to enable learners to learn.

Issues for e-tutors

Working as an online e-tutor brings not only new roles and working methods but also new issues. Key issues that need to be considered include:

- issues around virtual space and power
- issues about responsiblility
- issues about boundaries
- issues about style (directive vs facilitative)
- issues about computer misuse
- issues about copyright
- issues about plagiarism
- handling challenging situations.

In a traditional teaching room the e-tutor is often working from the front and the physical layout of the room often identifies the central position of the e-tutor. In an online environment the e-tutor takes up the virtual space in the same way as learners. At first glance, apart from names there is very little to differentiate e-tutors and learners. However, unlike the learners, the e-tutor may well be the only person in the group who has the technical rights to set up and organize this space – on *WebCT*, for example, e-tutors can organize their own virtual work-space and select colours, icons and other design features. In addition, for learners who are very new to online work, the e-tutor is likely to have the most experience of online teaching and learning, and be the most skilled in this environment. Their authority within the micro-learning environment and their higher knowledge and skills level, can immediately raise issues of power and control. In the context of an e-tutor working with a community of learners – e.g. a developing community of practice – then it becomes harder for the e-tutor to be an equal member of the community.

Rohfeld and Hiemstra (1995) suggest that the online e-tutor needs to accept responsibility for facilitating the group discussions so that they stay on track and group harmony is maintained. They also suggest that the e-tutor is responsible for contributing specialist knowledge and weaving together different discussion threads.

The online e-tutor is likely to face a range of dilemmas about boundaries. Goodyear (2000) describes these as boundaries around the e-tutor as:

- leader
- designer and establisher of learning settings
- repository of knowledge
- representative of the organization, e.g. public library, university
- evaluator/assessor (keeper of rewards and punishments).

There is no simple solution to these dilemmas and the e-tutor needs to continually revisit and reflect on these issues. Goodfellow (1999) explores the conflict in roles between the constructivist, facilitating and knowledge construction roles and the role as assignment-marker and learner supporter which he says 'forces the e-tutors into the position of expert and assessor.' Goodfellow argues that this conflict expresses itself in e-tutors' increased workload as they attempt to resolve these contradictions.

Associated with the issue of boundaries is an issue of style and where on the continuum of directive vs facilitative style the online e-tutor should operate. There is no simple answer to the question, although a more directive style is likely to be more useful with new and inexperienced online learners, while a more facilitative style is more appropriate to more mature learners and those with experience.

Another issue that sometimes arises with e-learning (and other ICT-based programmes) is the issue of computer misuse, e.g. through hacking, viruses or access to unacceptable materials. It is really important that e-tutors understand their organization's policies on computer misuse. These need to be brought to the attention of e-learners at the start of the e-learning programme, and this is standard practice in educational organizations, where new students are advised of the computer usage policy as a part of their induction process. If individuals do break these policies (either inadvertently or deliberately), then it is important to deal with them in an appropriate manner. Many organizations publish their computer misuse policy on their website, so it is worthwhile obtaining a copy and reading it.

Copyright issues are considered in Chapter 8 and, as with computer misuse, it is important to know and understand the principles of copyright with respect to e-learning programmes. If in doubt, then obtain advice and support from library and information professional bodies such as ALA, AALA and CILIP.

At the time of writing, plagiarism is a hot topic in education organizations. Plagiarism refers to the passing off of other people's intellectual property as one's own. It is very easy for students to access documents on the internet and then 'cut and paste' whole or parts of documents and attempt to pass them off as their own work. Library and information workers are often asked for advice on tracking down source documents that have been 'cut and pasted' into student's work. Frequently, selecting a section of the text under scrutiny and using it as a search phrase in a search engine will help identify the original document. In the UK, JISC (www.jisc.ac.uk) is carrying out extensive work on plagiarism, and from 2002 it is supporting a project that will explore the use of software to automatically check students' work. This is likely to become common practice in educational organizations in the near future. Library and information workers in educational institutions frequently play a central role in the education of students and staff on the issue of plagiarism.

As in face-to-face learning situations, e-tutors are likely to experience challenging situations. It is worthwhile being prepared for these situations and developing a range of strategies for handling them. Examples of situations that arise include:

- flaming (the online equivalent of road rage)
- quiet students or lurkers (sometimes called 'browsers')
- dominant students
- online work fizzling out.

Here are some example situations where new or potential e-tutors might like to consider and identify strategies for handling them. There is no 'right' answer for each of these situations. However, time spent thinking about your response may help the e-tutor to be prepared for similar situations in real life!

Challenging situations

Situation 1 Irate student

Example e-mail:

> Grrrr. It has taken me 4 hours to get online. I have had little or no help from the college. Now that I'm online I am finding the level of discussion inane. I have come on this course to learn about project management, NOT to have a meaningful relationship with other students. (I am happily married though my wife is sick of the amount of time I am spending on the course.) Don't expect me to contribute.

How do you handle this situation?

Situation 2 Over-enthusiastic learner

Week 3 of the course. You are managing a discussion group involving six information workers. They are working together on a mentoring programme. One participant (John) responds to everyone else's contribution and has taken to sending long responses with quotes from the books that he is reading. You notice that contributions from others are getting smaller.

How do you handle this situation?

Situation 3 Quiet student/browser

Week 3 of the course. You are managing a discussion group involving 12 library and information workers from different organizations. Eight of them contribute regularly, while two of them have not made any contributions.

How do you handle this situation?

Situation 4 Challenging student

Example e-mail:

> I am getting increasingly fed up with this course. I am expected to read up all the materials for myself and some of them are more than 3 years old. I wish we had traditional lectures and seminars. That way the tutor works too! I don't think library staff should be tutoring us – their job is to issue books! The fees are expensive and I don't think I'm getting value for money.

How do you handle this situation?

Situation 5 Sexist comment
Example e-mail:

> *Has anyone read the project management book by Stevens. I think it provides the best introduction to the subject. I was surprised as it is written by a woman. Bob*

How do you handle this situation?

Situation 6 Using discussion group as a bulletin board
In your information skills discussion group a number (three out of 12) students have started to use the group for buying/selling books, finding homes for kittens, and selling tickets to a rave.

How do you handle this situation?

When faced with a challenging situations e-tutors need to consider:

- whether or not to intervene
- when to intervene
- how to intervene – what organizational policies and procedures need to be taken into account
- how to intervene – in group or in private? If private, then is it best to use e-mail, phone or face-to-face?
- what the likely short- and long-term implications of the intervention are – for the individuals, the whole group and the e-tutor
- whether or not to get help or support, e.g. from a colleague or specialist such as a disabilities officer.

Chapter 9 contains a case study that was used in an e-learning programme to help information workers consider a range of challenging situations and how to handle them in practice.

Working with a co-tutor
Co-tutoring involves working with other colleagues, e.g. other information workers, IT specialists, trainers, teachers or lecturers and jointly delivering the e-learning programme. Co-tutoring offers a number of advantages:

1   Different tutors bring their own personalities, knowledge and skills, and experiences to the programme. Pairs or trios of tutors working together can

provide a much richer learning environment than any single individual.

2   Different tutors will have different virtual voices and this provides a variety of experiences for the learners. Again the presence of different voices with different tones and perspectives provides a more stimulating learning environment than the voice of an individual tutor.

3   The workload can be shared, with individual tutors taking responsibility for the development of resources, maintenance of the learning environment and introducing new activities.

4   Individual tutors can take responsibility for individual learners and/or small learning sets. This shares the workload and also enables the e-tutor to focus in depth on particular learners, learning groups or activities.

5   Tutors can provide each other with support and feedback.

6   Tutors can provide each other with back-up, e.g. during holiday periods.

Probably the most important factor contributing to successful co-tutoring is the need for the co-tutors to share the same or similar values and beliefs about learning and e-learning. This will help to ensure that that there are no irreconcilable differences during the programme. When starting to work as a co-tutors, it is worthwhile spending time discussing how the tutoring team will work together, and also clarifying individual roles and responsibilities. It is important to build time into the e-learning programme for e-tutors to discuss current issues regularly and decide how they will be handled. This is important as it enables the e-tutors to present a professional and co-ordinated presence on the e-learning programme and it can also deter e-learners from attempting to play one e-tutor off against the other.

Quotation from an e-tutor

Working with my colleague Denis worked well. We divided the work out between us and I took responsibility for all the learning resources while Denis provided the detailed text for the online activities. In reality we checked and amended each other's work.

Online we had 10 learners and we tutored five each. They were often involved in group activities, e.g. evaluating a website, and each of us took responsibility for one group. This cut our workload and meant that there weren't too many messages to read. Even so, some days I had 20-30 messages to read. They were a very enthusiastic group!

We found that we needed to meet once a week (we both work in the same information unit) and this helped us keep on track with the pro-

gramme. Occasionally, if we were uncertain about a message that we wanted to send out, then we would send it to each other for feedback. I found this really useful, e.g. with one message I wanted to send out Harry said that the tone was a bit sharp and irritable so I toned it down. In hindsight this was really valuable as I think if I'd sent my original message it would have come over as very negative.

Overall I recommend co-tutoring – it provides valuable help and support, and it means that the learners get a much better learning experience.   Jane (information researcher)

Becoming an e-tutor

Becoming an online tutor does not happen overnight or as a result of a simple staff development process. Experience and discussions with colleagues suggests that it is a process that is likely to involve time in adapting to and evolving an e-tutoring style. In addition it may involve some of the following learning processes:

- experience of e-learning as an e-learner
- working in e-learning teams
- involvement in e-learning activities outside the organization
- working with a mentor.

E-tutoring experiences from library and information workers

Initially I found that I was going online into the discussion group several times a day. It began to eat up my time. I am now quite strict and only access the discussion group 3–4 times a week. The students know when I am likely to go online. This has saved me a lot of time and it has encouraged them to become more independent.   Barbara

I felt lost and didn't know what to expect. I teamed up with an experienced tutor and became a 'browser' on his discussion group. This showed me that I was on the right lines.   David

One big mistake I made was that I used the online discussion group and e-mail to manage situations that would have been best handled over the phone or face-to-face. I now think about whether or not an electronic

144

response is the best kind of response to a particular situation before I reply to a student's e-mail or message. Rob

I only got to grips with being an online tutor after I'd taken part in an e-learning course myself. Becoming an e-learner helped me to find my online voice and it showed me different ways of tutoring. My tutors were excellent and I still use them as role models. I've now got an internal image of good and bad tutoring and I use this as my guide. Chris

Staff are likely to experience a change process as they move into becoming an online e-tutor. Boud (1981) describes a typical change process involving the following stages:

- the entry stage
- the reactive stage
- the proactive stage
- the integrative stage.

At the **entry** level, e-tutors become familiar with the systems and their possibilities for learning, and the first stage of this may involve familiarization with technical systems and technical support from IT help desks. This is often followed by induction and familiarization workshops and events with opportunities to explore current good practice. This first stage may take place online, or it may be offered as a blended solution involving face-to-face workshops and online activities.

At the **reactive stage**, e-tutors become familiar and competent in the basics of online learning and teaching so that they develop the skills required to carry-out the pedagogical, social, managerial and technical activities and processes outlined earlier in the chapter. This may involve a range of different development processes and activities, and these may also be used in the **proactive stage**. The differences between these two stages is the amount of autonomy an e-tutor will take in these activities and processes.

Information workers may develop their e-tutoring knowledge and skills through:

- technical support from IT help desks
- online workshops and activities
- work within learning sets of colleagues
- co-tutoring
- exploring current good practice, e.g. visits to other e-learning sites, reading

- networking and other professional contacts
- use of reflective journals
- constructive feedback on own practice, e.g. through peer observation
- mentoring.

Progress through the reactive to the proactive stage may be led by the developing e-learner, or it may be guided and supported through a structured staff development process or by processes such as mentoring. As e-tutors develop their confidence and competence, and become pro-active e-tutors, then they will move into the **integrative stage** – they will have integrated their new knowledge and skills with their existing practice, and will be able to offer leadership in the development and provision of e-learning programmes within information units.

Developing e-tutoring skills

There are an increasing number of workshops and programmes designed to enable library and information workers to develop their online tutoring skills. These vary from free programmes, available on the internet, through to specially designed programmes aimed at a specific cohort of information workers. Increasingly individuals are gaining experience as e-learning students before they start online tutoring.

Career progression

I wanted to move on in my job and perhaps move into a library in a college. I decided that online learning and teaching would really help my curriculum vitae and help my career to progress. I signed up for an Open University programme T171 You, your computer and the internet. This gave me all the skills I needed to be confident about online learning and I also learnt about the technical aspects of the computer and internet. I've now started applying for jobs and at a recent interview I was really pleased to be able to talk about issues such as lifelong learning, public access to IT in libraries, and the internet as an information source in an informed way. I didn't get the job but I did get very good feedback. I'm really confident that I'll move into a new job soon.

Irene (reference librarian in a UK public library)

Four examples have been selected below to demonstrate the different ways in which library and information workers develop their skills as e-tutors. It is interesting to note that, although some of these programmes were initiated by library and information services, each of the programmes is open to people involved in teaching and learning activities, ICT, library and information work, and educational development. As the design, development and delivery of e-learning programmes tends to be a collaborative process, so is the training and development of e-tutors.

The first example demonstrates an in-house staff development programme aimed at staff in a learning resources department (a converged service made up of library, ICT, media and language support staff) and also academic staff. The second example is an in-house programme aimed at information services and academic staff in a university. This programme is of particular interest as it is validated at Masters level and also for Associate Membership of the Institute for Learning and Teaching. The third example is an innovative Masters programme in e-learning, which regularly attracts participants working in the library and information profession. The last example is *LeTTOL* – an accredited e-learning programme based in the further education sector in the UK.

One of the outcomes of these programmes is that they enable relatively small groups of professional practitioners to establish themselves as communities of practice. Some of these communities may extend beyond the life of the formal learning group.

Online tutor programme

The following programme was designed and delivered to a number of different learning resources staff at the University of Lincoln during 1999/2000.

Aim

To pilot a staff development programme to equip learning resources staff to support online learning

Learning outcomes

By the end of the programme participants will have:

- experienced being a member of an online collaborative learning community
- explored the use of virtual learning environments to support experiential learning
- applied a theoretical model of online learning in practice
- designed, implemented and evaluated an online learning session

- reflected on the learning processes

Learning methodologies

Two half-day workshops (one at the beginning and one at the end of the programme); online workshops; independent learning. The programme is built around an expectation of 20 hours of participant learning time spread over a six-week period. Participants receive a printed guide to online tutoring.

Topics covered

- introductions; introduction to the programme
- introduction to the virtual learning environment facilities
- becoming an online tutor; changing tutor roles
- tutor and student experiences of online learning and teaching
- the five-stage model of online learning
- planning and delivering online learning activities
- development of a checklist of good practice
- evaluation

Essential resources

- Salmon, G. (2000) *E-modelling*, Kogan Page.

Evaluation

Twelve staff started this workshop and four withdrew, giving reasons of workload and time pressures. This workshop was evaluated using a paper-based questionnaire and also an informal discussion in the final workshop. Key findings from this evaluation were:

1 The workshop had met the expectations of six out of eight completing participants.
2 Most relevant learning points from the event: 'time to learn how to use the virtual learning environment', 'gained a sense of the process of online learning', 'how to manage an online learning group'.
3 Improvements to the workshop: 'more time – needed longer time between each of the workshops'; 'next time run it over 12 rather than six weeks, reduce the amount of reading'; 'opportunity to observe a "model" workshop would be appreciated.'
4 Other comments: 'time and heavy workload prevented me from fully participating in the online activities', 'found it impossible to log on

regularly (need to change working habits?)', 'VLE not easy to use
– very slow'.

Masters level module in e-learning in higher education

The Information Services department at Birmingham University have
launched an innovative part-time e-learning programme for information
services staff, education development workers and also academic staff.

The module covers the underpinning knowledge necessary for participants to undertake all aspects of online learning and teaching in
higher education. This includes coverage of the underpinning theoretical content that currently informs online learning and teaching in higher
education. Participants develop their knowledge and skills in developing and using teaching tools and resources in a managed learning
environment; online tutoring; design and development of online learning materials or programmes; and assessment of online learning. The
participants engage in and experience a number of different approaches to online learning – i.e. collaborative, problem solving and co-operative
learning sets. They apply the processes of critical evaluation and reflection to their online work.

Fig. 6.2 *Home page for the e-learning in higher education module*

E-learning and teaching

The aim of this programme is to develop e-learning practitioners in higher education. The module is delivered over 32 weeks through four online workshops and two face-to-face sessions:

- Induction session (face-to-face)
- Portfolio building session (face-to-face)
- Workshop 1 Introduction to online learning and teaching
- Workshop 2 Online tutoring
- Workshop 3 Design of online learning resources
- Workshop 4 Assessment of student learning.

The four online workshops enable participants to:

- gain direct experience of networked learning by using web-based conferencing to support communication on the course
- identify how students interact with electronic multimedia from a practical and pedagogic perspective
- work within a community of practice and engage in reflective practice.

The typical pattern of workshops is to provide:

- tutor guidance throughout the workshop
- specific online activities, e.g. case studies, visiting and evaluating e-learning activities and sites, online seminars, followed up by feedback, discussion and de-briefing
- guest 'speakers' through online conferences
- online seminars
- participants carrying out specific group activities that enable them to experience working in different types of e-learning groups (collaborative, problem-solving and co-operative)
- e-learning practice with associated self/peer/mentor/tutor observations, followed by review and reflection processes
- opportunities for independent study and networking, both within and outside the university, by electronic means and also face-to-face
- reflection on practice, both as student and practitioner, captured through the use of a learning journal
- completion of a summative review and reflection on their learning throughout the whole workshop.

The participants receive a range of support materials, including a student guide to the workshop (including reader), a guide to reflection and also online resources (accessible from their *WebCT* site).

Assessment is based on a portfolio containing examples of participants' online activities, including their work as e-tutors. In addition, participants are expected to maintain a learning journal.

Successful completion of the programme enables participants to gain 20 credit points towards the university's certificate in teaching and learning in higher education. It has also been validated by the Institute for Learning and Teaching (ILT) to enable people who successfully complete the module to gain Associate membership of the ILT.

Evaluation

At the time of writing, the programme is being delivered to the first cohort, who are a mixture of 17 information services and academic staff. Initial feedback about the programme is very positive, as learners have found it to be relevant to their work and to have helped the development of their skills as e-tutors. The programme involves co-operative and collaborative group work and this has led to an increased understanding of the different perspectives of information services and academic staff. One important feature of the programme is that it has led to the development of a virtual community of practice, and this is likely to influence the organization long after the end of the programme.

Key issues that have been identified during the programme are:

- the need to be realistic about the amount of time individuals can commit to the programme
- the need to provide one-week breaks at regular intervals so that learners can have a break from the programme
- the need to provide a long period of online socialization time (the second stage in Gilly Salmon's model), even when the learners know each other in a face-to-face environment; this time is important as it enables individuals to develop and feel comfortable with their virtual voice
- the need to provide a wide range of support to e-learners, e.g. technical help, tutorial support, mentoring support.

Masters programme in e-learning

The MEd in E-learning (previously called MEd in Networked Collaborative Learning) by action research is a two-year part-time course provided by the University of Sheffield. It is built around the principles of action learning, research and problem-based learning. The philosophy of the course emphasizes 'the implementation of innovatory online practice by creating a supportive and creative online research learning where participants can feel free to experiment and "learn by doing", while constantly holding a critical perspective on their practice and the theory underpinning it.' (McConnell, D., 2000, 220).

The course is delivered entirely online and participants come from all over the world. Each year a small number of library and information professionals take part in this programme, working alongside colleagues from different parts of the educational world (schools, colleges and universities), as well as independent trainers and consultants. The programme is built around a series of workshops, where participants negotiate their own study topics and projects with their peers and tutors. This means that information professionals can choose topics relevant to their own interests and workplace. Examples of subjects explored within the programme include: information literacy, the development of a web-based information skills programme, and time management for e-learners who are information workers.

Feedback from a participant

The programme was excellent and enabled me to develop my online learning and teaching skills. It also gave me a really good understanding of the theory of learning and teaching. I enjoyed the group work and have made some new friends. The main difficulty was that I was the only library person in the group and at times I felt that the other students didn't really understand my perspective. Two years is a long time and I had had enough of the course by half way through the second year. I did achieve my learning outcomes and I would recommend the course to anyone who wants an in-depth understanding of e-learning.

Claire (tutor librarian)

LeTTOL

QUILT (Quality in Information and Learning Technology) is a multi-faceted staff development programme aimed at making further education college staff enthusiastic about new technology and designed to help them incorporate it into their work. The *QUILT* model has influenced the form of the National Learning Network (see Chapter 1). One of the original *QUILT* projects, *LeTTOL* (*Learning to teach OnLine* at www. shefcol.ac.uk/lettoll), started as a consortium of South Yorkshire colleges, and now reaches learners around the world. It won the 1999 Becta Beacon Award for information learning technologies.

The online programme equips participants to teach learners online, support learners using e-mail and conferencing, manage online learning provision, employ the internet as a resource for teaching and learning, and apply appropriate learning methods in the design of online learning materials. The majority of course activities, including tutor support, peer inteaction and assessment, take place online. The course is accredited by the UK Open College Network.

> *I took part in the LeTTOL programme as I wanted to be able to support students at the college where I am the librarian. I loved the course. It was hard work but exciting. It was great 'meeting' people from different professional backgrounds. I made new contacts, e.g. with college lecturers, and we are still in touch and exchange resources. The course gave me new skills, new friends and it was like a breath of fresh air to my career. I've got much more involved in ICT at college and feel I have gained a lot from the experience.*
>
> John (college librarian)

Guidelines for establishing a staff development process

Salmon (2000) describes a staff development programme based on the five-step model and identifies a list of criteria for training e-tutors:

1 Enable new e-tutors to experience online learning before they start e-tutoring for real.
2 Ensure that as much as possible of their learning is online.
3 Keep the focus on online skills (rather than, say, technical issues).
4 Keep the training simple and don't over-complicate.
5 Provide an environment suited to e-tutors with a wide range of prior skills.
6 Check the training programme before going live – ideally, check it with novice online e-tutors.

7 Provide a minimum of print-based materials.
8 Provide clear information about the expected time requirements of the programme.
9 Make sure the programme is accessible – any time, any place.
10 Build in technical support and enable e-tutors to develop their technical skills
   as the programme develops.
11 Ensure the online e-tutor trainers model excellent online e-tutoring skills.
12 Include different types of knowledge – strategic, declarative and procedural.
13 Offer plenty of opportunities for e-tutors to explore their attitudes to online
   learning.
14 Enable e-tutors to interact with one other.
15 Ensure that the goals of the programme are visible.
16 Use familiar metaphors to explain online e-tutoring.
17 Spot people needing extra support and intervene promptly.
18 Build in reflection.
19 Monitor and give feedback on the work of the online e-tutor trainers.
20 Ensure on-going development of the online e-tutor trainers.

Additional themes that need to be covered in staff development programmes
include:

* a need to explore the context (subject, department) and underlying pedagogic approaches of e-tutors
* a need to consider learning styles (of both e-tutors and learners)
* a need to consider online working, e.g. time management, information overload.

Summary

Online tutoring is a rapidly developing field with a growing number of library and
information practitioners. There is currently a wide range of useful practice in online
learning and teaching, and there is no 'right' way of e-tutoring, although there is
a growing body of accepted practice. The practice of e-tutoring highlights the importance of tutors becoming involved in pedagogical, social, managerial and technical
aspects of online learning. Moving into e-learning involves getting to grips with
a range of new issues, and one approach to working as a new e-tutor is to work
with a co-tutor. Finally, the development of effective online e-tutors is likely to
involve a range of development processes and activities. Many e-learning programmes for e-tutors and aspiring e-tutors are established to enable library and

information workers, educational developers and academic staff to work and learn together. This process may be a transformational one, leading to new values and beliefs, and a change in underlying paradigms about learning and teaching. It can also lead to the development of communities of practice.

Recommendations for online e-tutoring

This list was provided by Goodyear (2000).

Pedagogical recommendations

1. Have clear objectives – decide on your goals for using on-line learning
2. Encourage participation – by being visible on-line and providing opportunities to which learners can respond
3. Maintain a non-authoritarian style – learners need to feel their presence (and their contributions) are valued
4. Be objective
5. Don't expect too much – on-line learning especially for those new to it can be demanding in terms of time to read and navigate around the on-line space. Allow learners time to explore, not always to be making contributions
6. Don't rely on offline material – especially if your learners are at a distance and may have difficulties accessing the materials
7. Promote private conversations as well – encourage the learners to form alliances with their peers, eg through e-mail.
8. Find unifying threads – threads that help bring apparently disparate ideas together, to help learners find new links between ideas, etc
9. Use simple assignments – because overly complex procedures can be difficult to understand especially if explained in a text
10. Make materials relevant – so that learners can see the links between using the on-line environment and the support materials
11. Require contributions – do expect that learners who have opted to learn in this way have responsibilities to participate. It is what this type of learning is about.
12. Present conflicting opinions – so that learners have to engage with alternate viewpoints, and that might encourage them to (re)consider their own views.
13. Invite visiting experts – bring in external visitors to your on-line space, to stimulate discussions and to bring in other valued viewpoints
14. Don't lecture – the on-line environment can promote a flattening of relationships between e-tutor and learner in which learners contributions are

valued, but not if you adopt a didactic style of presence

15. Request responses – by setting questions that require answers/comments from the learners. This can help learners see opportunities for them to be responsive and visibly active on-line.

Social recommendations

1. Accept lurkers – people need time to browse and explore and it's not necessaily helpful to have everyone feel they have to say something every time, especially if someone else has captured the essence of your response in their message already

2. Guard against fear – learners may lack confidence and feel intimidated online; especially if there are lots of messages from vocal and apparently highly knowledgeable members in the group

3. Watch the use of humour – it can be difficult for people to appreciate humour in text, especially irony and sarcasm. Humour should be used with caution.

4. Use introductions – so that people know who else is on-line, and can find ways to get to know each other, background interests, experience, etc.

5. Facilitate interactivity – encourage learners to communicate with each other, to send contributions that foster interaction.

6. Praise and model the behaviour sought – show by example the way you expect learners to interact on-line.

7. Do not ignore inappropriate behaviour – if necessary remove, and certainly contact the person responsible, preferably privately

8. Expect that flames may occur – especially in large groups, and among those who have not met face-to-face. Take action immediately to restore confidence among other group members.

Managerial recommendations

1. Encourage informality as appropriate – create spaces for informal chats and socialising eg as cafes

2. Distribute a list of participants – so people know who else will be on-line

3. Be responsive – act on the messages learners send, and at least acknowledge if you can't deal with the request/question immediately

4. Provide for administrative responsibilities – on-line environments require levels of administration and management that should be part of your resource planning

5. Be patient – often people need time to respond and have other commitments

6. Request metacommunications eg on the course – to see how people are viewing the on-line environment, so that remedial actions can be taken where necessary

7. Synchronise and resynchronise the group – from judgments about how successfully they are working together, through your ongoing monitoring of the on-line environment

8. Be mindful of proportion of e-tutor contributions to the conference – do not overly fill the space with your presence, which may suggest domination of the discussions

9. Take procedural leadership - by signalling in your actions on-line what is required of others

10. Use email to prompt – to signal to those not participating that their presence is encouraged

11. Be clear

12. Don't overload – particularly in a new course where participants may well feel phased by too much information

13. Change misplaced subject headings – so that a clear signal is given about the content of messages

14. Handle digressions appropriately – suggest an alternative space for that discussion or possibly that it is off-target

15. Vary participants' amount of contribution – eg by giving periods of more and less intense responsibilities

16. Appoint learner leaders – to help learners develop skills of leading and, e.g. skills of managing a group based activity

17. Allow yourself preparation time – to get opening messages on-line, to prepare resources required, etc

18. End the sessions – by explicitly stating a closure, possibly by adding a summary

19. Make use of experienced e-tutors – who will have reasonable expectation of what is required from them and will have developed strategies for helping encourage effective ways of participation.

7

Successful e-learning

Introduction

The experiences of e-learners can vary hugely depending on the philosophy and structure of their e-learning programme. Learners using interactive learning materials may find that their experience is familiar and rather similar to print-based independent study. In contrast, individuals involved in working with an online group of learners and tutor(s) are likely to be involved in working in collaborative groups that only meet online, acquiring new learning strategies (both individually and collaboratively), constructing knowledge and meaning, and becoming part of a virtual community of practice.

The purpose of this chapter is to explore factors that enable successful e-learning in a networked learning situation involving learning groups. It explores this issue from a number of perspectives:

* skills required to become an e-learner
* preparing to become an e-learner
* learning to learn and e-learn
* e-learning experiences
* practical advice to new e-learners.

Scenario

Patsy is an academic librarian whose workload appears to be constantly growing. She has recently been asked to manage projects ranging from developing a website to introducing a new induction programme for 1500 new students. She would like to develop her project management skills but has little time available to attend a course. She hears about an online course via an e-mail discussion group and sends for further information. Two weeks later she is enrolled on the course and online.

The project management course involves working through a printed booklet, which takes a week. Then Patsy has access to an online tutorial group (made up of three LIS staff and two MIS staff) that gives her help and support as she works through a practical exercise based on her new student induction programme. She finds that she can log into the discussion group most days. If she has a quiet evening or reference desk duty, then she often goes online and catches up with the discussion group. Four weeks later, Patsy has completed all the planning and is ready to implement her new induction programme.

In the course evaluation she writes:

This course has really improved my approach to project management. I can now see where I was going wrong and in future I'll follow the project management guidelines. The online group was great – lots of help and support. It was fun too. It was great being able to log into the group at times when it was convenient for me. It meant I could fit it in around my other work. I was worried about the time it would take to learn to use the virtual classroom but as I was used to sending e-mails I found that it only took a few minutes.

Skills required to become an e-learner

Individual staff and library or information unit customers normally require some basic IT skills before they can become successfully involved with an e-learning programme. At a minimum level they need very basic IT skills – the ability to use a mouse and familiarity with a Windows environment. Most e-learners find it useful to be able to type and ideally to use word-processing software, and also to send and receive e-mails.

Many libraries and information units provide ICT skills training to their staff and customers. In some situations this is through face-to-face workshops, such as Computing for the Terrified, while in others it is by other means. For example, providing workshops on topics such as e-mail, genealogy, surfing the net, or helping children with their homework, is often used as a technique for encouraging adults to return to learn, enhance their ICT skills and use library facilities.

E-mail for retired people

Margaret Kendall (2000) describes the use of e-mail as a starting point to enthuse people and motivate them into using a computer. She describes the use of introductory e-mail sessions as a means of engaging people of retirement age in the use of ICT. Once they become comfortable with sending e-mails to friends and family, then they begin to explore information available on the internet. Sometimes this then leads them into participating in an e-learning programme.

Preparing to become an e-learner

Individuals come to e-learning with a variety of experiences of traditional face-to-face situations; some people have had very positive experiences while for others the experience, sadly, has been negative. A small but growing number of people are developing their experiences as e-learners. Our experiences of traditional educational situations means that we know what to expect in these situations and have internalized the behaviours and processes that take place in face-to-face educational situations. E-learning involves learning in completely different ways and often the only contact with others is through text-based messages. This means that e-learners need to spend time getting to grips with the new environment, developing online communication skills and learning new approaches to learning. This process is described in Gilly Salmon's model (see Chapter 5) as the first two stages: access and socialization.

Learning to learn and e-learn

The concept of 'learning to learn' developed in the mid 1990s, and led to the widespread use of programmes in schools, colleges and universities to enable individuals to identify and strengthen their learning skills. Increasingly, 'learning to e-learn' is becoming established as an idea, and the importance of enabling individual learners to develop their strengths in e-learning is seen as crucial to the success of many learning programmes. High drop-out rates are often associated with e-learning programmes, and one approach to combating the problem is to introduce learners to the basic skills of online learning. There are a number of strategies that can be used to facilitate the initial experiences of e-learners:

- face-to-face induction courses
- print-based induction programmes
- taster e-learning programmes
- online quizzes and development tools.

Face-to-face induction courses

Many e-learning programmes, and particularly in-house programmes, run face-to-face induction sessions. The outline programme below was used on an induction programme for information services and academic staff starting the e-learning in higher education module at Birmingham University.

The induction session

Aims

The aim of the induction session is to ensure that all participants are prepared to start the e-learning module.

Learning outcomes

By the end of the first induction session you will be able to:

* identify other participants and their areas of interest and expertise
* explain the structure and outline content of the module
* explain the assessment strategy
* access and use basic *WebCT* features.

Background information

The induction session will include a range of activities and opportunities through which participants can get to know each other, the tutors and the module co-ordinator. A review of the module, its delivery and assessment will give the opportunity for any questions or concerns to be raised. An hour-long IT-based session will introduce the managed learning environment and the module's *WebCT* facilities. Participants who may be unfamiliar with virtual conferencing or discussion rooms (for example) will be able to see how these are accessed and used. Key facilities and sources of support for the module will be identified and discussed (including the tutoring and mentoring arrangements); a guide to Workshop 1 and a guide to reflective practice will be distributed, and the next stages of work on the module will be identified. There will be the opportunity to raise and discuss questions on any of these aspects of the module.

Indicative programme

1   Introduction; housekeeping arrangements; session learning outcomes

2 Introductory activity
3 E-learning in HE – the module
4 Break
5 Portfolio assessment – description of the requirements
6 Module support (tutors, mentors, administration, WebCT)
7 Introduction to WebCT
8 The next stage
9 Final questions and close.

One of the activities used during this induction session was an e-learning inventory. The purpose of this inventory was to help participants focus on different aspects of e-learning and to start off discussions about becoming an e-learner. These discussions were also helpful in informing the tutors about participants thinking about and attitudes to e-learning. The e-learning inventory is presented in Figure 7.1.

E-learning Inventory

The aim of this inventory is to help you to consider your approaches to learning and using online learning tools at the outset of this module.

Introduction

What are your initial expectations about this E-learning module?

Section one: IT Skills	Low			High
1 How much do you enjoy working and learning online?	1	2	3	4
2 How do you rate your *WebCT* skills?	1	2	3	4
3 How do you rate your internet searching skills?	1	2	3	4
4 How do you rate you web design skills?	1	2	3	4
5 How much experience of using conferencing tools have you had?	1	2	3	4

Section 1. Score _____

Please write any comments on section one here.

Fig. 7.1 *E-learning inventory*

Section two: Collaborative learning	not very			very
6 How important is it for you to be part of a learning group?	1	2	3	4
7 How important is it for you to work in a friendly and supportive group?	1	2	3	4
8 How important is it for you to discuss your experience and ideas with others?	1	2	3	4
9 How important is it for you to give and receive feedback?	1	2	3	4
10 How important is it for you to socialize within your learning group?	1	2	3	4

Section 2. Score _____

Please write any comments on section two here.

Section three: Independent learning	not very			very
11 How important is it for you to work independently?	1	2	3	4
12 How important is it to you to select your own learning activities?	1	2	3	4
13 How important is it to you to be able to plan your own goals and timescales?	1	2	3	4
14 How comfortable are you with managing your own learning time?	1	2	3	4
15 How important is it to you to 'do it your own way'?	1	2	3	4

Section 3.Score _____

Please write any comments on section three here.

Section four: Reflection	never	rarely	sometimes	always
16 Do you question basic ideas, processes or models?	1	2	3	4
17 Do you stand back and look at your learning experiences from different perspectives?	1	2	3	4
18 When you have finished learning about something, do you think back about how effective your learning process was?	1	2	3	4
19 Do you change the way you go about learning new things as a result of thinking about past learning situations?	1	2	3	4
20 Do you discuss your reflections with others?	1	2	3	4

Section 4.Score _____

Please write any comments on section four here.

Fig. 7.1 *E-learning inventory* (continued)

Print-based induction programmes

For some people, using print-based induction materials to an e-learning programme is an anathema. However, they do have the advantage of enabling the new learner to read about their new programme and become familiar with it without needing to go online. For some people they can provide a familiar reassurance.

Many organizations provide print-based induction materials which may be provided to the e-learner as a printed guide, or the learner may be required to print out or download the material from the computer. Individual information workers or teams may provide these materials. Sometimes the organization will provide print-based induction programmes. The University of Lincoln, for example, provides printed guides to new e-learners (and also e-tutors) via their *Virtual Campus.*

National schemes often provide accessible induction materials. Learndirect, for example, provides a print-based course called *How 2 Learndirect*. The estimated duration of the course is five hours and it provides learners with an introduction to Learndirect and Learndirect learning. It covers six main topics: learning, study skills, qualifications, using ICT, learning online, and what next? These are presented through a series of practical activities, case studies and quizzes. At the time of writing this was a free course.

Taster e-learning programmes

Many organizations have developed taster courses to help learners get to grips with e-learning, e.g. Learndirect and Open University. Jim Flood (2002) of the Open University (www.corous.com) says:

> *Dropout rates for online programmes are worryingly high and can range as high as 80% giving the incorrect impression that online learning is not effective or successful. The main problem is that the internet is an unfamiliar learning environment, without a teacher there to give advice. Learners often lack confidence when it comes to using the technology and feel very isolated if they are thrown in at the deep end with no support and explanation. 'Learning to learn online' is designed to hold the students' hands as they become acclimatized to the online learning environment, as well as helping them to develop the*

practical skills they need to learn effectively, and work collaboratively online.

Use of online quizzes and development tools

Many learning portals include checklists, quizzes and online guidance to new e-learners. These are useful as they enable new e-learners to start thinking about their approaches to learning in this environment. One example is *What makes a successful online student?* from the University of Illinois and available on www.ion.illinois.edu/IONresources/onlineLearning/StudentProfile.html (accessed 28 April 2002). This site gives clear guidance on the qualities of being a successful online student; it has links to an online quiz, 'Self-evaluation for potential online students,' and an article, 'What every student should know about online learning,' by John Reid. Figure 7.2 shows part of the University of Ulster e-learning website at http://campusone.ulst.ac.uk/whatis.shtml (accessed 5 May 2002). This website is well worth visiting as it contains guidance and self-assessment quizzes

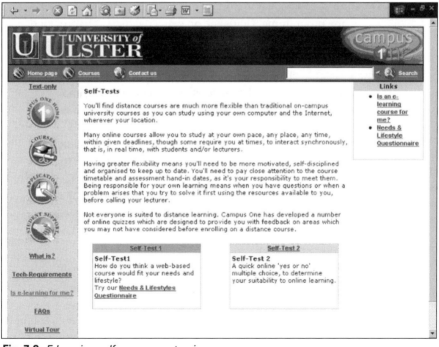

Fig. 7.2 *E-learning self-assessment quiz*

for students who are embarking on e-learning programmes.

The example below has been adapted from information presented on the University of Ulster website and used as part of the e-learning in higher education module induction programme mentioned earlier in this chapter.

Tips for succeeding online

1   **Find out how the programme is designed**. Make sure you know how the programme is designed by reading the participant handbook and workshop guides.

2   **Be prepared to participate online several times a week**. Taking steps to avoid feeling isolated is extremely important when learning at a distance. You should try as much as possible to contribute and share your ideas on the subject you are studying with your peers and tutors.

3   **Don't be afraid to speak up if you are having problems**. It is very important that you speak up if you are having difficulties. If you don't understand something, it is likely that several others will be having similar problems.

4   **Organize your time**. It is important that you set aside time for working on the programme. Guidance on dates/deadlines are provided on the *WebCT* site. You should try to set yourself realistic milestones or deadlines and should try not to fall behind.

5   **Find a suitable place to study**. You should find a suitable place to study that is free from distractions. This is particularly important when you are involved in online conferences, which can require intense concentration.

6   **Apply what you learn**. You will gain the opportunity to apply your learning in the group activities and your own e-practice. This will help you to integrate ideas and e-practice.

7   **If in doubt then ask**. Post a message on the group WebCT site or send an e-mail to your tutor (if it is a personal matter). You will normally receive a reply within 48 hours.

These tips are adapted from the University of Ulster website on: http://campusone.ulst.ac.uk/whatis.shtml

E-learning experiences

The practical realities of e-learning mean that e-learners need to

- manage their learning time
- develop skills in reading and following threads
- develop an online voice
- adopt different roles and responsibilities.

In this section, the topics are explored from a learner's perspective (the tutor's view was presented in Chapter 6).

Managing e-learning time

> The successful student needs to be able to enter their on-line learning environment several times a week, read and respond to messages. In traditional learning environments student can identify blocks of time for their learning activities. In on-line learning environments students need to access their learning environment regularly, e.g. 4 times a week. If they do not do this then they are likely to lose the thread of what is being said and 'fall behind the group'.
>
> (Cooper and Smith, 2000).

E-learning involves a new approach to time management as e-learners take part in ongoing asynchronous discussions as well as scheduled face-to-face sessions, conference or chat sessions, not to mention independent study. They need to log into the virtual learning environment three or four times a week to keep up-to-date with, and take part in, ongoing asynchronous discussions. These need not be long sessions. Sometimes 5–10 minutes is sufficient to read and provide quick responses to messages. Messages that require a more in-depth response can be dealt with there and then, or at a later time.

During the first few weeks of an e-learning programme, e-learners are likely to find that they will need to adjust to the demands of the programme.

Comments from e-learning students

I found it hard to fit the e-learning course into my working week. I nor-

mally manage to log into the discussion group 2–3 times a week. My late night duty is on a Thursday and if we are quiet then I normally get a lot of work done then. I can't rely on a quiet Thursday night and sometimes I have to catch up over the weekend. Jane

Using WebCT to catch up with messages usually gets me enthusiastic about tackling some other part of the work, too, and depending on my week, I can do the work in little bits or great chunks. John

Initially I felt as if I needed to be online all the time and felt overwhelmed. The course 'took over' my life. I now keep an eye on how much I am online and limit my access. Basically I limit my own time online and fit it in and around other priorities. I find the online socialization, and particularly the virtual pub, a real motivator and often visit them before the learning sets. Chris

If I miss more than a few days then I find that there can be 50–60 messages waiting for me. This is really frustrating and quite demotivating. I now log in every day – even if it's only for 10 minutes, this helps me to keep on top of the work and means that I don't dread entering WebCT and finding lots of messages waiting for me. Sam

Initial research (Allan, 2002) suggests that e-learners tend to manage their time in two distinct ways: some people plan their time using diaries and log in at regular times; other people log into the virtual learning environment as and when their time permits, i.e. they are opportunistic. New e-learners are advised to spend a little time thinking about how they can manage their time.

Developing skills in reading and following threads

The online student also needs to be able to read a large number of messages and become 'comfortable in trying to make sense of jigsaws of text'.

(Cooper and Smith, 2000).

Sometimes people feel overwhelmed by the number of messages that they need to read. In lively groups or conferences, someone may return from a few days' holiday and be faced with 100+ messages. This means that e-learners need to develop skills in skim reading and identifying key messages, analysing relatively large amounts of information and then synthesizing a number of different ideas and perspectives (this particular skill is called weaving). Many e-learners find it easier to do this if they keep up-to-date with the messages and print out key messages. Online summaries, e.g. from the e-tutor or a volunteer, are a useful means of managing the information contained in messages.

Developing an online voice

As online learners students need to be able to create and project their online voice and this involves developing a writing style that is appropriate to the online environment and also confidence in posting messages.
(Cooper and Smith, 2000).

Netiquette is the term used to describe online communications – here are some general guidelines in good online communication practice.

1 Thank, acknowledge and support people freely.
2 Acknowledge before differing.
3 Speak from own perspective.
4 Avoid flaming spirals.
5 Use emoticons to represent feelings, e.g. :-) (a grin!).
6 CAPITAL letters are equivalent to shouting – don't use them.
7 Be cautious when quoting other messages while replying to them – don't over-quote as this leads to very long messages.
8 Send messages to the appropriate forum and thread.
9 Keep messages short. Longer messages need to be used as an attachment so people can choose to read them at leisure.
10 Don't respond to a message if you are experiencing strong negative feelings. Give yourself time to cool down. Then respond.

There are many guides to netiquette available on the internet. Some useful starting points include Alexander (2000), and also www.albion.com/netiquette and www.jade.wabash.edu/wabnet/info/netiquet.htm.

Here is an example of a brief guide to netiquette written by students.

E-learner guide to netiquette

This guide was constructed by three groups of information workers as part of an e-learning activity.

Group A
Follow the STOPP code:

- Short – brief and quick
- TOlerant – of other people's ideas and understanding
- Polite – civil, in good taste
- Positive – clear, decisive and certain.

Group B
Follow the MUCH guide:

- make your answers   Meaningful
- try to be   Understanding
- always be   Constructive
- and make the comments   Helpful.

If we use MUCH, then we'll get the most out of the discussions.

Group C
It is important to:

- welcome everyone as they arrive
- encourage participation and ask others what they think
- let others know when you are going to be 'absent'
- accept that individuals arrive at the conference at different times (we all have different pressures on us at any one time)
- accept different/changing levels of participation.

Advice to new e-learners

The following advice was given to a group of information workers starting a new e-learning programme:

Plunge in and get involved in the group. Adopt a friendly and informal style. Notice what works well and repeat these successes. Don't be too concerned about getting it right or posting 'perfect' messages. Occasional typing errors are a normal part of online communications. Over time you will find that you develop and become very comfortable with your online voice.

Adopting different roles and responsibilities

E-learners will find that their roles and responsibilities are more closely aligned with learners who are involved in resource-based learning, problem-solving learning or action learning sets than with people studying in an environment that relies on traditional learning and teaching activities such as lectures. In essence, the e-tutor is likely to move from being the 'sage on the stage' to the 'guide on the side' and this shift is accompanied by e-learners taking on more responsibility for their own learning and also the overall learning process. Some people find this a little disconcerting at first, while others relish the freedom to take a more active role in their learning process. Goodyear (2000) summarizes these changes in Figure 7.3.

Traditional student roles	E-learning student roles
Passive recipients of knowledge	Constructors of their own knowledge
Memorizers of facts and models	Complex problem solvers
Viewing topics from tutors' perspectives	Seeing topics from multiple perspectives
Members of a seminar group – may be little collaboration or interaction	Members of a collaborative learning team
Little control	Shared control with the students as fellow-learners
Little power	Shared power with the students
Little emphasis on students as independent learners	More emphasis on students as autonomous, independent, self-motivated managers of their own time and learning process

Fig. 7.3 *Change in student roles*

Practical advice to new e-learners

E-learning is still a relatively new way of working for many people. The following practical advice was prepared by e-learners as part of a course activity in which they were asked to give their advice to new e-learning students:

1   Plan a set programme and stick to it .
2   *Don't* let the messages accumulate – getting back into things can be terribly frustrating. If you realize that's why you're not doing the work, bite the bullet and mark the messages as read to make a fresh start, rather than feeling you're lagging behind for months. If something is important, you can always find it later, when things quieten down.
3   Be opportunist and never disregard the value of 15 minutes here or there.
4   Take it easy to start with! Make the most of the medium and set aside time when you know you are free and responsive to participate.
5   Discover your own pattern with regard to accessing *WebCT*. Experiment with a mix of methods, e.g. working on and offline. Use opportunities when you have an unexpected 'free' 15 minutes.
6   As regards the online part, try, if possible, to log in every day to keep abreast of and on top of messages. In terms of the offline component, set aside a certain amount of time each week.
7   Think about it on three levels – (1) where you can fit in day-to-day communications; (2) when in the week you are most likely to get reading done (I aim for three slots or so, usually, including at least one during the week-end); (3) look at the deadlines and work out in what chunks to complete the work.

Summary

This chapter explores the practical realities of group-based e-learning from the students' perspective. New e-learners need to have basic ICT skills. They are then likely to experience a 'learning to e-learn' programme to help them become confident in tackling their e-learning programme. Once learners start working with others in a networked learning environment, then they need to develop their skills in managing their learning time, reading and following threads in discussion groups. They also need to develop their online voice and presence. Working as an e-learner involves adopting different roles and responsibilities from those of a traditional learner, as e-learners are required to be more autonomous. Overall, new e-learners are likely to experience a period of change as they adapt and develop relevant skills and become familiar with the new demands of this form of learning. It is important that they are supported through this transition period.

8

Design of e-learning programmes and activities

Introduction

The purpose of this chapter is to provide basic guidelines on developing e-learning programmes. Increasingly, library and information workers are involved in the development of e-learning programmes and there are a variety of reasons for going down this route.

An e-learning survey of 500 organizations by The Epic Group (2001) identified the following top five factors in deciding to make use of e-learning:

1 making learning more accessible
2 reducing training delivery time
3 reducing the cost of training
4 delivering a wider range of training content
5 improving knowledge retention.

Other factors for deciding to make use of e-learning included:

- interest at senior management level
- exploiting the organization's internet and intranet facilities
- seeing for yourself how valuable online e-learning can be
- demonstrating the use of leading-edge technology
- demand from users.

These findings match the situation found in many library and information units, where staff want to provide flexible access to learning opportunities and to meet the learning needs of large numbers of people who may be located in different towns, cities or countries. They may want to offer 24/7 (24-hour, 7-days-a-week) learning opportunities within their service. Some information workers may initiate or become involved in e-learning collaborative projects, e.g. within the profession or with a community group. Sometimes the motivation for getting involved in these kinds of projects is that they can provide access to additional funding to develop innovative activities.

Information workers may become involved in organizational e-learning activities and may work collaboratively with staff development or training units to provide new learning opportunities in the workplace. For example, an information worker in a financial services company in the City of London is involved in a collaborative project for developing a blended induction programme for new staff at their offices in both the UK and USA. She brings her information searching skills, ICT skills and general knowledge of learning and training to the project and, as a result, is able to ensure that the services and activities of the information unit have a high profile in the induction programme.

Sometimes a motivation to develop virtual learning materials comes from a desire to promote a professional appearance or to 'keep up with the Joneses'. Alternatively, there may be a personal motivation – individual information workers may want to develop and demonstrate their up-to-date skills and, possibly, gain a new post or promotion.

This chapter starts with an introduction to the five stages of the design and development process and then each stage is explored in detail.

The design and development cycle

The e-learning project may be the responsibility of an individual project manager, a training officer within an information unit, or individual workers. E-learning projects are often the responsibility of a special unit or team (perhaps created for this particular purpose) and may involve individuals from different professional backgrounds working together. Teams involving library and information staff, ICT staff, educational developers, tutors or trainers, and subject specialists are very common. Conversely, in voluntary organizations and school libraries this process may be carried out by an individual librarian or an enthusiastic volunteer.

The development process for an e-learning programme is similar to that for any other learning event. The process is a cyclical one and involves five stages:

- needs analysis
- design
- development
- delivery
- evaluation.

Whether the project is a major one that will run over a number of years and involve a multi-professional team, or it is a small-scale project involving an individual information worker, the project leader will need to go through the design cycle to ensure that the e-learning provision is:

- relevant to the needs of the organization/unit/individual
- appropriately designed, developed and delivered
- evaluated to ensure continuous improvement.

Needs analysis

The first stage of the design process is that of analysing the current situation and gathering information. This involves consulting a number of different people and resources, and using your findings to develop answers to the questions below. The basic starting point is to think about the current situation and to ask the following questions:

1 Why is there a need to develop this learning programme ?
2 Why is there a need to deliver it using e-learning?
3 How will the proposed programme meet the aims and objectives of the library and information service?
4 How would the development of the programme serve the needs of the library and information service?
5 Who are the potential learners – numbers, their background, ICT background, entry knowledge and skills?
6 How would the development of programme serve the needs of customers and/or staff?
7 What are the draft aims and learning outcomes of the programme?
8 What will be the underlying pedagogical approach of the programme?
9 What type of structure do you have in mind? Will it include producing interactive learning materials, or a structured programme involving learning groups and/or a blended approach of face-to-face and e-learning?
10 A brief description of the type of programme you have in mind.
11 Is there a budget? And if so then what is it?
12 Who will be working on this project?
13 How much time have you got? Work out a rough figure for the next six months.
14 Does the programme already exist?

E-learning and teaching

There are a number of people who are worth consulting about the proposed e-learning programme:

- senior/top management
- middle managers and team leaders
- internal customers
- external customers
- intended participants themselves
- colleagues in other LIS.

Hackett (1997) provides useful guidelines on this consultation process and identifies three principles to guide your choice:

1 Consult until you are confident that there is a real need for the e-learning programme and that you know what the need is.
2 Consult the people who know most about the need.
3 Consult the people who should be supporting the e-learning programme and its outcomes.

Identifying requirements

It is crucial to the success of the e-learning programme to identify its purpose and what will be achieved. This will then inform the design, development and evaluation of the programme. There are a number of ways in which this can be expressed:

Aims

These are a broad statement of what the programme aims to achieve. The aims will answer questions such as:

- What is the purpose of this programme?
- What is the programme intended to achieve?

Example aims

1 The aim of this programme is to enable new staff to use basic ICT tools
2 The aim of the e-learning programme is to encourage young people to read and use information resources.

3   The aim of the induction programme is to enable new staff to find their way around the virtual learning environment.

4   The aim of the e-learning programme is to enable students to access and evaluate information resources.

5   The aim of the e-learning programme is to promote mentoring in the library and information community.

Learning outcomes

Learning outcomes specify what someone will gain from the programme. It is important to specify the learning outcomes accurately and clearly, as they form the basis for the content of the programme and also all assessment activities. Outcomes must describe things that you are able to demonstrate that you have learned. It is therefore helpful to avoid the use of words which describe non-observable states of mind, i.e. vague or woolly words. It is important to specify learning outcomes so that they are measurable, as this means it is possible to assess what has been learnt.

Example learning outcomes

By the end of the unit learners will be able to:

*   print out a report
*   explain how to carry out the issue procedure
*   list the main functions of the system
*   send an e-mail with an attachment.

When you are writing learning outcomes it is useful to:

*   use clear English
*   use specific words such as explain, produce, write, evaluate
*   avoid general words such as develop, understand, know.

Table 8.1 (Rowntree, 1990) gives guidance on the use of verbs when writing learning outcomes.

Table 8.1 *Language and learning outcomes*

Avoid words like	Use words like
Know	State
Understand	Describe
Really know	Explain
Be familiar with	List
Become acquainted with	Evaluate
Have a good grasp of	Identify
Appreciate	Distinguish between
Be interested in	Analyse
Acquire a feeling for	Outline
Be aware of	Summarize
Believe	Represent graphically
Have information about	Apply
Realize the significance of	Assess
Learn the basics of	Give examples of
Obtain a working knowledge of	Suggest reasons why

E-learning in higher education module

Aim

The purpose of this module is to provide you with the knowledge and skills you need to develop as an e-learning and teaching practitioner.

Learning outcomes

On completion of this module you will be able to:

- demonstrate knowledge of the underpinning theoretical content that currently informs online learning and teaching in higher education
- critically evaluate online learning and teaching tools and resources within a managed learning environment
- demonstrate good practice in supporting online learning and teaching
- demonstrate good practice in developing online learning materials and programmes, including the use of online assessment tools
- apply the processes of critical evaluation and reflection to your work.

For an example of a mentoring programme for information workers see pages 179–81. Additional examples of aims and learning outcomes are presented in Chapter 4.

Producing a programme outline

A programme outline is a relatively short document (often less than 1000 words) that summarizes the key features of the proposed e-learning programme. It is a useful document as it can be used to:

- obtain management support and agreement for the programme
- brief the project team
- form the basis of marketing materials.

The programme outline is likely to contain information organized under the following headings:

1 **Programme outline**:
   - aims and learning outcomes
   - level
   - tutor(s)
   - intended audience – who, numbers, entry requirements/pre-requisites, ICT skills
   - hardware and software required to access the programme
   - outline programme (session headings/topics)
   - learning and teaching strategies
   - learning resources
   - assessment strategy
   - indicative reading
   - progression pathways
   - links with other programmes.
2 **Programme management**
   - induction and learner support
   - technical requirements
   - library and other learning resources
   - accreditation details, including internal and external moderation, appeals procedure
   - quality assurance policies and procedures.

Mentoring programme for information workers

Aims

The aim of the online mentoring programme is to enable information professionals to establish successful mentoring schemes within their library and information service.

Learning outcomes

By the end of the programme participants will be able to:

- explain the benefits and challenges of workplace mentoring schemes
- identify the role and responsibilities of mentors and mentees
- evaluate the advantages and disadvantages of using virtual communications as a tool within the mentoring process
- identify and establish an effective mentoring scheme within their workplace
- review and evaluate a mentoring scheme
- reflect on their own practice in supporting workplace learning.

Level

Accredited at Level 4 (undergraduate level).

Tutor(s)

James Smith, Philippa Clark.

Intended audience

Library and information workers, who may be team leaders, middle managers, people with responsibility for training and development. As part of this programme involves e-learning, all participants must have basic IT skills, e.g. use of internet, word-processing and e-mail.

Hardware and software requirements

PC with access to internet.

Outline programme

The programme consists of two face-to-face sessions and three online sessions. It runs for six weeks:

Session 1 (face-to-face) – introduction to the programme, introduction to mentoring and the mentoring process, module assessment, the virtual learning environment (*WebCT*).

Session 2 (*WebCT*) – evaluation of existing programmes. Use of WebCT in the mentoring process.

Session 3 (*WebCT*) – collaborative group work on the report.

Session 4 (*WebCT*) – guest 'speaker'.

Session 5 (face-to-face) – review and evaluation of the programme. Action planning.

Learning and teaching strategies

Face-to-face sessions: mini-presentations, case studies, practical small group activities.

E-learning: collaborative group activities, guest speaker, discussion and conference room activities.

Independent learning: reading and research.

Learning resources

Participants will be provided with a printed open learning resource. Access to additional resources is through the *WebCT* site.

Assessment strategy

Collaborative report. Learning journal.

Indicative reading

Clutterbuck, D. (1997) *Mentoring*, CIPD.

Salmon, G. (2000) *E-moderating*, Kogan Page.

Progression pathways

Successful completion of this programme enables candidates to progress to a university certificate programme or a work-based learning degree.

Law on the 'Net: A Distance Ed Course for Non-Law Librarians

[Used as marketing material and obtained from www.infopeople.org/]

* What is V.C. §23103?
* Can my landlord charge me an additional security deposit for my guide dog?
* I need the form to change my name.

Traditionally, many non-law librarians have avoided legal questions either because their libraries lack legal resources or because they lack expertise in finding legal materials. Today, legal issues are so intertwined with daily life that they are virtually impossible to avoid, and the internet has made legal resources available to even the smallest library. Users need assistance in finding the appropriate legal information, whether it is the text of a law referenced in a newspaper article, a court ruling needed for a school assignment, the name of a lawyer, or practical assistance in handling their own legal matters.

Workshop description

This four-week workshop will be taught via distance education using the web. It consists of four one-and-a-half to two-hour modules. You can work on each module at your own pace, at any hour of the day or night. However, you will be expected to log in to the course each week to do that week's assignment.

This distance education course will cover the variety of legal resources available for legal research on the internet. We will cover both Californian and Federal sources for statutes, pending legislation, case law and regulations, as well as municipal codes.

During the course you will be doing exercises and taking quizzes. You will also participate in online discussion forums as part of the distance learning process. When you register, you will receive the URL to get to the course, and a username and password in your registration confirmation. Law on the 'Net will begin on May 21, 2002 and go until June 18, 2002.

Highlights

Using your web browser and your internet connection, you will log in to the *Infopeople Blackboard* distance education site and learn in the following areas:

Module One: Overview - What exactly is 'the law'? Where do I begin?
'The law' is not a monolith but rather the interaction of activities by our three branches of government. Learn the questions to ask to find out what users are really looking for and why *Findlaw* is not the only, and sometimes not even the best, starting place for legal research on the internet. Uncover other websites offering legal information to both lawyers and non-lawyers and discover what legal information is not available on

the internet. Learn about the county law libraries and what they offer to members of the public.

Module Two: California and local law

What happened to that bill legalizing the ownership of ferrets in California? What has the California Supreme Court been up to lately? Where can I find the form to adopt my stepchild? Can I open an adult book store next to a day care facility? After all, the kids can't read.

California has done a commendable job of making its laws available to the public via the internet. Learn the authoritative websites for information on California bills, statutes, cases and regulations. Learn where to find municipal ordinances for your own city and county and for cities and counties across California.

Module Three: Federal law – the weak link on the net

I'm doing a paper on the Supreme Court cases on the death penalty since 1990. Where can I find them? I'd like to read the text of the Fair Debt Collection Practices Act. Where can I find information about getting a green card?

Federal law can be found on the internet, but not in one neat package (or two or three or ...). Dozens of courts and federal agencies have put their materials on individual websites making comprehensive federal legal research a challenge. Learn who's put what on the web and how authoritative it is. Learn why checking the currency of the information is of particular concern with federal legal materials.

Module Four: Lawyers – where to find them; where to find out about them

- Is your brother-in-law's neighbor's son really a lawyer? Where did he go to school? Has he ever had disciplinary charges filed against him?
- Help! I need to find a Spanish-speaking attorney to help me patent my invention.
- I need Johnnie Cochran's e-mail address so I can ask him to speak at Career Day.
- How do I file a complaint against my attorney?

Finding a lawyer can be a challenging process and is often untaken during a stressful time. The internet has not only made the task much easier but has also greatly expanded the amount and types of information readily available to the public.

Workshop instructor: [name]

Who should attend

Any library staff members who are asked for legal information resources. *Note:* Infopeople's grant funding restricts participation in distance education courses to individuals currently working in California libraries.

Prerequisites

This course is taught over the web. You must:

- have an internet connection and either *Internet Explorer* (preferably IE 5) or *Netscape* (version 4 or higher – *not* 6)
- be able to save a file to your computer and print it out using Microsoft Word or a compatible word-processing program
- be comfortable navigating on the web and going back and forward in a website that uses frames
- have an appreciation of lawyer jokes.

If you are not comfortable with any of the above, please consider taking this course with a buddy who does meet these requirements. [Registration information is included here.]

Using existing programmes and packages

Using existing programmes and packages saves time, expense and stress; it also means that you are not re-inventing the wheel and can use other professionals' expertise. The main disadvantage of using existing programmes or packages is that they may not completely match your needs. Chapter 4 includes a checklist for evaluating web-based training materials.

Design

The design of an e-learning programme or package of interactive learning material involves taking the initial programme outline and beginning to work out the detail. This involves considering:

1 the aims and learning outcomes
2 what the learner must do to achieve the learning outcomes
3 the topics or themes
4 the detailed learning and teaching strategy
5 the assessment strategy
6 the overall structure, e.g. breakdown into modules
7 your content, exercises and activities
8 supporting materials, e.g. images, examples
9 the logical order and links between different materials
10 how the event will be delivered to the learner – the mix between face-to-face, e-learning; the mix between independent, co-operative and collaborative learning processes
11 approaches to ensuring that the programme is accessible to learners with additional needs
12 the total number of learner hours
13 the total number of e-tutor hours
14 the house style
15 any intellectual property issues
16 any pre- or co-requisites required by the learner
17 how the programme will fit in with other learning opportunities.

Development

This involves taking the proposed programme and producing all the relevant documentation, learning resources, setting up the learning environment, establishing the necessary learning support systems, providing management and administrative support. Different tasks and processes are likely to be carried out by different team members, and the project co-ordinator will have the task of ensuring the different parts of the package are produced on time.

The following areas need to be considered in depth:

- learner support
- content
- learning design
- approaches to learning
- assessment
- navigation
- usability
- introducing text, sounds and images

- storyboard
- using ICT tools
- technical issues
- copyright
- house style
- pilot programme
- accessibility.

Learner support

At this stage you need to consider how the learner will be supported through the learning process. The types of support that need to be considered include:

- induction support
- use of technical systems
- technical help support
- tutorial support
- peer support
- mentor support.

The types of support will vary depending on the kind of programme. For example, an online training package that will typically involve 30 minutes' learning time will probably be supported via online explanations and help menus. In contrast, a 30-week e-learning programme that is based on co-operative and collaborative group work is likely to require extensive support of different types.

It is important to consider the provision of learner support in depth, and to identify and clarify the preparation required to provide learner support. The following questions need to be answered:

1   How will you deliver the support mechanisms?
2   If they are to be system or paper-based, then who will develop and produce them?
3   If they are to be delivered by people, then are those people available and will they require training and development?
4   What resources need to be developed and produced?
5   What will it cost?
6   How will the support process be introduced to the learners?

Content

There are a number of different ways of handling content in an e-learning pro-gramme. A common approach is to divide the content into chunks. Figure 8.1 shows a commonly used approach to doing this. It involves dividing the programme into a hierarchy: programme, module, unit, section. Different organizations will use different terms for the different levels within a programme – an alternative is book, chapter, page, paragraph. Each level of the hierarchy will typically have its own list of aims and learning outcomes; at the programme level these are very gen-eral, while at the section level they are very specific. A key point in planning programmes is to use the simplest structure possible.

Approaches to learning

This section explores two different approaches to learning: content-driven and process-driven.

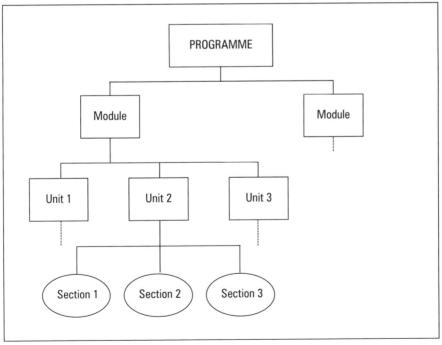

Fig. 8.1 *Producing an overall structure*

Content-driven

Many traditional e-learning programmes that are built around the use of interactive learning materials focus on presenting the content in an interesting and engaging way, and enabling the learner to engage with the material through a range of different learning activities and assessment processes. These e-learning programmes may be used for individual independent learning or as additional support to another programme – e.g. the use of internet tutorials may be used to support face-to-face instruction. The underlying principle of many of these programmes is that of presenting a pre-digested set of knowledge using behaviourist principles (see Chapter 5).

The checklist in Table 8.2 sets out the characteristics of good-quality content-driven programmes and it can be used to inform content developers.

Table 8.2 *The characteristics of good-quality content-driven programmes*

		Yes	No
1	Overview and summaries		
2	Content divided into meaningful chunks		
3	Content arranged in a logical order		
4	Choice of routes within materials		
5	Content written in an accessible style and at the right level		
6	Technical terms explained and supported by a glossary		
7	Lively, stimulating and enjoyable		
8	Uses visual images and sound		
9	Includes relevant activities		
10	Includes opportunities for feedback		
11	Accurate and up-to-date		
12	No spelling or grammatical errors		
13	Supported by additional (optional) learning resources		
14	Complies with copyright legislation		

Process-driven

In this model, the learner works with others, e.g. peers and tutor, and this is an essential part of the learning process. The content is presented using summaries and basic frameworks, and then the learners are taken through a series of activities or processes to enable them to engage with the ideas, apply them to a relevant situation and construct knowledge as they achieve their learning outcomes. The underlying principle of many process-driven programmes is knowledge construction (see Chapter 5).

The five-stage model presented in Chapter 5 provides a framework for developing a process-driven learning programme. A key issue for designers is to identify the progression path of their learners – many information skills programmes can be successfully completed by development to Stage 3 (information exchange), while professional development programmes are likely to involve movement to Stage 5.

Process-driven e-learning programmes need to be structured to enable learners to work through the five stages. Salmon (2000) identifies the following typical activities:

Stage 1 Access and motivation
- ensure that the online group is set up with a welcome message
- ensure learners know how to access the online group
- open and close the discussion group (at the start and end of the unit).

Stage 2 Online socialization
- lead a round of introductions with, perhaps, an online ice-breaker
- welcome new team members or late arrivals
- provide a structure for getting started, e.g. agreement of group rules, netiquette
- if individuals break the agreed group netiquette, then tackle them (either privately or through the discussion group)
- wherever possible, avoid playing 'ping pong' with individual group members and ask other people for their opinions and ideas
- encourage quieter members (sometimes called 'lurkers' or 'browsers') to join in
- provide summaries of online discussions – this is called weaving and involves summarizing and synthesizing the content of multiple responses in a virtual group.

Stage 3 Information exchange
- provide highly structured activities at the start of the group life
- encourage participation
- ask questions
- encourage team members to post short messages
- allocate online roles to individual members, e.g. providing a summary of a particular thread of discussion
- close threads as and when appropriate
- encourage the online group to develop its own life and history; welcome shared language, metaphors, rituals and jokes.

Stage 4 Knowledge construction
- provide more open activities

- facilitate the learning process
- pose questions for the group to consider
- encourage group members to question theory and practice
- encourage the group to develop its own life and history; welcome shared language, metaphors, rituals and jokes.

Stage 5 Development

- encourage group members to lead discussions
- encourage group members to transfer their skills to other areas of their work
- support individual 'risk'
- encourage reflection on different learning processes (individual and group).

Process-driven e-learning programmes are likely to involve a mixture of individual, co-operative and collaborative activities. There is an extensive range of learning activities that can be used in this type of programme, and these are explored in more detail in Chapter 9.

Table 8.3 *The characteristics of good-quality process-driven e-learning programmes*

	Yes	No
Clear and relevant learning outcomes		
Learners experience a learning process that takes into account the five-stage model (access, socialization, information exchange, etc.)		
Learning activities clearly link to learning outcomes		
Clear description of learning activity		
Learning activities are relevant and authentic		
Activities lead to a clearly defined result, e.g. report, summary, website, power point presentation		
Arrangement of learning activities into a logical sequence		
Balancing the amounts of individual activities and group activities		
Includes opportunities for feedback		
Includes opportunities to summarize and reflect on learning experiences		
Realistic timescale (remember holiday periods)		
Provision of basic learning resources		
Supported by additional (optional) learning resources		
Appropriate tutor-support is available		
Accurate and up-to-date		
No spelling or grammatical errors		
Complies with copyright legislation		

Learning design

Both content-driven and process driven e-learning programme will need to use a variety of approaches to satisfy the needs of individual learners. In Chapter 5 the implications of current theories of learning and knowledge were outlined and these implications are summarized below in the following checklist:

Checklist of the implications of models of learning and teaching for the design of e-learning environments, programmes or activities

Motivation

1 Identify and present clearly the goals and learning outcomes.
2 If possible, link these to qualifications and/or progression in the work-place.
3 Provide an accessible virtual learning environment.
4 Provide effective learner support.
5 Provide constructive feedback.

Models of learning

6 Provide visual, auditory and practical experiences:
   - use visual images – diagrams, graphs, photographs, mindmaps
   - introduce auditory experiences – sound clips, discussions, telephone support
   - introduce activities – quizzes, developing and producing a product such as a website.
7 Provide different learning activities
   - for pragmatists – case studies, practical tips and techniques
   - for activists – activities, opportunities to socialize
   - for reflectors – opportunities to stand back and think, learning journals and reflective activities
   - for theorists – background information and links to additional learning materials.

Reflection on learning

8 Provide opportunities to practise working with new skills and knowledge.
9 Provide opportunities to synthesize and integrate ideas.
10 Provide opportunities for reflection, e.g. during and at the end of programmes or activities.

11 Encourage learners to stand back and reflect on different aspects of e-learning programmes, e.g. individual or group processes, their feelings about e-learning, implications of their experiences for their studies or work.

12 If you are involved in establishing e-learning programmes that lead to a qualification, then include reflective practice as part of the assessment strategy, e.g. online reflective activities or learning journals.

Learning as a social activity

13 Select learning processes that include group work, e.g. co-operation and collaborative activities.

14 Ensure that prospective e-learners are clear about the types of learning activities involved in independent or group learning situations.

15 Identify the sources, types and levels of support within the e-learning programme.

16 Identify the roles of peers, colleagues and mentors in the e-learning programme.

17 If you are using a group-learning process, then start off with collaborative group activities, as this can enhance motivation, group bonding and also generate supportive relationships that will facilitate learning throughout the programme.

Knowledge and competence

18 Identify the approach to knowledge that is required in the particular e-learning programme.

19 Ensure that the e-learning programme matches the underpinning theory of knowledge

Approaches to learning

20 Identify the underlying approach to learning, e.g. behaviourist or constructivist, and ensure that the programme is congruent with this approach.

Five-stage model of learning

21 Use the Gilly Salmon five-stage model as a framework for design.

22 Ensure that there is technical support built into the delivery process.

23 Ensure that learners who access e-learning programmes from library and information services have access to appropriate technical support.

Learning to learn

24 Provide e-learners with access to support in becoming e-learners.

25 Build in 'learning to learn' activities early in the programme.

26 Ensure that staff who support e-learners understand the different demands made by an e-learning programme.

Communities of practice

27 Consider whether or not you wish to develop an online learning community.

28 If you decide to establish an online community, then identify the relevance of a community of interest or a community of practice.

29 If you are establishing, developing and maintaining a community of interest, then consider using a mail list, bulletin board or similar tool. Establish clear boundaries and follow existing good practice in running and moderating such a community.

30 If you are establishing, developing and maintaining a community of practice then consider using McDermott's 10 critical success factors. (McDermott, 2000).

Assessment

Assessment involves finding out how much an individual or group has learnt, and it can take place before, during, at the end of or after an e-learning programme. Assessment enables learners to recognize their achievement and areas for development, and it also enables e-tutors, designers and the LIS to evaluate the e-learning programme and identify areas for improvement. The design of assessment activities and processes involves considering the following questions:

- what learning outcomes are going to be assessed?
- what are the assessment criteria?
- what assessment strategy will be used?
- what type of assessment activities will be included in the programme?
- how will they fit into the timing of the overall programme?
- how will the assessment process be communicated to the learners?
- how will feedback be provided to the learners?
- how will the assessment activities be recorded?

Asessment can involve a wide range of activities, e.g. use of computer-assisted assessment where learners complete question sets and the whole assessment process is administered via the VLE, and individual or small group acitivies that typically result in the development of a product such as a report, website, or review. Assessment activities are explored in more detail in the following chapter.

Navigation

At any stage in the learning programme, learners need to know where they are, how they got there and where they can move to next. It is important that the materials are organized in a logical way and that guidance is available. The following facilities are often used to organize learning materials and guide learners:

- home page with site map
- search tools
- help facility
- headings
- menu of contents
- index
- glossary
- hotlinks
- bookmarks.

One useful practice is to present the whole programme and highlight completed units, work-in-progress and forthcoming units. This enables learners to visualize their progress within the whole e-learning programme.

Many virtual learning environments provide these facilities as a standard set of authoring or tutor tools. This means that it is relatively simple for information workers and e-tutors to prepare their learning programme, and it means that they don't need to develop specialized technical skills.

Usability

It is really important that the e-learning programme is readable and easy to use. There is nothing worse than being faced with indigestible chunks of dense reading material in a very small font. Factors that need to be considered include:

- text should be legible against the background
- use of appropriate font style and size

- text should be surrounded by sufficient space – 'white space'
- text should be divided into appropriate-sized chunks, e.g. 5–6 points per chunk
- long pages should include a table of content and a 'back to top' button
- lists and bullet points rather than large blocks of text
- minimal horizontal scrolling
- maximum accessibility, e.g. provide large font versions, and provide text of audio tapes.

It is also important that the text is accessible to a diverse group of learners. Further information on this topic is available from *The Web Accessibility Initiative* at: www.w3.org/TR/WAI-WEBCONTENT/.

Introducing text, sounds and images

It is relatively simple to use software packages to integrate a wide range of materials into an e-learning programme (this topic was outlined in Chapter 5). The following features are relatively easy to add to authored material:

- document files
- *PowerPoint* files
- audio files
- image files
- video files
- animation files.

Document files using PDF (Portable Document Format) are created and read in *Adobe Acrobat*. They are widely used as a means of distributing documents on the internet. PDF file links allow content to display PDF files in a new window. Images that have been created outside the word-processing software and held as GIF or JPG files can be included in the document. Images can be included as a background as well as in the foreground of the screen. Audio files can be played as clickable links or background audio that starts as soon as a page is loaded or on the closedown of a section. Shockwave/Director movies can be made in *Macromedia Director*, and *Shockwave* (.dcr and .swf files) can be included in the content.

There is a balance to be achieved between providing a multimedia presentation and providing e-learning materials that are readily and quickly accessible. It is important to consider the needs of diverse users, e.g. people who have impaired hearing, and to provide alternative formats, e.g. scripts to accompany audio clips and captions on video clips. Examples of accessible media-rich materials can be found at http://ncam.wgbh.org/richmedia/showcase.html (accessed 24 April 2002).

Storyboard

A storyboard is used in content-driven interactive learning materials as a means of presenting the materials to be delivered in a narrative form. It normally includes a screen-by-screen outline of the screen content and layout audio script, visual images and graphics, and a description of the interactions or activities presented on that screen. The storyboard is a crucial document, and it will normally be checked by a subject specialist and an editor before it is approved. The storyboard is then used as the basis for the development process by the materials production team.

Using ICT tools

The following tools are commonly used to create e-learning materials and manage the learning process:

* HTML editors (*HoTMetal_Pro, HotDog, PageMill* etc.)
* website development tools (*FrontPage, DreamWeaver, NetObjects Fusion* etc.)
* computer-based training authoring tools (*Asymetrix ToolBook, Macromedia Authorward, IconAuthor, TopClass* etc.)
* curriculum management and training record systems (*NetG SkillVantag Manager, Asymetrix Librarian, Macromedia Pathware, TopClass* etc.)
* virtual learning environments (*WebCT, Blackboard, The Learning Web, Virtual Campus, Lotus Learning Space, TopClass*).

It is worth identifying the tools available within your organization and the technical support available. Information workers are likely to have access to organizational ICT systems and support services, and while this may mean a lack of choice about the choice of specific tools, it will mean that there is likely to be in-house technical assistance available. It is well worthwhile exploring the tools available and identifying any additional tools that need to be obtained, and also individual training requirements. Many e-learning projects include ICT workers on their teams, and this can be a really effective method of ensuring that the most appropriate technologies are used with a minimum of stress and wasted effort.

Technical issues

A range of technical issues need to be considered at the development stage. Enthusiastic technical people sometimes want to develop learning environments that demonstrate currently available and developing technical features. While these can be impressive, they can also put up huge barriers to e-learners, who may be accessing the system from a relatively old PC using a fairly standard modem.

The following guidelines can be used to develop learning environments that are accessible to everyone:

1 Ensure that the program runs on all supported brands and versions of browsers and browser add-ons such as plugs.
2 Check that the program runs on all supported types of computer at the minimum supported specification.
3 Ensure that the program is free of software bugs and broken links.
4 Minimize the time taken to load images, applet, movie, audio file or document. If the delay is more than 10 seconds, then give an estimate of the time to download and also reasons why the download will be helpful. Provide alternatives where possible, e.g. the script of an audio file.
5 Ensure that videos display without break-up.
6 Ensure that audio clips are free from hisses and other extraneous noises.
7 Make sure that page refresh is quick so that the learner's attention is held throughout the process.

A useful source of standards for developing and maintaining e-learning materials is the Institute of IT Training (www.iitt.org.uk/), who informed the development of earlier parts of this chapter.

Copyright

Copyright is a complex issue and it is really important that programme developers don't accidentally or intentionally infringe copyright legislation. There are very good guides to copyright legislation available, such as that on the JISC website www.jisc.ac.uk, and guides such as those written by Cornish (2001).

Some basic rules in the development of e-learning materials and programmes include the importance of clearly labelling, dating and identifying all learning materials. It is important to obtain written permission if you are using other people's intellectual property, e.g. images, text, sound, animation, list of URLs. Key points to cover when writing for permission include:

- bibliographic references for the required material
- lists of the pages, screens and frames
- details of material in preparation: outline materials, audience, size of audience, proposed usage (e.g. three times per year), life span (likely to be two years), proposed use (e.g. educational, not-for-profit, commercial)
- details of the organization, e.g. public, private or third sector.

House style

It is important that the e-learning programme is presented using a house style, as this enables the whole programme to look very professional, and learners aren't distracted or confused by the use of a number of different styles. The majority of organizations have their own house style for use in electronic and printed communications, and it is important to identify in-house guidelines covering issues such as typeface, font size, and the choice, size and use of logos. Practical problems can arise, e.g. if the organization's house style is inappropriate for an e-learning programme. This can then result in delicate negotiations by the project leader with the appropriate staff, e.g. marketing people.

The use of a graphic designer is invaluable in ensuring that the e-learning programme is presented in an accessible way. Although this adds an extra cost to the overall project, the author's experience is that it is well worthwhile, as the introduction of the professional skills of a designer with appropriate ICT skills can enhance the e-learning programme and make it highly attractive to the learner.

It is also worthwhile involving an overall editor who will check that:

- the content, activities and resources all meet the overall aim and learning outcomes
- the materials all demonstrate the required level and language
- house style has been applied consistently
- the learning materials 'hang together' as a coherent whole.

Pilot programme

If possible, it is worthwhile piloting the e-learning programme with a small group of learners. This will help to identify any problems in the programme and it will also enable the identification and correction of any errors or problems. Having a trial run on exercises and activities also enables the developers to obtain a sense of the learning experience and whether or not it is manageable, e.g. in terms of time, resources, type of activity.

It is often not possible to run a pilot programme and in this instance it is worthwhile asking colleagues, particularly those whom have not been involved in the project, to give their feedback on the e-learning programme. Again, this feedback will enable the developers to improve the programme.

Delivery

The moment of truth! Delivering a new e-learning programme can be an exciting and challenging process. Once the programme starts then the programme leader or e-tutor is likely to be involved in a number of distinct activities

- monitoring the virtual learning environment, learner and tutor activities
- monitoring the use of the support systems, e.g. technical support
- informing the programme team of developments
- networking with LIS key staff, e.g. senior managers.

Monitoring the virtual learning environment involves checking the different parts of the environment and ensuring that the right information is available at the right time. The large virtual learning environments provide tracking tools that can be used to identify the following types of statistics for both learners and tutors:

- number of times logged into the system
- number of messages read
- number of messages posted
- performance on assessment activities such as quizzes.

As well as this quantitative data, it is worthwhile obtaining information from the learners themselves and this can be obtained indirectly by reading messages and identifying current issues such as time issues, and also by direct methods such as using questionnaires, interviews or focus groups (see the final section in this chapter).

It is useful to obtain information from the e-tutor and to find out what is working well, and also any areas for change and improvement. If the e-learning programme is used by library and information unit customers, then it is worthwhile checking with staff such as those on service points for feedback they may have obtained by informal means.

The support systems, e.g. technical help and online reference desk, may also be monitored, and this provides information about the impact of the e-learning programme on existing support services and also areas for potential change or clarification within the programme. An example of the kinds of changes introduced into e-learning programmes in library and information services as a result of this type of monitoring include:

- introduction of a face-to-face induction session so as to provide additional ICT support
- introduction of a printed manual to highlight key information about getting started as an e-learner
- provision of additional technical support in the evening when many e-learners in academic environments are carrying out their learning activities
- change in the presentation of learning resources so that they are identified as essential viewing or optional activities.

The information obtained from all of these monitoring activities needs to be fed back to the programme development team and a summary may also be prepared and circulated to senior management.

Accessibility

All groups of learners are likely to include disabled individuals and it is important to consider how e-learning programmes can be made accessible to everyone. This can involve using assistive technology to facilitate access to learning resources and teaching materials; examples include Electronic Braille displays and speech output systems. It also includes designing learning materials and programmes so that all students can access them. Barnes and Seale (2002, 3–4) describe the importance of using Universal Design Principles so that e-learning programmes and resources:

- are developed with consideration of the needs of a diverse population
- are not described as being anything more than easy for everyone to use
- are always accessible (but because accessibility has been integrated from the beginning of the design process, they are less likely to be noticeable)
- benefit everyone, not only disabled people.

Phipps, Sutherland and Seale (2002) in their publication *Access all areas: disability, technology and learning* provide an up-to-date book that summarizes the current situation with special reference to the needs of learners in colleges and universities.

Evaluation

This section is concerned with evaluating the e-learning programme to ensure that it meets its stated aims and learning outcomes, and also the changing needs of the library and information service. Evaluation involves gathering information about the e-learning programme and then using this information to measure the value of the programme.

What should be evaluated?

Evaluation of e-learning is likely to focus on three main issues:

- learning and its impact on the LIS
- the learning environment and learning materials
- the learning process.

Learning and its impact on the LIS

A very popular and simple evaluation model is that used by Kirkpatrick (1994), which evaluates learning programmes and events at four different levels:

- reaction
- learning
- changes in behaviour
- impact on the library and information service.

The reaction to the e-learning programme is how learners feel at the end of a unit, workshop or whole programme. This is their immediate response without time for detailed reflection on the event or to apply their learning in another context. The next level of evaluation is concerned with the knowledge or skills someone has learnt as a result of the programme. What impact has the programme had on the learner's behaviour in the workplace? This is effect of the e-learning programme on the learner's behaviour. The final level of evaluation is the impact on the library and information service – is the programme helping it to achieve its business objectives?

Different people may be involved in the evaluation process, e.g. learners and their co-learners, e-tutors, workplace colleagues, team leaders and managers. Involving a number of different people obviously improves the quality of the evaluation process, and it also increases the cost (in both time and other resources).

An important decision is whether or not to include the evaluation process as an integral part of the e-learning programme (e.g. all evaluation activities to be carried out as learners work through the programme), or to carry out the evaluation using alternative means such as e-mail, paper-based tools or face-to-face sessions. In the early stages of running a programme it can be really useful to include face-to-face evaluation sessions, as this sometimes produces richer information. Issues that had not previously been considered can then be picked up and explored in more detail.

E-learning programmes are typically evaluated using a wide range of tools available. Table 8.4 is adapted from Hackett (1997).

Table 8.4 *Tools for evaluation*

	Reactions	Learning	Behaviour	Impact on LIS
Online or paper-based questionnaires or reports	*	*	*	*
Team leader questionnaires or reports	*	*	*	*
Online assessment activities		*	*	
Customer survey			*	*
Employer survey			*	*
Interviews	*	*	*	*
Performance appraisal		*	*	
Observation		*	*	
Team/unit performance indicators				*
LIS performance indicators				*
Senior management opinion	*	*	*	*

Example evaluation forms

The first example shows an e-mail sent out to information workers involved in an e-learning project management course.

Evaluation request using e-mail

From: Jules Johnson
To: Projman123
Subject: Evaluation of e-learning project management course

Hello everyone,
Well done for completing the course. Thank you for your enthusiasm, commitment and humour (!) during this programme. As it is the first time we have delivered this course by e-learning it would help us if you could give us your feedback by answering the following questions:

1   Did the programme meet your expectations?
2   What were your learning outcomes from the programme?

3   How will you use your new knowledge and skills in your information unit?
4   What were the best parts of the course?
5   What were the worst parts of the course?
6   How could we improve the course?
7   Any other comments?

Thank you for this feedback – please send it by the 15 April. Do remember to keep in touch and let me know how your work-based projects progress.
Best wishes, Jules

The second evaluation form was used to collect information (using a webform) about a face-to-face induction event for an e-learning programme.

E-learning induction programme: evaluation form

The purpose of this questionnaire is to help us to evaluate the induction session. Your feedback will provide us with valuable information.

1   What did you hope to get out of the induction session?

2   General comments about the session:

3   Please indicate your evaluation of the session (poor = 1, excellent = 5):

Trainers ☐	Information provided ☐
Printed resources ☐	Group discussions ☐
Activities ☐	WebCT session ☐

4   What was the most useful part of the session?

5   How could the session be improved?

6   As a result of the induction sessions what are your expectations about the module?

7   Any other comments?

E-learning and teaching

Learning environment and materials

Evaluating the learning environment and materials typically involves answering the following questions:

Learning environment

1   Is the learning environment easy to access?
2   Do security systems work without being too cumbersome?
3   Is the structure and layout of the learning environment intuitive?
4   Is the design of the environment attractive and visually pleasing?
5   Is it possible to take different routes through the learning environment?
6   Do all facilities (e.g. links, quizzes, surveys) work?
7   Is it up-to-date?

Learning materials

1   Are they easy to access and quick to download?
2   Is there a clear statement of aims, learning outcomes or objectives?
3   Do they arouse the learner's interest?
4   Do they use clear language?
5   Is the content organized into manageable chunks?
6   Is the content relevant?
7   Do they provide a variety of routes through the materials?
8   Do they use supporting images and diagrams?
9   Are there opportunities for learners to practise, e.g. activities and quizzes?
10 Is there personalized feedback?
11 Is the material up-to-date?

Learning process

Evaluating the learning process may involve exploring aspects of the e-learning programme such as:

- the development of virtual communication skills
- the development of e-learning to learn skills, e.g. time management
- the use made of learning materials
- the use made of virtual communication tools, e.g. e-mail, discussion groups, chat rooms

- the balance of independent, collaborative and/or co-operative working
- specific learning activities and processes
- peer support and e-tutor support
- other support processes, e.g. technical help desks, mentor support.

The following form was used to evaluate time management issues of information workers involved in a work-based e-learning programme.

Time management

The purpose of this questionnaire is to enable us to improve our support processes for information unit staff taking e-learning programmes. All answers will be treated as confidential and will be used to help us develop our support systems for e-learners.

1 Do you use your own computer, a computer at work, or a mixture of own/work computers to access *WebCT*?

2 All participants were allocated one hour a week to work on this course while at work. Were you able to use this time for study? Please comment on your answer.

3 How did you manage your time with regard to your e-learning programme?

4 Please outline any time management issues you have experienced during your e-learning programme?

5 What were your main barriers to finding time for the e-learning programme?

6 What time management advice would you give to someone starting out on an e-learning programme for the first time?

7 How could we improve the support we give to the next group of information staff taking this course?

8 Any other comments?

Thank you for completing this questionnaire.

Results of evaluation

The findings from the evaluation process may result in a number of different outcomes:

- the e-learning programme is abandoned
- the e-learning programme is re-designed – new learning objectives, new structure, new content, new methods, new tutors
- the preparation work is re-designed – new briefing material, new pre-course work
- the virtual learning environment is re-designed – new virtual learning environment, re-organized site, change in navigation, change in design
- the e-learning process is changed – new activities, fewer activities, new timing
- no change.

Summary

The design cycle involves a needs analysis, design, development, delivery and evaluation. There is no simple solution or prescription for designing effective e-learning programmes. Success depends on researching and responding to the following factors:

- organizational and individual learning needs
- setting realistic aims and learning outcomes
- incorporating key design principles in interactive learning materials and learning processes
- using an appropriate balance of independent and group-based learning activities
- applying relevant models of e-learning such as the Gilly Salmon five-stage model
- incorporating principles of learning
- developing and piloting practical and sustainable learning programmes and activities
- evaluating the programme or activity and using this feedback to improve it.

9

E-learning activities

Introduction

The aim of this chapter is to explore a range of common e-learning activities and to provide examples of how they are used in practice. E-activities are like any other learning activities, i.e. they are used to facilitate the learning of a particular subject or process, and they also enhance the learners experience and professional practice. E-learning activities include assessment activities, e.g. online quizzes. Information workers who are involved in online learning and teaching activities may be involved in developing or delivering e-activities.

E-activities can be divided into four groups depending on the relationships between the learner(s) and e-tutor, as shown in Table 9.1 (Goodyear, 2000).

The chapter is divided into three distinct sections. The first section on e-learning activities considers the background and reasons for using activities, and provides a brief summary to their design. It includes a table summarizing a range of common e-learning activities, with their main advantages and disadvantages. E-tutors may find this table provides a guide to the types of activity they can use when developing programmes. The second section includes a brief description of specific types of e-activities, followed by examples or guidelines for their use in library and information e-learning situations. The final section considers e-learning assessment activities.

E-learning activities and exercises

Effective e-learning activities are those that mobilize, engage and enable learners to develop their knowledge and skills. Salmon (2000) discusses the concept of mobilization, which involves generating interest and motivation in taking part in the activity. Once learners are mobilized, then they can engage with the learning processes, which 'involve cognitive processes such as creating, problem-solving, reasoning, decision-making and evaluation. In addition, students are intrinsically motivated

Table 9.1 *E-learning activities: e-learner and e-tutor relationships*

Types of activity	Examples
Individual activities – learners work by themselves and then discuss work with tutor.	Holding an online interview and providing feedback
	Investigation and feedback on electronic or printed resources
	Investigation and feedback on workplace activities or projects
	Reading and response to articles in online journals
	Writing reports or reviews
Learner–tutor activities – learner works with tutor on a joint activity.	Development of learning contracts
	Discussion and feedback
One-to-many techniques – tutor or visitor disseminates information or ideas to a large group, e.g. 1 guest speaker to 1000 students.	Online lecture
	Virtual visitor
Many-to-many techniques – learners and tutor(s) work together.	Brainstorming
	Case studies
	Discussion groups
	Debates
	Project groups
	Role plays
	Simulations or games

to learn due to the meaningful nature of the learning environment and activities.' (Kearsley and Schneiderman 1998). Effective e-learning activities are those that enable individuals or groups to work on authentic tasks or situations. E-learners, like all learners, need to know that their learning activities are relevant and have some meaning for them. This means that they need to be focused on a current issue or need rather than on an abstract task.

The preparation of e-activities is similar to the preparation process for face-to-face activities and involves focusing on the following aspects of the e-activity:

- purpose or aim
- learning outcomes or objectives
- participant numbers
- overall structure of the activity
- interaction structure
  — collaboration requirement (including deadlines)
  — process and outcome
  — time required by learners and tutor

- preparation of learning resources
- identification of additional resources.

Table 9.2 summarizes commonly used e-learning activities, and highlights their advantages and also potential problem areas.

Specific examples of e-learning activities

The examples included in this section cover the most commonly used e-learning activities currently used in library and information e-learning programmes.

A wide range of activities and exercises can be used to enable e-learners to develop their knowledge and skills, and also to learn from each other. Activities may be carried out individually or in groups.

Individual activities

Individual e-learning activities include:

- investigating a website and providing feedback
- completing a question set
- reading and responding to an article or report
- evaluating a website, service or learning environment
- holding an online interview and providing feedback
- producing a product or report, e.g. website, set of guidelines.

The following example activity is adapted from the Open University course T171 *You, your computer and the net*. This introductory course provides a first step in e-learning for approximately 12,000 students each year. This activity enables students to start developing their information skills and it relies on resources developed from a wide range of LIS across the world. This is an individual activity although it could easily be adapted for group work, e.g. by asking a small group of learners to produce a website that critically evaluates a range of websites relevant to their studies.

Table 9.2 *E-learning activities*

Activity	Characteristics	Reasons for use	Advantages	Potential problems
Brainstorming or wordstorming	Individuals pool ideas and generate new ideas/options. A 'quick' activity, and therefore probably best carried out in a chat or conference room.	Enable ideas and new perspectives to be identified. Useful for focusing learners on a new topic.	Quick and simple method.	Individual learners may not engage with the activity.
Case studies	Learners are presented with a particular situation and are typically asked to explore it and develop 'solutions'.	Enable individuals to explore different situations from a range of different perspectives. Enable learners to share ideas and experiences, and construct their knowledge.	Case studies can be closely related to workplace situations. Can be used to prepare learners for future situations.	Time-consuming to develop. May not be perceived as 'real' and therefore not valued. Individual learners may not engage with the activity.
Debates	Structured or unstructured discussion based on two or or more different *perspectives*.	Enable learners to explore issues or ideas. Enable learners to share ideas and experiences, and construct their knowledge.	The best debates are lively, based on real-life issues and concerns. Involve all learners.	Debate may become a slanging match. Use of abusive language. A few participants may dominate. Quieter group members may feel intimidated.
Discussion groups	Structured or unstructured discussions. May be based on a specific issue or set of ideas.	Enable learners to explore issues or ideas. Enable learners to share iideas and experiences, and construct their knowledge.	The best online discussions are lively, based on real-life issues and concerns. Involve all learners.	Discussion peters out or is unfocused. Learners don't participate or hijack discussion. Individuals dominate. They are not inclusive.

Table 9.2 *E-learning activities (continued)*

Activity	Characteristics	Reasons for use	Advantages	Potential problems
Exercises	Typically a tutor sets up and facilitates exercises that involve pairs, trios or larger groups of e-learners working together on a specific task, e.g. producing a set of guidelines, reviewing a website.	Enable learners to work in a focused way and benefit from the sharing of experience, ideas and support.	Can be highly motivating and satisfying experiences. Individuals learn from each other. Products may be of higher quality than if produced by individuals.	Time needs to be spent on working out how to work together. Individuals may opt out or be freeloaders.
Icebreakers	Relatively short activities that enable learners to get to know each other, become familiar with the technology and environment, and start the learning process.	To 'break the ice' at start of a new e-learning programme. Enable learners to start to develop their online voice.	They give individuals an opportunity to become familiar with e-learning. Individuals can join in as they access the technology (makes it easier for late arrivals to get going).	Some people don't join in. A few participants dominate. Quieter group members may feel intimidated. Some people may find it frustrating, i.e. they want to get started with the content of the course.
Project groups	In co-operative groups, individuals work on their own task and share ideas, feedback and give support. In collaborative groups, the group works on a whole group project.	Can be based on workplace projects. Enable multidisciplinary or multiprofessional teams to work together. Help to develop team working and virtual communication skills. Encourage sharing of experience, ideas and support.	Can be highly motivating and satisfying experiences. Individuals learn from one another. Products may be of higher quality than if produced by individuals.	Time needs to be spent on working out how to work together. Individuals may opt out or be freeloaders.

Table 9.2 E-learning activities (continued)

Activity	Characteristics	Reasons for use	Advantages	Potential problems
Role play	Individuals may take on a specific role, either in a text-based environment or in a MUD or MOO environment (see Chapter 2). They then explore the role and the consequences of selected kinds of action. Needs to be facilitated by an expert.	Enables individuals to explore different situations from a range of different perspectives.	Provides practical experience in handling particular situations. Time to reflect and learn from experiences.	Individuals don't engage with the role play. Individuals engage too closely with it – this is potentially dangerous, particularly if individual learners have mental health issues.
Simulations or games	A group follows a set of rules or a situation that simulates a real-life situation. May be facilitated by an e-tutor or group member(s).	Enable individuals to experience a 'real-life' situation. May provide experiences that are hard to work on in real life.	Provide practical experience in handling particular situations. Time to reflect and learn from experiences.	Time-consuming to develop. May not be perceived as 'real' and therefore not valued. May be difficult to relate experiences to workplace.
Team-building activities	A group takes part in an activity that involves every-one (the online equivalent to outward bound training). The discussion and reflection on the activity is more important than the actual activity itself.	Enable e-learners to experience and become familiar with online group work.	Learners can develop online netiquette skills and gain experience of good practice in team work.	Individuals don't engage with activity and may perceive it as a waste of time. Learners don't participate or individuals dominate.

212

Table 9.2 E-learning activities (continued)

Activity	Characteristics	Reasons for use	Advantages	Potential problems
Virtual visitor or guest speaker	Typically a tutor invites an experienced practitioner or someone with specialist expertise to visit the online group, either synchronously or asynchronously, for a set period of time.	Introduces specialist knowledge. Opportunity to explore different perspectives. May be used to emphasize particular perspective.	'Breath of fresh air'. Provides 'excitement' and 'difference'. Provides additional ideas, experiences, perspectives.	Technical issues, e.g. problems with access to site. Virtual visitor doesn't prepare for visit and misreads culture of group. Virtual visitor hijacks session and leads it into unwanted areas. Virtual visitor usurps tutor's role. Learners don't engage with activity and 'ignore' virtual visitor. Learners don't accept virtual visitor. Unrealistic expectations (tutor, virtual visitor or learners).
Virtual visits	A group of e-learners may visit another group and share their experiences, using chat or discussion groups.	Opportunity to explore different perspectives.	'Breath of fresh air'. Provide 'excitement' and 'difference'. Provide additional ideas, experiences, perspectives. Enable learners to experience different VLEs.	Time needed to set up and organize visit. Technical issues, e.g. problems with access to site. Problems with different groups of learners developing rapport. Visit becomes a social rather than a learning experience. Unrealistic expections (tutor, virtual visitors or learners).

Individual information skills activity

Introduction

In this exercise you will work individually to find some websites relating to the subject of Module 1, and evaluate the information in them.

Outcomes

The exercise should help you with the following:

- developing skills in using the web as a resource
- developing skills in evaluating content on the web
- developing skills relevant to the first assignment.

Background

As you will know, one of the good things about the web is also one of the bad things – namely, anyone can publish (almost) anything. This means that the web is an excellent information resource (for example, many academics publish their papers on the web), but also that you may have to work through a lot of information to find what you want. And how do you judge the material you find? The usual publication route, when a journal, magazine or book publisher agrees to publish material, has some form of quality control built in. We know, for example, that an article in an academic journal will usually have been reviewed by peers, so one has a certain level of faith in its arguments and factual statements (although of course errors do arise). This is not the case on the web, so you must bring your own judgement to bear.

The activity

In this exercise you will look at a site, and produce a brief summary on various aspects of it. This will give you practice in writing for your assignment, give you an opportunity to consider the issues relating to reliability on the web, and a chance to put these into practice.

Here is what you should do for this exercise:

1   Read through one of the resources on evaluating web material provided below.
2   Look at Assignment 1 Question 1.
3   Search the web for relevant sites on the subject of Assignment 1 Question 1
4   For one site produce a summary which answers the following

questions (this is a different set of questions from those posed in the assignment, but this should help you in that task).

5   How easy was it to find your way around the site?

6   What was the 'look and feel' of the site like? Did you like it? Did the design get in the way of the content? Did the design match the tone of the content?

7   What was the writing style like? Was it friendly, academic, humorous, factual, commercial, etc.?

8   Who do you think is the audience for the site? Is it the general public, professionals in that field, academics, children, etc.? Does the style (in terms of both presentation and writing) match this?

9   How reliable is the information on the site? Is it likely to be biased in any way?

10 You may like to share your summaries with other members of your tutor group.

Resources to help with this activity

Evaluating web material at http://unfccc.int/resource/library/criteria.html. This site lists five criteria for evaluating web resources.

Evaluating web resources by Jan Alexander and Marsha Tate, reference librarians at Widener University in Pennsylvania, USA. Includes information on how to evaluate advocacy web pages, business web pages, news web pages, etc. Available at www2.widener.edu/Wolfgram-Memorial-Library/webevaluation/webeval.htm.

The internet detective, an interactive tutorial on evaluating the quality of internet resources. *The internet detective* has been developed to benefit the academic research community in the European Union. It may be used freely for non-commercial academic and research purposes. Available at www.sosig.ac.uk/desire/internet-detective.html.

Web evaluation criteria by Susan E. Beck, Head, Humanities and Social Sciences Services Department, New Mexico State University Library, available at http://unfccc.int/resource/library/criteria.html.

Evaluating web sites: criteria and tools, from Cornell University Library, Cornell University, USA, available at www.library.cornell.edu/okuref/research/webeval.html

UCLA guide on evaluating web material, available at www.library.ucla.edu/libraries/college/help/critical/index.htm

This is an example of a very good e-learning activity. It is clearly presented in a readable and friendly style. There are clear learning outcomes and the activity is clearly described and broken into manageable chunks. The activity is closely linked to a forthcoming assignment and this is likely to encourage learners to take part in it. Finally, a range of readable resources are hot linked to the activity giving students a choice of background reading matter.

Group activities

There are many different kinds of group activities. The two specific examples considered here demonstrate the use of frequently asked questions and a learning-styles activity. Other group activities may involve case studies, project groups and team-building activities, and these are all explored later in this chapter.

Frequently asked questions

Frequently asked questions (FAQ) lists on websites, databases or 5 x 3 card records are a common method of responding to common queries or concerns. They provide a useful devise for focusing individual or small-group online activities. E-learners can be asked to prepare and present a list of FAQ based on their own learning experiences. Typical examples include:

- preparing a list of FAQ for new members of LIS staff
  (LIS staff induction programme)
- preparing a list of FAQ for new sixth-formers
- (information skills module for sixth-formers)
- preparing a list of FAQ for using *WebCT*
  (LIS staff learning to use *WebCT*)
- preparing a list of FAQ for using HTML
  (LIS staff learning to use html).

Asking e-learners to develop FAQ lists is a useful method for consolidating learning, assessing learning, sharing experiences, and preparing resources that can be used by future learners. It also doesn't need to be a very time-consuming activity as, by their very nature, the answers to FAQs tend to be short.

Learning-styles activity

The example activity below was used in an e-learning programme aimed at library and information staff in a college. It includes the following elements:

- individual activity using an online questionnaire
- group activity based on findings from individual activity
- reflection and use of a learning journal
- a link to a face-to-face workshop.

E-activity on learning styles

This activity was included in the early stages of an online discussion group for library and information staff in a college. Below is the learning outcome for the activity and a series of messages from the tutor. These messages show how he started and closed the e-activity.

Learning outcome
By the end of this activity staff will be able to explain and apply the Honey and Mumford model of learning styles to online learners.

Structure of the activity
This activity is introduced in week three of the programme. All the e-learners will now be working online and will have gone through online introductions using an icebreaker. They have also developed a set of online ground rules.

The messages
Message 1: Introduction to learning styles
> Hi
>
> We are now going to move into a very important subject on the course; the topic of learning styles. Most of us have a preferred way of learning, e.g. when I am faced with a new computer system I like to 'have a go' and will learn by trial and error and experimentation. This is in contrast to a friend of mine who will read the manual and follow all of the instructions step by step. This difference is related to us having different preferred learning styles.
>
> This may be a new concept to some of you and it is perhaps a familiar idea to others. Whatever your experience of learning styles the first activity involves you in identifying your own learning style.
>
> What you have to do
> What you need to do is complete the online learning style ques-

tionnaire (you will find it in the learning resources section of the online system). Complete the questionnaire and identify your pre-ferred learning style. Obtain a printout and think about the results.

If possible then please complete this activity by 1 March when I'll post a message giving you the instructions for the next part of the activity.
bfn
James

Message 2: Implications of learning styles

Hi

Well done for completing the questionnaire. The next step is to find out who has which learning style preference. Please would you each send a message into the group stating:
Your learning style preference
What you like about online learning
What you dislike about online learning.

Many thanks. I'm looking forward to finding out the type of mix we have in this group. Every group is different and differences in learning styles help to make learning exciting.
bfn
James

Message 3: Working in groups

Hi there

Thanks for the interesting information about the likes/dislikes in the group. Areas of similarity I noticed include: activists got very very frustrated if the IT systems went wrong; reflectors liked having time to think before sending a reply; theorists wanted more information and reading. So that we can explore this theme of similarity and dif-ferences in more detail I propose that we set up four learning sets (red, green, blue, orange – not very original names but feel free to choose your own names) in which you explore learning styles in more details. I have assigned people into the following groups:

Red - John, James S, Ann, Tina, Sarah
Green - James T, Russell, Jane
Blue - Janice, Marg, Andy,
Orange - David, Peter, Wendy,

You will notice that you have been grouped according to your learning style preferences.

What you need to do
As a group discuss and decide responses to the following questions:

1   What helps you to learn via the online discussion group?
2   What stops you from learning via the online discussion group?
3   How do these findings relate to the model of learning styles?
4   You will find it helpful to do some background reading. Articles 6,7 and 8 in your reader are the key ones.

You will need to decide your group response and submit it to the main discussion group within 7 days, i.e. by Thursday 12th.
I look forward to hearing from you all. Do contact me if you have any queries. Has anyone worked out my learning style?
Best wishes
James

Message 4: Group working

Hi there
I hope your online discussions on learning styles are going well. One final question:
Review your online discussion (red, green, blue, orange) group learning processes. How do these reflect your learning styles?
Please would you discuss this question and answer it in your reply to the whole group.
Remember that your reply needs to be in by 16th March.
bfn
James

In response to this message, individual learners input a variety of messages and these were then discussed by the whole group. Tentative conclusions were weaved by a group member. The final message in this activity was then posted by the tutor:

Message 9: Learning journal

Hi
We are now getting to the end of this activity. Thank you all for par-

ticipating. Thanks in particular to Ann for your weaved summary. You really picked up the key points and also highlighted the complexity of the area. I liked the way you concluded with a list of partially answered questions.

Remember the learning journal? You might want to include work from this activity in it. Some questions you might want to consider include:

- *What have you learnt from this activity?*
- *How will you use this learning in your life as an online student?*
- *How will you use this learning in your training room activities?*
- *You might want to write this up in your learning journal.*
- *Remember to reflect on your entry. How has your own learning style affected how and what you wrote? What about re-writing it from the perspective of someone with a different learning style?*

This now formally closes this activity. There is now a break in the discussion group e-activities to give you all time to prepare for the one day workshop. The workshop guide will give you all the necessary background information and reading. Do get in touch if you have any queries.
BFN
James

Brainstorming

Brainstorming is a problem-solving technique that involves quickly generating and sharing ideas without censoring them. It is often used in face-to-face sessions as a means of focusing on a particular issue, generating a wide range of options and/or raising the energy in a group. In face-to-face sessions it is often carried out over a very short time span, e.g. a few minutes.

Brainstorming in an e-learning environment involves group members working in a chat or conference room and typing in ideas very quickly. They don't respond or comment on other people's ideas during the process. It enables people to generate ideas freely and also to build on other people's ideas as one idea triggers another. It also allows simultaneous contributions.

Carol Glover (2002) suggests that individuals become anxious when brainstorming in a group, and that this can limit the effectiveness of the technique. One way around this problem is to give people advanced warning about the use of this technique. This enables them to start brainstorming alone before bringing their ideas to the group.

Case studies

Case studies are a useful method of enabling e-learners to focus on a particular situation, and to explore it and develop 'solutions'. They take some time to prepare, as the e-tutor needs to collect appropriate materials and examples, work out an appropriate case study, and then mentally 'walk through' the case study and the likely processes that the learners will engage in as they work on the materials. The best case studies are those based on real situations that are closely linked with the learners' experiences. The following case study was successfully used on an e-learning module for information services staff. While some of the learners expressed their surprise at the types of situations that were introduced into the case study, they were all based on recent experiences within a higher education institution.

Case study: Working with diverse groups

Aim

The aim of this activity is to enable you to explore issues about working with diverse groups of learners.

What you will need to do

Read the guide to online tutoring. This will provide you with an overview of e-tutoring.

Working in your teams, explore and discuss the case study. Some questions to prompt discussion are included at the end of the case study.

The e-learning group in the case study is clearly not working well. What actions would you take as their e-tutors to resolve some of the issues identified in the case study? What type of learning activity would you introduce to get the group working together? How would you take into account the individual differences portrayed in the case study?

As a result of your work each team needs to produce a set of guidelines on working with diverse groups. These guidelines will be used for a training programme for new e-tutors.

Please present your results to the whole group by 11 March.

Case study

Two of you have been asked to take over an e-learning group (12 members) at very short notice as the group's two e-tutors have both gained promotion and moved to new pastures. The two e-tutors took a team approach to the group: one offered expertise in IT and the internet (she is based in LIS) while the other offers subject expertise. The e-learning group (NewSkills Group) is a 40-week long programme and it enables participants to develop their IT, communication and online skills in the context of a specific subject. It is a Level 1 programme.

Information obtained from WebCT Discussion group and e-mail

You begin exploring the group discussion for and discover that there are a wide range of issues in the group that need tackling. As you read through the messages you print out significant ones and make your own notes. Here are your findings:

Janet

Although the group is now 6 weeks old, Janet appears to have read less than a third of the messages. She has posted 10 messages (most group members have posted between 50 and 100) and these are all very short and supportive of other people's work. She hasn't contributed new ideas or helped develop discussions within her small group work project.

> *Hello everyone,*
>
> *I agree with all the comments made by John and Susan. I'm still not clear about what we have to produce as a group report. Does anyone know?*
>
> *Janet*

Terry

Terry is a very active group member. She appears to log on every few hours. Terry tends to answer everyone's queries and has strong opinions. She caused an upset with the following messages:

> *Hi everyone*
>
> *Time is short! Would everyone make sure they put the right subject heading on their messages. It is netiquette and helps me to file everything away.*
>
> *Thanks.*
>
> *Terry*

Hi everyone

I've read the documents and understand the task. I suggest that James and Andy do the research, I'll collate their findings and write the first draft. Jane could edit it and make sure I don't make any typos. I think this is the best way of going forward. It builds on our strengths. (I won't mention what happened in the first activity). When will you produce the first draft J and A?

Terry

James

James appears to be progressing well. He is online three or four times a week and works well in a group. His messages are always very supportive.

Andrew

Andrew has only posted a few messages. They are very short and you are concerned about his literacy skills. Is he dyslexic?

Hi

OK about reading. Will search for more dotumets. Im confused about actiwity help

Andy

Susanne

As you are working through the site an e-mail arrives from one of the students, Susanne.

Hello,

I understand you are the 2 new tutors for the NewSkills Group. I am very unhappy about the group. I contacted the old tutors (by e-mail) and they seemed to ignore me. I am being bullied by two of the women. They ignore me, patronise me and put me down (read the messages and you'll find this is true). One of them thinks she is better than me and offered to teach me how to use WebCT – she sent me 3 e-mails to my home address offering help. Is she a stalker? Can you sort them out. I don't want to work in a group with them. Will you throw them off the course? Otherwise I'll use the university's equal opportunities policy and take you all to court. You have 3 days to reply to this e-mail.

Susanne

Jane

Jane appears to be working well on the programme. You are concerned about her workload as she has posted a number of messages that suggest she is stressed out. Unfortunately there has been no response to these messages. Here is an example message posted at 1.05 am:

Hi

Sorry this is late. Working til 10 pm again last night. My cat died this morning too. Back to work now.

Jane

Adrian

Adrian seems to be hanging around the edge of the group. He reads messages but rarely inputs anything of value to the group activities. Terry called him a 'freeloader' when she worked with him. He ignored her comment. Adrian has suggested that group members visit his personal website so that they can see how 'a good website is designed'. You visit it and, to your horror, discover that it contains pornographic material. You are sickened by the images you see. You wonder if other students have visited it. There is no mention of it in the discussion group.

Anne

Anne appears to be working through the programme with ease. Her messages are friendly and supportive. She often gives help and support to others.

Sam

Sam only logs on once a week as he can only access *WebCT* at the weekend. He does contribute a lot during the weekend but often seems to be out of step with the group work. He is obviously doing a lot of reading and thinking. His contributions are really high-quality.

Russell

Russell is an active member of the group and often helps to get the team work moving forward. He is obviously technically very skilled but is careful not to use jargon or introduce ideas that are very much in advance of the course. He has given a lot of his time to help others overcome technical issues.

Elizabeth

Elizabeth is concerned about the amount of work involved in the course and also the cost of being online. This is her latest message:

> Hi
>
> *I am getting fed up with this course. There are too many messages to read and a lot of them are about social chit chat rather than the WORK. I came on the course to get a qualification and learn more about IT. I dind't come here to make new friends (I've got enough friends anyway and I hardly have time to see them). Could everyone cut out the chat and get on with the work.*
>
> Liz

Victoria

Vicky is struggling to keep up with the reading but is fully involved in all the team activities. She is really good at supporting others and often brings a 'down to earth' approach to the work. She uses a lot of appropriate humour in her team work.

Prompt questions

Having read the messages, you need to explore and discuss your findings within your group. Here are some prompt questions to start off the process:

1   How can the e-tutors sort this out?
2   That porn site was revolting. Isn't there a policy about offensive materials within the university? Should the e-tutors report it to the police? Should the e-tutors discuss it with a colleague? What issues are involved in this situation?
3   How could the e-tutors handle the alleged bullying situation?
4   What other issues are present in the group? How could they be handled?
5   What issues will the e-tutors handle? What issues will they leave to the group to handle?
6   How could the e-tutors keep this group working together?

This activity generated a lot of discussion, and also research into the parent organizations' policies and procedures. Discussions focused around the following themes:

- the need to prioritize and deal with the pornography issue and the alleged harassment situation first
- the need to follow formal procedures, e.g. computer misuse, harassment and bullying
- whether to intervene or let matters resolve themselves
- whether to intervene in discussion groups or whether a private response is more appropriate
- the need to differentiate between typographic errors and dyslexia, and the importance of diagnostic tools and support for individuals with special needs
- the need for e-tutors to have support and back-up from their institution.

The guidelines produced by the e-learners enabled them to summarize their findings and it provided them with a useful tool for use in their information service.

Discussion groups

In e-learning programmes discussions are normally focused around a specific activity or current theme. The e-tutor's role is normally to start off the discussion and, if necessary, provide background learning resources. Once the discussion has got started, the e-tutor will facilitate it using skills described in detail in Chapter 6. Below is an example message posted by an academic librarian as part of an information skills module (Neil is the tutor):

Message: referencing sources

Hello everyone,

Neil has asked me to help you learn how to reference your work. The aim of this activity is to help you get high marks in your first assignment.

For most of your assignments you will need to research and consider other people's ideas. When you use these ideas in your own written work, you must credit the sources within the main body of your assignment and also provide detailed information about the source in a bibliography. This is called information citation and is an essential part of academic practice.

If you are unsure of what referencing involves then look at the example article [*hotlink*] - in particular notice the list of references at the end and also the way there is a connection between the ideas mentioned in the article and the reference, e.g. on page 3 (final paragraph) Dewar quotes Virginia Griffin (1988) and this will lead you to a reference listed in alphabetical order at the end of the paper. Spending 10 minutes

examining the way this paper uses references will really help you to get
it right in your assignment.

There are 2 key questions we will explore in this discussion:
* Why is it important to reference work?
* How do you reference work?

So does anyone want to get the ball rolling? Why is it important to
reference work? How do you reference work?

best wishes

Alison

This message started off a discussion involving:

- students sharing horror stories (examples of plagiarism that resulted in students failing their course)
- experienced students pointing new students to library guides on referencing and providing their own examples of how to do it
- sharing other resources on plagiarism, e.g. an online test (http://education-indiana.edu/~frick/plagiarism)
- someone preparing a list of reasons why is it important to reference work:
  — a moral issue about cheating and intellectual honesty
  — a netiquette issue about giving credit to other people's work where it is due
  — a learning issue – the need to identify and separate your own and other people's work – you will then be able to reflect on and learn about their own learning experience.
  — an academic issue – if you reference someone else's work, your reader will be able to look up the source.
- someone shared a metaphor (original source Open University) relating plagiarism to driving and speeding:

*Many people speed, some accidentally and some deliberately,
but no one wants to be caught speeding. If detected then the
penalty will vary from a small fine to loss of licence depending
on the particular situation. These penalties occur whether or
not we meant to speed. To make sure we do not break the law.
we need to know what the posted limit is and concentrate on
keeping within it. This is particularly true if driving abroad
when you might not know the local rules. Increasingly tutors*

are using detection equipment similar to speed cameras, and
can detect plagiarism both minor and major. Educational
institutions and examination awarding bodies have the power
of the court to deduct marks or expel the student.

Icebreakers

Online icebreakers are similar to those used in face-to-face situations. They help a new group to 'break the ice' and start to get to know each other. In an online environment they also give people the opportunity to become familiar with the technology and also develop their online voice. As with face-to-face icebreakers, it is important that the activity is acceptable to the group and also that they can see its relevance to their learning programme.

Here are two example icebreakers:

Icebreaker from an undergraduate information searching module tutored by an information skills librarian

Hello everyone,

Welcome to the information searching module. As you know this is a new course and one that is taught entirely online. This may be a new experience for most of you – don't worry you will soon become familiar with the way it works.

The purpose of this activity is to start to get to know each other and to become familiar with the Blackboard conference facilities.

Please would you introduce yourself to the others by typing in a message introducing yourself and saying:

Your subject

Why you have chosen this module

What you want to get out of this module

How often each week you intend to visit the Blackboard site

Where you will be studying, e.g. library, flat, hall

Any concerns you have about studying for the module

How you like to relax, e.g. sport, soaps etc.

Once you have sent off your message then take the time to read all the comments made by everyone as a means to get to know your fellow learners and tutor. Respond to other people's messages in your group. You will start to build threads of messages or online conversations where different people are contributing, commenting on and asking questions about one theme.

A few key rules about online discussions: keep it friendly, keep it informal, don't worry too much about spelling or other typo errors. I'm looking forward to getting to know you all. I'll be dipping in and out of the 'conversations'.

This activity starts on 10 February and runs until the 17 February.

All the best

Chris

Icebreaker from an e-learning module aimed at LIS and academic staff

Hello everyone,

It was good to meet you all at the induction workshop. What we are going to do now is start the online work. To help us get going please would you send a message in which you introduce yourselves by identifying:

- your main learning point from the induction workshop
- your expectations about working online
- any concerns you have about working online
- when you think you'll be coming online, e.g. lunchtime, early evening etc.

Please would you respond to each other's messages and use this as an opportunity to find out more about each other.

The next activity will be posted on 20 September.

Best wishes,

Jane and David

Team-building activities

While icebreakers are a useful technique for helping e-learners to get to know each other it is sometimes worth spending additional time getting to know each other and becoming confident about working online. The following desert exercise (source unknown) has been used by the author during early stages in a number of e-learning courses for library and information workers.

Desert exercise – introductory message

Hello everyone,

Here is the next group activity. You may find it helpful to print out these instructions for further reference. I hope you enjoy the activity.

The purpose of this activity is to enable you to:

- develop your skills in online group work
- develop online threads on particular discussion topics
- discover some of the advantages and disadvantages of online group working.

The exercise:

Your group was attempting to cross the Sahara Desert and your mini-bus has broken down. You are able to obtain 5 from the following list:

torch (4 battery size)	bottle of salt tablets(1000)
jack-knife	1 quart of water per person
sectional air map of crash area	book entitled *Edible Animals of the Desert*
plastic raincoat	2 pairs of sunglasses per person
magnetic compass	2 quarts of 180 proof vodka
bandage kit with gauze	1 overcoat per person
45 calibre pistol	cosmetic mirror
parachute (red and white)	

What you need to do

Individually, you need to identify your top five items and your reasons for selecting them. You need to share your thinking with the group.

Then working as a team you have to select your team's top 5 items. The selection should be based on consensus i.e. a group decision making process. Consensus is difficult to reach. Therefore, not every ranking will meet with everyone's complete approval. Try, as a team, to make each ranking one with which all team members can at least partially agree. Here are some guides to use in reaching consensus:

- Avoid arguing for your own individual judgements.
- Approach the task on the basis of logic.
- Avoid changing your mind only in order to reach agreement and

avoid conflict. Support only solutions with which you are able to agree somewhat, at least.

- Avoid 'conflict-reducing' techniques such as majority vote, averaging or trading in reaching decisions.
- View difference of opinion as helpful rather than as a hindrance in decision making.
- View your initial agreement as suspect.

I will be popping in at regular intervals although I won't take part in the activity unless you want to ask me specific questions.

Once you have decided your top 5 team items then post a team message with the subject name '5 items' by 27 April.

Best wishes

Barbara

This activity enables individual learners to get involved in a group process and it is the type of activity that many people are familiar with in face-to-face training sessions. This type of activity may take 7–14 days to complete online, and it is really important to allow enough time for everyone to take part and have a real discussion.

Desert exercise – e-tutor's response at the end of the activity

Hello everyone

Well done for succeeding with the task and delivering a list of 5 items by the deadline. I was very impressed with the way you worked and noted the following really good practice:

- acknowledging each other's messages
- backing your ideas up with brief explanations
- keeping your messages relatively short
- asking for ideas, asking for agreement
- using other information sources, e.g. experience, TV programmes, internet
- appropriate use of humour
- a volunteer producing summaries of findings
- completing the task on time
- creative ways of using materials present, e.g. mirrors.

This is an excellent start to the e-learning course. Well done. You will find that the skills you have developed here will be very useful in your first assignment.

If you have been quiet during this exercise (and I am aware that there are many reasons for this, e.g. half term holiday, pressures of day job, teething problems with the technology) then my suggestion is that you do get more involved in the next activity. This is important as you will need to use some of your messages in your assignment. Do contact me if you have any queries or concerns.

The definitive list

So, what is the definitive list? Here are the top 5 items from the 'experts':

Mirror	Torch
Overcoat	Parachute
Water	

The torch and mirror were for signalling purposes. Overcoat to keep warm. Parachute to signal and also keep warm.

What to do next?

You might like to think about what you have learnt from this activity. Also, what helped the exercise to work well and how could it be improved? You could share these thoughts in this general discussion area.
The next activity will be posted on 10 May.

Finally

Well done. You have got off to a brilliant start to the course.
Barbara

This message praises the learner's work, it identifies good practice, it includes individuals who have been 'quiet' and it gives the recommended answer. It also points the learners to a general discussion area and explains when the next activity will be posted. This desert exercise may be referred to later on in the same course, e.g. as an example in discussions about netiquette, group working or using a diverse range of sources.

Project groups

E-learning programmes often include project work as this enables individuals to work on specific activities that are often directly related to their workplace. Problem-solving projects are popular and important as they enable people to share ideas and expertise and perhaps develop innovative solutions to problems. The types of projects that groups could be working on include:

- development of a website
- development of learning resources
- production of a report or journal article.

Project management e-learning course for information workers

The author ran an e-learning programme on project management for information workers and this involved a blended mix of face-to-face and virtual workshops. Co-operative groups were set up in which participants worked in small groups on their own workplace projects. They used standard project management tools, e.g. *MS Project*, and gained help, support and encouragement from each other as well as their tutor. The types of projects that participants worked on included:

- implementation of a new integrated information system
- development of a digital learning resource centre
- development of a departmental website
- production of a new set of printed resources
- closure of a learning resource centre.

Overall, the participants achieved the following outcomes:

- they learnt standard project management skills and techniques
- they applied their new knowledge and skills to workplace information projects
- they developed new virtual communication skills
- they internalized the experiences of an e-learner
- they developed as a community of practice.

Virtual visitors

Virtual visitors may be invited as special guests on library and information staff development programmes, formal learning programmes or to enhance special events. They may be information workers with particular experiences or expertise, e.g. an information officer with experience of using a particular system, customers who are willing to share their perspectives on the service, or individuals who can share a particular perspective such as the experience of using a library service as a hearing impaired customer.

As with face-to-face encounters the organization of virtual visits involve a fair amount of preparation. In particular, the organization of synchronous sessions can be particularly demanding and stressful, as they depend on everyone having access to a working virtual environment at the same time. The following guidelines (prepared with the help of Dina Lewis) may be used to help organize and support virtual visits.

Guidelines for virtual speakers

1 Clarify aims, outcomes and expectations of visit.
2 Prepare for visit, e.g. read course documents, read previous discussions, read participant biographies, discuss purpose of visit and expectations with tutor(s).
3 Minimize introduction of additional reading materials.
4 Provide a photo of yourself.
5 Provide links to websites etc. that you have been involved in.
6 Provide any reading materials in advance.
7 Introduce yourself and clarify expectations, e.g. how often you will log into discussion, total length of time you will be online.
8 Spend some time establishing rapport, e.g. acknowledge comments made by learners, make connections with their work, earlier stages of programme.
9 Focus discussion on an authentic situation or activity.
10 Include time for closure and say 'goodbye'.

Guidelines for tutors

1 Make contact with virtual visitor several weeks before visit.
2 Negotiate fees and expenses.
3 Clarify aims, outcomes and expectations of visit.
4 Ensure that virtual visitor's contribution to the online group is timely.

5 Provide visitor with guidelines.
6 Provide learners with background information and photo of visitor.
7 Provide learners with aims, outcomes and expectations of visit.
8 Integrate visit with learning activities – make it an integral part of the course and, ideally, link it with assessment activities.
9 Introduce visitor in the discussion group, keep a low profile.
10 Thank the visitor in discussion group and also by private e-mail.

Guidelines for learners

1 Identify aim, learning outcomes and expectations of visit.
2 Identify what you can gain from visit.
3 Prepare a list of questions you want to discuss with visitor.
4 Read introductory material, including visitor biography.
5 Welcome visitor and help them to obtain a 'quick snapshot' of you.
6 Participate in discussions and be supportive of visitor.
7 Thank visitor at end.

Assessment activities

Assessment involves finding out how much an individual or group has learnt as a result of the e-learning programme. The assessment of learning is an important part of all organized learning activities, including both face-to-face and online learning experiences. Traditionally, formal assessment, e.g. through marked assignments, is a process that library and information workers are not always involved in. However, everyone involved in delivering learning programmes is involved in informal assessment activities. For example, a face-to-face trainer will observe the faces of delegates and listen to their comments to assess whether or not they have learnt key ideas.

Assessment can take place at a number of different times during the learning programme:

1 **Diagnostic tests** at the start of the module or programme – these help individuals and tutors to assess their starting point and the need for either pre-programme activities or to accelerate through the programme.
2 **Formative assessment activities** during the module or programme – these enable individuals and/or tutors to assess progress on the programme and the need for additional work.
3 **Summative assessment activities** at the end of the module or programme –

these enable the individual learner and/or tutor to identify whether or not the learning outcomes have been achieved.

4   **Post-programme assessment activity** after the end of the programme – these enable the individual learner and/or tutor to assess the retention of knowledge and skills, and the transfer of learning to another environment, e.g. workplace.

Individual learners find assessment activities helpful as they enable them to chart their own progress, identify their new knowledge and skills, and also any gaps; they feel a sense of achievement, and this can be a very motivating experience. In addition the assessment process can lead to academic or vocational awards or credits. Assessment activities provide opportunities to give feedback and this may be carried out automatically or by a tutor. The assessment activities can also be used to evaluate the e-learning programme, and to identify any areas that need developing and improving.

Content-driven assessment

Many interactive learning materials provide assessment activities based around the use of question sets. This involves developing a range of questions or activities that will enable the learner to identify whether or not they have achieved the learning outcomes of the programme. Many integrated learning environments provide automatic question set facilities that enable individual tutors to present an assessment activity without needing any specialized technical knowledge. Alternatively, polling software (see Chapter 2) can sometimes be used to set up and administer assessment activities. Table 9.3 provides a summary of content-driven assessment activities. The following example shows the use of a simple true or false question set in the *Netskills TONIC* programme that is described in Chapter 2.

Exploring the internet – Netskills quiz

Instructions

In this module, you have learned a few underlying concepts which are common to most internet navigation tools. Can you say which of the following statements are true or false?

Make your selections from the checkboxes and drop-down menus. When you have answered all the questions, select the 'Am I Right?' button. Your attempt will then be graded and feedback given for questions that you may have answered incorrectly.

Example questions included:

Question Number 1:

Client software acts as a go-between for you and the information server.

True ☐

False ☐

Question Number 4:

HTML is a language for writing and editing video- and audioclips:

True ☐

False ☐

Example obtained from: www.netskills.ac.uk/TonicNG/

Process-driven assessment

In process-driven assessment activities, learners may be asked to work individually or in collaborative or co-operative groups. In this kind of assessment activity

Table 9.3 *Content-driven assessment activities*

Type	Key features	Advantages	Disadvantages
Test questions	Question presents the learner learner with a list of possible used to assessand they must choose the correct answer, e.g. true/false, matching, multiple choice.	Can be used to test both simple and complex learning. Very efficent – can cover content at a great depth.	Can be time-consuming to design. Can encourage rote learning. Learners can guess the correct answer!
Interpretive exercise	Learners are presented with a a situation, e.g. case study. They are then asked a series of questions (completion or test questions) about the material.	Can be used to assess complex learning, e.g. application of principles, identification of cause–effect relationships, understanding of complex information. Can be used to identify underlying assumptions. Can be used to assess application of theory to practice. Offers challenging and interesting assessment activities.	Can be very time-consuming to design. Learners may not transfer ideas or skills to their workplace.

learners are asked to demonstrate that they have achieved the learning out-comes of the programme through a wide range of activities including:

*   production of products such as websites, reports, essays
*   evaluation of products, e.g. websites
*   working in groups can lead to assessment activities that involve self, peer and tutor-assessment
*   demonstration of reflective practice, e.g. submission of individual messages from a discussion group supported by a reflective commentary, use of learning journals.

These approaches are summarized in Table 9.4.

The advantages of these types of assessment activities are that they can be used to assess complex learning and the application of theory to practice. They can be extremely motivating and lead to great strides in learning. However, they can be very time-consuming to develop and some learners may find them rather challenging. If learners are new to a particular kind of assessment activity, then they will need to learn how to do it before they can engage in the activity.

Group assessment activities

The assessment activities below were used with a group of library and information workers who undertook an e-learning module on mentoring delivered by their local university. The aims and outcomes of the programme are presented in Chapter 8. Successful completion of the ten-week programme involved successfully completing a learning journal and also a group report. On successful completion of the programme participants achieved a university certificate of 30 credits at Level 4.

Group report – setting up a workplace mentoring scheme

This is a small group activity and you will be assigned to work with two colleagues from your own library and information unit.

The assignment is to produce a written report in response to the following terms of reference:

Write a report aimed at the director of your library and information department. The aim of the report is to identify the potential role of mentoring within your department and how a mentoring scheme could be established. You need to think about the following issues: benefits of mentoring, role of the mentor and mentee, key features of successful

Table 9.4 *Process-driven assessment activities*

Type	Key features	Advantages	Disadvantages
Production of products, e.g. report, website	Individuals or groups produce a product to a specification.	Authentic activity, linked with workplace or 'real' learning situation.	Learners need to have appropriate levels of information literacy. May be very time-consuming for learner. May be very time-consuming for tutor – design and also actual assessment.
Evaluation of products	Individuals or groups evaluate a product to a specification.	Authentic activity, linked with workplace or 'real' situation.	Learners need to have appropriate levels of information literacy.
Self, peer and tutor assessment	Individuals follow a specific process and provide typed feedback.	Learner obtains useful feedback from a range of sources. Can be very motivating.	Learners need to know how to give con-structive feedback. If individuals break rules, then it can be a very damaging experience.
Reflective commentary	Individuals reflect on an activity and link their experiences with theory.	Learners develop critical thinking skills. Learners link experiences to practice. Learners develop a better understanding of themselves.	Many learners are unfamiliar with this type of activity. Learners may approach the activity at a surface rather than a deep level. Can be time-consuming to design in a way that will work.
Learning journal	Learners keep a personal journal (paper, word-processed) at regular intervals. They reflect on specific events, and consider the event, the positive/ negative aspects of it, their learning from the event, and what they will do differently as a result of their reflection.	Enables learners to reflect and think about their progress and development. Over time a development pattern becomes clear. It can lead to transform-ational learning.	Many learners find it really difficult to keep a learning journal. It becomes a chore.

schemes, challenges to setting up the scheme, recommendations for action. The report will be no longer than 2000 words.

What you need to do

1 Work through *Theme 3: Learning resource 1: Mentoring in the workplace.* This will provide you with the detailed information about mentoring. It will also provide hot links to example schemes and mentoring activities within the information profession.

2 Remind yourself about key skills in report writing. You will find it helpful to review *Theme 1: Learning resource 3: Report writing.*

3 Check the assessment criteria, before you start working on this assignment (see Table 9.5).

4 As a group, decide how you are going to work together. Produce a group action plan.

5 You will need to produce a first draft of your report.

6 Remember to edit your work. It is often helpful to ask a friend or colleague to read your report and give you feedback on it.

7 After you have responded to the feedback, then it is worthwhile double-checking that you have met all the assessment criteria before handing your work in.

8 Remember to reflect on this group process in your learning journal.

Table 9.5 *Assessment criteria for a written assignment*

Poor-quality report	Good-quality report
Introduction is limited or muddled.	Clear introduction to report describing its aim and outcomes, scope and context.
Unclear or vague definition. Benefits are sketchy and don't relate to information work practice.	Mentoring is clearly defined and described. Benefits of mentoring are clearly outlined and linked to current practice/ issues.
Unclear or muddled description of mentor/mentee. Confusion with role of others, e.g. manager, coach, training officer.	Clear description of role of mentor/mentee.
Work is descriptive and lacks evaluative comments.	Clear description of mentoring process. Evaluation of key features of successful schemes.
Few or no recommendations. Recommendations do not relate to content of report.	Clear set of recommendations that logically follow on from content of report.
Report is poorly guided and is difficult to follow.	Presentation of the report is clear, logical, with well-labelled sections.

Report lacks visual images.	Report includes appropriate visual images, e.g. diagrams.
The language and style are inappropriate for the audience.	The langauge and style are appropriate for the audience.
There are grammatical and spelling errors	Grammar and spelling are correct.
Report does not meet professional standards of presentation.	Overall presentation of the report is professional.

Learning journal

This will be a working document (you may select your own form and structure, e.g. hand-written, Word document, HTML). It demonstrates your development as a reflective practitioner. It may be used to record reflection on the learning activities in the module, the face-to-face workshops and online learning activities, feedback from peers, mentor and/or tutor.

Assessment criteria

Good-quality learning journals will demonstrate many of the following characteristics: a range of entries; clarity and good observation in the presentation of events or issues; evidence of speculation; evidence of a willingness to revise ideas; honesty and self-assessment; thoroughness of reflection and self-awareness; depth and detail of reflective accounts; evidence of synthesis, analysis, evaluation etc.; relationship of the entries in the journal to any relevant coursework; theories etc.; match of the content and outcomes of the journal work to module aim and outcomes; reflection on the reflective processes.

Self-assessment activities

Many e-learning programmes incorporate self and peer assessment activities. Self-assessment activities may include completing and thinking about the results of a simple profiling tool. This is demonstrated in Figure 9.1, taken from the University of Ulster website at http://campusone.ulst.ac.uk (accessed 6 May 2002). This type of self-assessment tool is relatively simple to create with an automatic scoring facility incorporated. It can be used as a standalone self-assessment tool or as part of a programme. The role of self-assessment activities in learning to e-learn programmes is explored in Chapter 7.

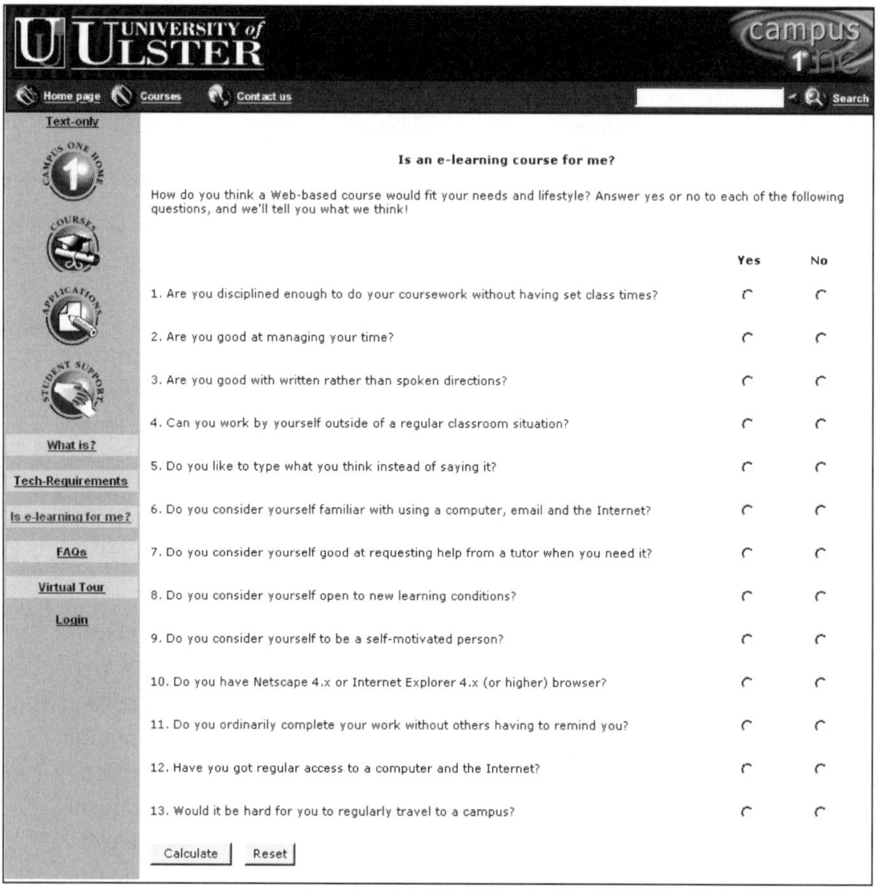

Is an e-learning course for me?

How do you think a Web-based course would fit your needs and lifestyle? Answer yes or no to each of the following questions, and we'll tell you what we think!

	Yes	No
1. Are you disciplined enough to do your coursework without having set class times?		
2. Are you good at managing your time?		
3. Are you good with written rather than spoken directions?		
4. Can you work by yourself outside of a regular classroom situation?		
5. Do you like to type what you think instead of saying it?		
6. Do you consider yourself familiar with using a computer, email and the Internet?		
7. Do you consider yourself good at requesting help from a tutor when you need it?		
8. Do you consider yourself open to new learning conditions?		
9. Do you consider yourself to be a self-motivated person?		
10. Do you have Netscape 4.x or Internet Explorer 4.x (or higher) browser?		
11. Do you ordinarily complete your work without others having to remind you?		
12. Have you got regular access to a computer and the Internet?		
13. Would it be hard for you to regularly travel to a campus?		

Calculate Reset

Fig. 9.1 *Self-assessment activity from the University of Ulster*

Peer assessment activities include individual learners giving feedback to a group of learners or an individual learner. This may be an informal or a formal learning process. This is a useful learning tool as it means that e-learners develop their skills in giving and receiving feedback in an online environment. It also means that there is a greater sharing of knowledge, skills and different perspectives. Peer assessment activities do need to be introduced with care so that the learners know what is expected of them and how to give constructive feedback. If this type of assessment process goes wrong, e.g. individual learners give negative and destructive feedback, then it can be extremely damaging both for individuals and for the whole learning group.

Designing an assessment process

If you are involved in designing an assessment process, then it is worthwhile thinking about the overall assessment strategy. The following principles were developed from work by Graham Gibbs (1999) and can be applied to library and information e-learning programmes:

1 Link the assessment activity directly to the learning outcomes.
2 Integrate the assessment activity with the learning process rather than as an additional feature.
3 Ensure that there are explicit and clearly defined assessment criteria.
4 Ensure that the assessment activities are directly relevant to the information or library context .
5 Use a diverse range of assessment activities to accommodate different learning styles.
6 Provide prompt and meaningful feedback. Use the feedback to provide additional learning opportunities.

Summary

A diverse range of activities may be used to engage and mobilize learning in a virtual environment. Individual and group learning activities may be used to ensure that e-learners achieve their learning outcomes. It is really important that these are authentic and relevant to library and information work. Different types of assessment activities may be used to assess learning and also enhance and enrich the learning process.

E-learning and the LIS profession

10

Implications of e-learning and teaching

Introduction

Chapter 10 looks at the implications of e-learning for the library and information profession. E-learning is making an impact on individual library and information workers, their service, and the information profession. In many ways the increased use of ICT and web-based learning technologies has created opportunities for the provision of new services and resources to customers, new opportunities for developing our careers, and also new ways of working within our organization or sector.

Implications for individual library and information workers

E-learning offers new opportunities and challenges for information workers and it is having an impact on individuals in the following areas:

- new learning opportunities
- new employment opportunities
- development of new skills
- new roles and responsibilities
- teleworking
- life/work balance.

E-learning does offer new opportunities for library and information workers to develop their knowledge and skills in a wide range of areas. Examples of these opportunities are described throughout the book. However, it is worth bearing in mind that in order to access e-learning, people need computers and affordable access to the internet.

There is a growth in employment opportunities associated with e-learning, and newspapers, magazines and internet job-search sites regularly advertise vacancies for people who can establish e-learning centres, manage integrated learning systems, create, develop and maintain websites, and also organize learning material content, establish and manage e-learning programmes, and support e-learners, as well as use their ICT skills in the management and maintenance of the ICT-side of e-learning.

Many of these activities involve traditional information skills (e.g. managing and administering integrated learning systems and services), while others involve the development of new skills (e.g. the design and development of e-learning materials and also e-tutoring). For some information workers it offers an opportunity to develop their knowledge and skills, and to get involved in working in new ways with new groups of people. It also offers new development opportunities for individuals and access to a wide range of learning opportunities. It also adds a pressure for all information workers to be confident and competent in the use of ICT.

The last few decades have seen vigorous discussions about the role of library and information workers and this has been accompanied by the development of their role into new learning and teaching activities. One indication of this development is the rise in courses and events to enable information workers to become effective trainers. National programmes such as the EduLib programme trained many staff, while others obtained teaching and training qualifications through programmes such as the City & Guilds 730 programme, Certificate in Training Practice from the Chartered Institute of Personnel and Development, or the Postgraduate Certificate in Education. This newly constructed professional boundary appears to be expanding to encompass e-tutoring. The professional literature and the electronic networks are currently buzzing with information and guidance on moving into e-learning.

Chapters 4 and 6 provide examples of e-learning programmes for library and information workers. The development of programmes on e-learning is a growth area and one of the features of this approach to learning and training is that it offers new opportunities for information workers to take part in collaborative learning programmes with other groups of staff, e.g. trainers, lecturers, multimedia specialists and educational developers. These opportunities for collaborative development mean that individual information workers will develop both their collaborative working skills and also their understanding of the perspectives of other professional groups. This seems to be an important development as collaborative and co-operative working is high on the agenda in organizations that are involved in multi-professional project teams and working across traditional boundaries.

Information workers are developing new roles and responsibilities within libraries and information units. Current vacancies show that there is a demand for individuals who will work across traditional boundaries, and this is often associated with the delivery of training and education programmes. Information workers may be based in an information unit and have a special responsibility for ICT or e-learning across their organization. In addition, many library and information workers have moved out of the information unit and are now managing learning centres, educational development centres or learning materials units. The development of a new staffing structure at the University of Lincoln in the later 1990s resulted in a new role of learning advisor – someone who works within an academic department as well as in the learning resources department to support student learning. Learning advisors, many of whom started life as library and information workers, are actively involved in e-learning. They may, for example, be taking on board responsibility for managing and maintaining virtual learning environments such as those associated with a particular programme of study, responding to staff and student queries via bulletin boards, or producing FAQ lists. This new role has meant that the Learning Resources department is now much closer to its customers and has a direct input into many learning and teaching development activities (University of Lincoln, 1998).

In many organizations e-learning means that library and information workers are working together in new ways with other professional groups, e.g. subject specialists, educational developers or ICT specialists. An example of this can be found at the University of Birmingham, where the Learning Development Unit (part of the Information Services department) manages many collaborative projects. These bring together staff from different parts of the university who work together on a range of projects. Informal discussions with colleagues suggest that e-learning provides a 'new territory' and a virtual space where there are opportunities for different types of working relationships. The development of e-learning programmes for different groups of professional staff (mentioned in chapter 6) means that it is very important for information workers to understand other professional perspectives and cultures, and also the demands of collaborative or co-operative working.

E-learning also offers new opportunities for library and information workers to work from home. There are a relatively large number of opportunities for employment in the design, development and delivery of e-learning programmes. Individual information workers may be involved in e-tutoring, e.g. for a local college or university or for a national organization such as Learndirect or the Open University. They may also be involved in the development of content and materials for e-learning programmes. This type of working opportunity offers new opportunities to specific groups of workers such as individuals with caring responsibilities, people with a disability that means travel to work is a challenge, semi-retired people, and also individuals who are geographically isolated. The author lives and works in rural East Yorkshire and regularly works on e-learning projects involving information workers and other staff located throughout the UK and also overseas. While teleworking typically brings the potential for professional isolation, the existence of the types of virtual communications described in Chapter 2 means that this no longer needs to be an issue.

One potential issue with e-learning is that it offers both opportunities and challenges to maintaining a healthy life/work balance. In some respects it can provide flexible opportunities that reduce time spent travelling or away from the workplace or home. Conversely, during the research for this book, the author found that e-learning added to the already demanding workload of some information workers. As discussed in Chapter 6, it is really important that e-tutors learn to diary and manage their time so that they don't become overworked by the ever-pressing demands of virtual activities.

Implications for library and information units

Information and library services are currently involved in rapid changes as a result of:

- decreased resources and new funding streams
- pressure for increased productivity and accountability
- electronic information delivery
- the importance of virtual communications
- demand for new services
- increased demand for 24-hour/seven-days-a-week services
- opportunities offered by e-learning
- the importance of ICT expertise.

Libraries and information units have responded to these challenges and often take a lead role within their organization. This can take place at a number of different levels:

- provision of access to ICT, e.g. The People's Network
- provision of access to ICT training – face-to-face and also by e-learning
- development and production of e-learning programmes and resources
- provision of funding to support e-learning, e.g. providing help desk technical support, and also providing virtual support using e-mail, virtual reference

desks, bulletin boards and chat rooms
- managing and taking part in collaborative e-learning programmes or projects
- working across traditional boundaries to support innovative programmes as part of lifelong learning or other types of government initiatives.

The development of these new services and activities is often associated with changes in the organizational structure such as the convergence of library, ICT and media staff, or the expansion of the information service to include educational development, training and/or e-learning.

Library and information workers in organizations that use virtual learning environments, e.g. colleges and universities, are likely to be involved with them at a number of different levels:

1 **Strategic level**
   - development of organizational learning and teaching strategy
   - decisions about the selection and purchase of VLEs
   - policy decisions about the organization's strategy and the overall operation of the VLE
2 **Operations level**
   - managing and administering the VLE, e.g. configuring the system, providing learning spaces for departments, programmes or tutors
   - managing and administering copyright and other intellectual property issues
3 **Teaching and learning**
   - setting up and establishing specific e-learning environments such as: design of site, design and development of materials, uploading of materials, identification of weblinks, organizing staff and student passwords
   - training staff and students in the use of the VLE, and also providing technical help and support
   - e-tutoring, either as a co-tutor on an academic or vocational programme, or tutoring their own programmes.

Implications for the profession

At a professional level, e-learning and teaching is changing initial and continuing professional education and training. It is becoming an integral part of both traditional face-to-face programmes, where it may be used to provide student support and also deliver specific modules. It also provides opportunities for professional development entirely through e-learning. The previous chapters, particularly Chapters 4 and 6, gave examples of the use of e-learning in initial and continuing professional development.

While many traditional library and information education and training providers are involved in e-learning, they are now facing competition from new providers, both within their own country and from across the world. It is very easy for an information worker in one country, e.g. England, to access and take a professional qualification in another, e.g. USA. This globalization of library and information education means that new international communities of practice are developing, and that individuals are developing knowledge and experience of professional practice in other countries.

Virtual communication tools (discussed in Chapter 2) have helped to accelerate and facilitate opportunities for information exchange, sharing of ideas and support within the library and information communities. This means that new ideas are quickly disseminated, and there appears to be much greater access to current information, controversies and debate. The development of communities of interest based around specific themes or topics means that there are relatively easy-to-identify channels of communication within the profession. In addition, the practice of archiving messages and postings means that relative newcomers to the field have access to older information and ideas. The use of virtual communication tools means that it is much easier (in theory anyway) for new entrants to the profession to take part in professional discussions and networks.

The recognition of the existence of communities of practice (discussed in Chapter 5) appears to provide a new theoretical framework around what is well established professional practice. The concept of communities of practice is a relatively new one, and as it is becomes better understood, then it may be possible to develop more effective communities to the benefit of the library and information profession. This concept is becoming part of the curriculum in professional development programmes. While some people may consider it a new name for the traditional activities of collaborative working and networking, it is certainly being explored in new ways, which may throw new light on professional practice.

The importance of learning and teaching (including e-learning) means that many information workers are now joining other professional groups such as the Institute for Learning and Teaching (ILT), the Chartered Institute for Personnel and Development (CIPD) and the Association of Learning Technologies (ALT). This enables individuals to develop their knowledge and skills about specific areas and it also provides new opportunities for networking. It is increasingly common for library and information workers to be members of a number of different professional groups, and this obviously causes some competition for organizations such as the Chartered Institute of Library and Information Professionals (CILIP).

Final comments

Many library and information units are involved in supporting and providing e-learning opportunities, e.g. in information skills or ICT skills. While e-learning and teaching is unlikely to replace face-to-face training and education, it is rapidly becoming an important additional delivery method and it offers new learning opportunities to many people. E-learning is an important method of delivering information literacy programmes and it is used by many library and information workers as a way of supporting students, both school or campus-based and distance learning.

E-learning offers the opportunity for information workers across different countries to work together and construct their own professional knowledge through virtual communities of practice. It requires information workers to develop new skills in the design and development of e-learning materials and programmes, new approaches to learning and teaching, online communication skills, and also new ways of working with each other.

In addition, e-learning is beginning to have an impact on the structure and functioning of information services, particularly those in educational organizations. E-learning is a rapid growth area, and one which is increasingly having an impact on library and information workers and their profession.

11
Resources

Introduction

The purpose of this chapter is to provide guidance to further resources on e-learning. It would be impossible to provide an exhaustive guide to information on e-learning, so this chapter provides a range of starting points that readers can use in their quest for further information. The materials are organized under the following headings:

- books
- e-journals
- websites
  - e-learning tools and technologies
  - e-learning programmes and materials
  - e-learning and teaching
  - design of e-learning programmes and materials
  - professional links, networks and resources.

Books

Higgison, C. A. (ed.) (2000) *Online tutoring e-book*, Heriot-Watt University and The Robert Gordon University, available at http://otis.scotcit.ac.uk/onlinebook/ (accessed 15 August 2002).

Jolliffe, A. et al. (2001) *The online learning handbook*, London, Kogan Page.

Laurillard, D. (2002) *Rethinking university teaching*, 2nd edn, London, Routledge.

McConnell, D. (2000) *Implementing computer supported cooperative learning*, 2nd edn, London, Kogan Page.

Murphy, D. et al. (eds) (2001) *Online learning and teaching with technology*, London, Kogan Page.

Phipps, L., Sutherland, A. and Seale, J. (eds) (2002) *Access all areas: disability, technology and learning*, Bristol, JISC TechDis Service and ALT.

Ryan, S. et al. (2000) *The virtual university*, London, Kogan Page.

Salmon, G. (2000) *E-moderating*, London, Kogan Page.

Simpson, O. (2002) *Supporting students in online, open and distance learning*, London, Kogan Page.

Stephenson, J. (ed.) (2001) *Teaching and learning online*, London, Kogan Page.

Weller, M. (2002) *Delivering learning on the net*, London, Kogan Page.

E-journals

Ariadne available at www.ariadne.ac.uk (accessed 31 May 2002).

Interactive educational multimedia available at www.ub.es/multimedia/iem/ (accessed 12 July 2002)

International review of research in open and distance learning available at www.irrodl.org/index.html (accessed 12 July 2002).

Internet resources newsletter available at www.hw.ac.uk/libWWW/irn/irn.html (accessed 31 May 2002).

JALN available at www.aln.org (accessed 31 May 2002).

Journal of computer-mediated communication, available at http://jcmc.huji.ac.il/ (accessed 12 July 2002).

Learning technology: Journal of the IEEE Computer Society, Learning Technology Task Force (LTTF) available at http://lttf.ieee.org/learn_tech/index.html (accessed 12 July 2002).

Websites

E-learning tools and technologies

ANGEL www.angel.ac.uk (accessed 31 May 2002).
ANGEL (Authenticated Networked Guided Environment for Learning) is a JISC-funded project aimed at integrating learning environments with digital library developments. Their home site provides access to key documents and news.

CDE Software Evaluation http://cde.athabascau.ca/softeval/R.htm (accessed 31 May 2002).

This site evaluates and provides additional information on collaborative tool software products. It is aimed at distance educators and their students. It covers many free products.

Comparison of online course delivery software products, available at www.marshall.edu/it/ciy/webct/compare/comparison.html (accessed 31 May 2002).

This site provides detailed comparisons of products such as *Blackboard*, *WebCT*, *WebMentor* and *TopClass*.

www.jisc.ac.uk

This site provides access to up-to-date reports and projects on virtual and managed learning environments. Its focus is further and higher education.

Web-based learning resources library available at www.outreach.ubk.edu/weblearning/ (accessed 31 May 2002)

This resource covers a wide range of software tools for web-based courses.

E-learning programmes and materials

The Big Blue available at www.leeds.ac.uk/bigblue/bigbluelinksusukaus.html (accessed 31 May 2002).

Presents information and links in information skills training for students in higher and post-16 education in the UK. It also provides links to relevant projects in Australia, USA and the rest of the world.

Cybertours provides a series of websites focusing on particular subject areas and including planning your school library webnet. It is available at www.inforsearcher.com/cybertours/ (accessed 6 April 2001).

The International Association of School Librarianship (IASL) provides a useful list of information skills and resources on the internet. This covers a vast range of websites from US, UK, Australia, Canada and other countries. It includes a brief description of the resources, which include tutorials and websites. It can be accessed at www.iasl-slo.org/infoskills.html (accessed on 6 April 2001).

Online tutorials, available at http://faculty.washington.edu/jwholmes/ tutorial.html (accessed 23 January 2002).

Lists a wide range of web-based information tutorials.

Teaching with the internet available at www.enmu.edu/~kinleye/teach/Intech.html.

Web-based learning resources library available at www.outreach.utk.edu/weblearning/ (accessed 31 May 2002).

This resource covers distance education course catalogues and other off-campus opportunities. The contents range from single web-based courses and resources to virtual universities.

World Lecture Hall, available at www.utexas.edu/world/lecture/.

E-learning and teaching

http://oubs.open.ac.uk/gilly

This is the website of Gilly Salmon. It provides access to her five-stage model of e-learning and also many articles and presentations.

http://musgrave.cqu.edu.au

This site provides access to articles, journals, books, conferences and people involved in collaborative learning.

www.outreach.utk.edu/weblearning/ (accessed 31 May 2002).

This site provides access to a wide range of resources on web-based learning. It is oriented towards higher education, and especially adult distance learning. It provides useful overviews and definitions of key concepts. It includes large numbers of links (organized under headings such as quality criteria and proposals, strategy and planning, newsletters and eZines in distance education, professional organizations and community listserves, and legal and copyright issues).

www2.ncsu.edu/unity/lockers/users/f/felder/public/ILSpage.html

This home page provides access to Felder and Soloman's work on learning styles. It includes general information, an online questionnaire and a supporting article.

Panitz, T. (1999) *A definition of collaborative vs cooperative learning*, available at www.lgu.ac.uk/deliberations/collab.learning/panitz2.html (accessed 3 October 2001).

TUC Learning Services, available at www.learningservices.org.uk/links (accessed on 30 June 2002).

This site provides access to a wide range of learning and development opportunities (both face-to-face and virtual) in the UK. Its coverage is broad and includes basic skills, equal opportunities and diversity, funding learning, and work-based learning.

UK online centres, available at www.dfes/gov.uk/ukonlinecentres (accessed 30 June 2002).

This sites provides information about UK online centres, and it also includes links to other government initiatives.

Web-based learning resources library, available at
www.outreach.utk.edu/weblearning (accessed 31 May 2002)
This provides an extensive range of resources. Its focus is higher education, particularly for adult distance learners.

Wegerif, R. (1998) The social dimension of asynchronous learning networks, *Journal of Asynchronous Learning Networks*, **2** (1), available at
www.aln.org/alnweb/journal/vol2_issue1/wegerif.htm (accessed 12 July 1999).

Yale University Library (2000) *The Adult Learner*, available at
www.library.yale.edu/training/stod/adlearner.htm (accessed 3 October 2001).
This site provides a useful overview of adult learning.

Zemke, R. and Zemke, S. (1984) *30 things we know for sure about adult learning*, available at
www.hcc.hawaii.edu/intranet/committees/FacDevCom/guidebk/teachtip
/adults-3.htm (accessed 3 October 2001).

Design of e-learning programmes and materials

ErgoLib for safer library computing, available at
http://library.ucr.edu/ergolib/ergolib.html (accessed 29 May 2002).
This site provides useful health and safety information.

Ferl *Designing online courses – good practice guidelines*, available at
http://ferl.ngfl.gov.uk (accessed on 24 April 2002).

New Opportunities Fund, nof-digitise Technical Advisory Service *Creating online learning materials*, available at
www.ukoln.ac.uk/nof/support/manual/learning-materials/ (accessed 25 April 2002).

Standards for developing and maintaining e-learning materials are available from the Institute of IT Training (www.iitt.org.uk/) (accessed 24 April 2002).

Professional links, networks and resources

ALN www.aln.org (accessed 31 May 2002).
This is the home page of the Asynchronous Learning Network. It provides access to a wide range of publications, online discussions, conferences and projects. It is a particularly useful resource for researchers into e-learning.

Australian Library Association www.alia.org.au/ (accessed 6 April 2002).

This site provides access to a wide range of activities, publications and links.

BUBL www.bubl.ac.uk (accessed 31 May 2002).

BUBL is an information service provided for the UK higher education community.

CAUL www.caul.edu.au (accessed 23 January 2002).

The CAUL (Council of Australian University Librarians) home page provides access to hotlinks on the development of academic information infrastructure and e-learning in Australia.

CILIP www.cilip.org.uk (accessed 5 May 2002).

This developing site provides access to information about professional development activities and opportunities within the UK.

Free Pint www.freepint.com/ (accessed 12 June 2002).

This site provides a wide range of information on topics such as internet searching, marketing and companies. It hosts discussion groups, newsletter digests, job search. It is aimed at the library and information community as well as internet researchers.

ICONnect www.ala.org/ICONN/onlineco.html (accessed 6 April 2001).

The site of the American Association of School Libraries, a division of the American Library Association, provides access to a variety of free online courses aimed at school library staff, and it offers skills in using the internet, integrating internet resources into the elementary curriculum and exploring the effect of technology on the role of school library staff.

IASL www.iasl-slo.org (accessed 23 January 2002).

The site of the International Association of School Librarianship. It provides access to a wide range of internet resources relevant to school librarians and young people and has an international coverage.

JISC www.jisc.ac.uk

This site provides access to up-to-date activities, events reports and projects on e-learning and its focus is further and higher education.

LTSN Generic Centre www.ltsn.ac.uk/genericcentre (accessed 31 May 2002).

The Learning and Teaching Support Network provides access to information and news on the use of ICT in higher education. It includes some very useful starter guides, e.g. *Using the www in learning and teaching*, and these can be downloaded in RTF format.

Librarian Links http://home.gwi.net/brhs/lib.html (accessed 31 May 2002).

This site provides access to a wide range of websites that are relevant to library and information workers involved in e-learning.

LibraryNet www.schoolnet.ca/Ln-rb/e/index.html (accessed 31 May 2002).

This site is a co-operative venture involving Canadian libraries and Industry Canada.

ScotFEICT www.scotfeict.ac.uk (accessed 31 May 2002).

This site is concerned with ICT in Scottish further education. It provides a range of useful resources, links and news.

UK Public Libraries Page http://ds.dial.pipex.com/town/square/ac940/ukpublib.html (accessed 31 May 2002).

This site provides access to UK Public Libraries, networking and useful links.

Telematics for Libraries www.cordis.lu/libraries/en/liblearn.html (accessed 31 May 2002).

This site provides access to mainly European projects, and reports on the general theme of telematics for libraries.

UKOLN www.ukoln.ac.uk (accessed 31 May 2002)

UKOLN provides a national focus of expertise in digital information management. Their website provides access to news, research and current awareness, events and services.

Etienne Wenger's home page www.ewenger.com (accessed 12 June 2002).

This is the home page of Wenger, who has developed many of the ideas and models behind communities of practice.

References

Alexander, G. (2000) *Netiquette, or social conventions of computer conferencing*, available at http://sustainability.open.ac.uk/gary/netiquette.html (accessed 8 October 2001).

Alexander, J. O. (1999) *Collaborative design, constructivist learning, information technology immersion, & electronic communities: a case study*, available at www.emoderators.com/ipct-j/1999/n1-2/alexander.html.

Allan, B. (1999) *Developing information and library staff through work-based learning*, London, Library Association Publishing.

Allan, B. (2002) *E-learners' experience of time*, MEd thesis, University of Sheffield, in preparation.

Allan, B. and Lewis, D. (2000) *E-tutor guide to online learning and teaching using the Virtual Campus*, Hull, University of Lincolnshire and Humberside.

Amber, L. (2001) *Virtual Training Suite: evaluation report. A report prepared by Lin Amber, University of Bristol Information Services, March 2001*. Available at www.vts.rdn.ac.uk/evaluation.htm (accessed 15 August 2002).

American Library Association Presidential Committee on Information Literacy (1989). Quoted in *A progress report on information literacy: an update on the American Library Association Presidential Committee on Information Literacy: final report, March 1998*, available at www.ala.org/acr/nili/nili.html (accessed 3 March 2002).

Anderson, D. (2001) CPD on a virtual campus: a critical overview of online distance-learning, *Impact*, (July/August), 62–4.

Association for Psychological Type (2000) *What is the Myers-Briggs Type Indicator?*, available at http://209.224.198.54/aptmbtiw.htm (accessed 12 July 2002).

Atkins, H., Moore, D., and Sharpe, S. (2001) *Learning style theory and computer mediated communication: paper presented at ED MEDIA 2001 Conference held 24–26 June 2001 in Tampere, Finland*, available at http://oufcnt5.open.ac.uk/~Hilary_Atkins/edmedia.htm (accessed 12 July 2002).

Barajas, M. and Owen, M. (2000) Implementing virtual learning environments: looking for an holistic approach, *Educational Technology and Society*, **3** (3), 39–53.

Barnes, D. and Seale, J. (2002) Accessibility and inclusivity in further and higher education: an overview. In Phipps, L. Sutherland, A. and Seale, J. (eds) *Access all areas: disability, technology and learning*, Bristol, JISC TechDis Service and ALT, 1–5.

Barnett, R. (1997a) *Towards a higher education for a new century*, London, University of London Institute of Education.

Barnett, R. (1997b) *Higher education: a critical business*, Buckingham, Open University Press.

Benjes-Small, C. and Just, M. L. (2002) *The library and information professional's guide to plug-ins and other web browser tools*, London, Facet Publishing.

Bishop, S. and Henderson, G. (2001) *Information literacy made Ezy: paper presented at Information Online 2001, Tenth Exhibition & Conference*, available at www.csu.edu.au/special/online2001/papers/working_online_111b.htm (accessed 3 April 2002).

Boud, D. (1981) Moving towards autonomy. In *Developing learner autonomy in learning*, London, Kogan Page

Boud, D. J., Keogh, R. and Walker, D. (eds) (1985) *Reflection: turning experience into learning*, London, Kogan Page.

Bradley, P. (1999) *Discussion lists, Usenet and archives*, available at www.philb.com/mail.htm (accessed 28 February 2002).

Bradley, P. (2002) *The advanced internet searcher's handbook*, 2nd edn, London, Library Association Publishing.

Broughton, K. (2001) Our experiment in online, real-time reference, *Computers in Libraries*, **21** (4), (April), 1–4, available at www.infotoday.com/cilmang/apr01/broughton.htm (accessed 12 November 2001).

Buttery, T. (2001) *Wilberforce College: OnLINM (Learning in the New Millennium)*, available at http://ferl.ngfl.gov.uk/display.cfm?resID=2524 (accessed 25 April 2002).

Chartered Institute of Personnel and Training (2002) *Training and development 2002: survey report*, London, CIPD.

Clutterbuck, D. (1997) *Mentoring*, CIPD.

Collins, A., Brown, J. S. and Newman, S. (1989) Cognitive apprenticeship. In Resnick, L. B. (ed.), *Knowing, learning and instruction: essays in honour of Richard Glasser*, Hillsdale, NJ, Lawrence Erlbaum Associates, Inc., 453–94.

Collins, M. and Berge, Z. (1996) *Facilitating interaction in computer mediated on-line courses*, available at http://star.ucc.nau.edu/~mauri/moderate/flcc.html.

Cooper, T. and Smith, B. (2000) *Reflecting and learning from experience of online tuition: implications for staff development and quality assurance processes to support learner learning in this medium: Open University Millennium Conference proceedings.*

Cornish, G. (2001) *Copyright: interpreting the law for libraries, archives and information services*, London, Facet Publishing.

Cox, S. et al. (2000) How to herd cats in Piccadilly, *Times Higher Education Supplement*, (14 April), 36–7.

Currier, S. (2001) *INSPIRAL. Investigating portals for information resources and learning. Final report*, available at http://inspiral.cdlr.strath.ac.uk (accessed 14 August 2002).

Curry, L. (1983) *An organisation of learning styles theory and constructs*, ERIC Document 235, 185.

Darrouzet, C and Lynn, C (1999) Presentation at the Creating a New Architecture for Learning and Development Capacity-Building Workshop, Tokyo, 9–18 August 1999, Asian Development Bank Institute, available at www.adbi.org/Forum/es/es990809.htm.

Davies, B. (2002) No title or subject heading, posting to VLE@JISCMAIL.ac.uk, 18 June 2002.

DeShane, A. and Mahaley, M. (2001) *Mentoring: an annotated bibliography*, 2nd edn, available at www.slabf.org/mentorbib.html.

Downey, B. (1996) *Email interaction: summary of readers' comments*, available at www.lgu.ac.uk/deliberations/eff-interactcomments96.html (accessed 14 August 2002).

Eales, S. (2002) College challenge *Library and Information Update*, 1 (2), May, 52–3.

The Epic Group (2001) *Epic e-learning survey 2001*, available at www.epic.co.uk/ (accessed 14 August 2002).

Felder, R. M. and Soloman, B. A. (1988) *Index of learning styles*, available at www2.ncsu.edu/unity/lockers/users/f/felder/public/ILSpage.html (accessed 12 July 2002).

Fewings, J. (1999) The 'rough and ready' reckoner learning styles questionnaire, *Brainwaves*, (Spring/Summer), 9–12.

Flood, J. (2002) Jim Flood quoted in Courses to beat high drop-out rate, *Information Management Report*, (April), 11–12.

Garratt, T. (1997) *The effective delivery of training using NLP*, London, Kogan Page.

Gibbs, G. (1999) Using assessment strategically to change the way students learn. In Brown, S. and Glasner, A. (eds) *Assessment matters in higher education: choosing and using diverse approaches*, Buckingham, SRHE and Open University Press, 411–55.

Glover, C. (2002) Storm in a teacup: brainstorming – the process of generating new ideas, *People Management*, **8** (7), 44–5.

Goodfellow, R. (1999) *Expert, assessor, co-learner: conflicting roles and expanding workload for the online e-tutor*, available at http://iet.open.ac.uk/pp/r.goodfellow/research02.htm (accessed 12 June 2002).

Goodyear, P. (1998) *New technology in higher education*, available at www.lancs.ac.uk/staff/erapmg/personal/new.htm (accessed 12 June 2002).

Goodyear, P. (2000) *Effective networked learning in higher education: notes and guidelines*, Networked Learning in Higher Education (JISC/CALT), **73**, copies available from http://csalt.lancs.ac.uk/jisc (accessed 12 June 2002).

Grave, L. et al. (2001) *Developments in teaching and learning – the library role, USTLG Spring Meeting, Wednesday 28 February 2001, Lanchester Library, Coventry University*, available at www.leeds.ac.uk/library/ustlg/spring01/sally/report.htm (accessed 12 February 2002).

Hackett, P. (1997) *Introduction to training*, London, CIPD.

Hislop, G. (2000) *Working professionals as part-time online learners*, available at www.aln.org/alnweb/journal/Vol4_issue2/le/hislop/LE-hislop.htm.

Honey, P. and Mumford, A. (1992) *The manual of learning styles*, 3rd edn, Maidenhead, Peter Honey.

Hunter, R. (2001) Personal communication.

INSPIRAL (2001) Project site, available at http://inspiral.cdlr.strath.ac.uk (accessed 14 August 2002).

Jensen, E. (1995) *Brain-based learning and teaching*, Del Mar, CA, Turning Point.

Johnson, H. (2001) Information skills, information literacy, *Library Association Record*, **103** (12), 752–3.

Kearsley, G. and Shneiderman, B. (1998) Engagement theory: a framework for technology-based teaching and learning, *Educational Technology*, (September/October), 20–37.

Kendall, M. (2000) Lifelong learning through computer-mediated communications: potential roles for UK public libraries, *New Review of Libraries and Lifelong Learning*, **1 (1)**, 81–101.

Kent, T. (2001) *WebCT at the University of Birmingham*, published as an eLib review feature, available at www.wish-uk.org/margold/features.htm (accessed 28 March 2002).

Kirkpatrick, D. L. (1994) *Evaluating training programs: the four levels*, San Francisco, CA, Berrett-Koehler.

Kolb, D. (1984) *Experiential learning as the science of learning and development*, Englewood Cliffs, NJ, Prentice-Hall

Library and Information Commission (1998) *Building the new library network*, available at www.lic.gov.uk/publications/policyreports/building/index.html (accessed 14 August 2002).

McBain, I. and Rowe, T. (2001) *Help for students and profile for the library: the WebCT student help desk at Flinders University Library: paper presented at Information Online 2001, Tenth Exhibition & Conference*, available at www.csu.edu.au/special/online2001/papers/working_online_111c.htm (accessed 3 April 2002).

McCabe, M. F. (1998) Lessons from the field: computer conferencing in higher education, *Journal of Information Technology for Teacher Education*, **7** (1).

McConnell, D. (2000) *Implementing computer supported cooperative learning*, 2nd edn, London, Kogan Page.

McDermott, R. (2000) *Knowing in community: 10 critical success factors in building communities of practice*, available at www.co-i-l.com/coil/knowledge-garden/cop/knowing.shtml (accessed 21 November 2001).

McLoughlin, C. and Lucas, J. (2000) *Cognitive engagement and higher order thinking through computer conferencing: we know why but do we know how?, Teaching and Learning Forum 2000* (proceedings contents).

Martin, A. and Rader, H. (eds) (2002) *Information and IT literacy: enabling learning in the 21st century*, London, Facet Publishing.

Mason, R. (2002) Review of e-learning for education and training. In *Networked learning 2002: proceedings of the Third International Conference on Networked Learning 2002. Jointly organised by Lancaster University and the University of Sheffield, and held at the University of Sheffield, Sheffield, UK, 26-28 March 2002*, 19–26.

Morrison, K. (1995) Dewey, Habermas and reflective practice, *Curriculum*, **16** (2), 82–130.

Nipp, D. (1998) Innovative use of the home page for library instruction, *Research Strategies*, **16** (2), 93–102.

O'Connor, J. and Seymour, J. (1994) *Training with NLP: skills for managers, trainers and communicators*, London, Thorsons.

Pagell, R. A. (1996) The virtual reference librarian: using desk top videoconferencing for distance reference, *The Electronic Library*, **14** (1), 21–6.

Papp, R. (2002) Student learning styles and distance learning, *International Conference on Informatics Education & Research . Proceedings of the 16th Annual Conference of the International Academy for Information Management. 14–16 December, New Orleans, Louisiana*, available at www.iaim.org/ICIER2001/icier2001.htm (accessed 15 August 2002).

Pennie, D. (2001) From virtuous to virtual: the collaborative development of information skills at the University of Hull, *Vine*, **122**, 17–21.

Rohfeld, R. W. and Hiemstra, R. (1995) Moderating discussions in the electronic classroom. In Berge, Z. and Collins, M., *Computer mediated communication and the on-line classroom, Volume 3: Distance Learning*, Cresskill, NJ, Hampton Press, 91–104.

Rowntree, D. (1990) *Teaching through self-instruction*, 2nd edn, London, Kogan Page.

Salmon, G. (2000) *E-moderating*, London, Kogan Page.

Sharp, J. (1997) *Communities of practice: a review of the literature*, available at www.tfriend.com/cop-lit.htm (accessed 21 November 2001).

Sloman, M. (2002) Don't believe the hype, *People Management*, **8** (6), 40–2.

Smith, A. (1998) *Accelerated learning in practice*, Network Educational Press.

University of Lincoln (1998) *Managing learning innovation conference report no 1, report of a conference 'Making it happen' held on 17–18 June 1997, Lincoln*, Lincoln, University of Lincoln.

Wang, F-K and Bonk, C. J. (2001) A design framework for electronic cognitive apprenticeship, *JALN*, **5** (2), available at www.aln.org/alnweb/journal (accessed 8 July 2002).

Wenger, E. (1997) *Communities of practice: learning, meaning and identity*, Cambridge, Cambridge University Press.

Wenger, E., McDermott, R. and Snyder, W. M. (2002) *Cultivating communities of practice*, Harvard, Harvard Business School Press.

Index